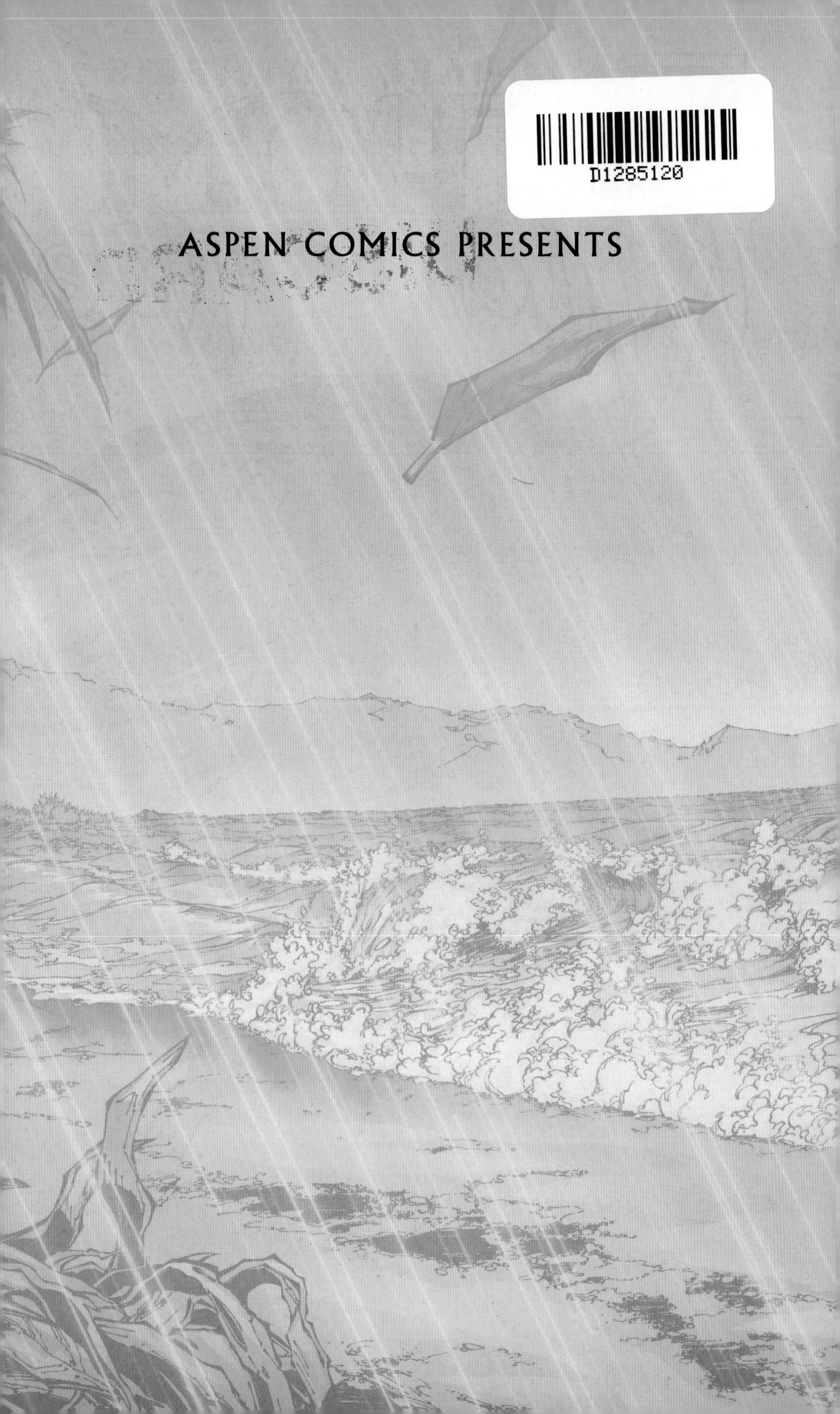
ASPEN COMICS PRESENTS

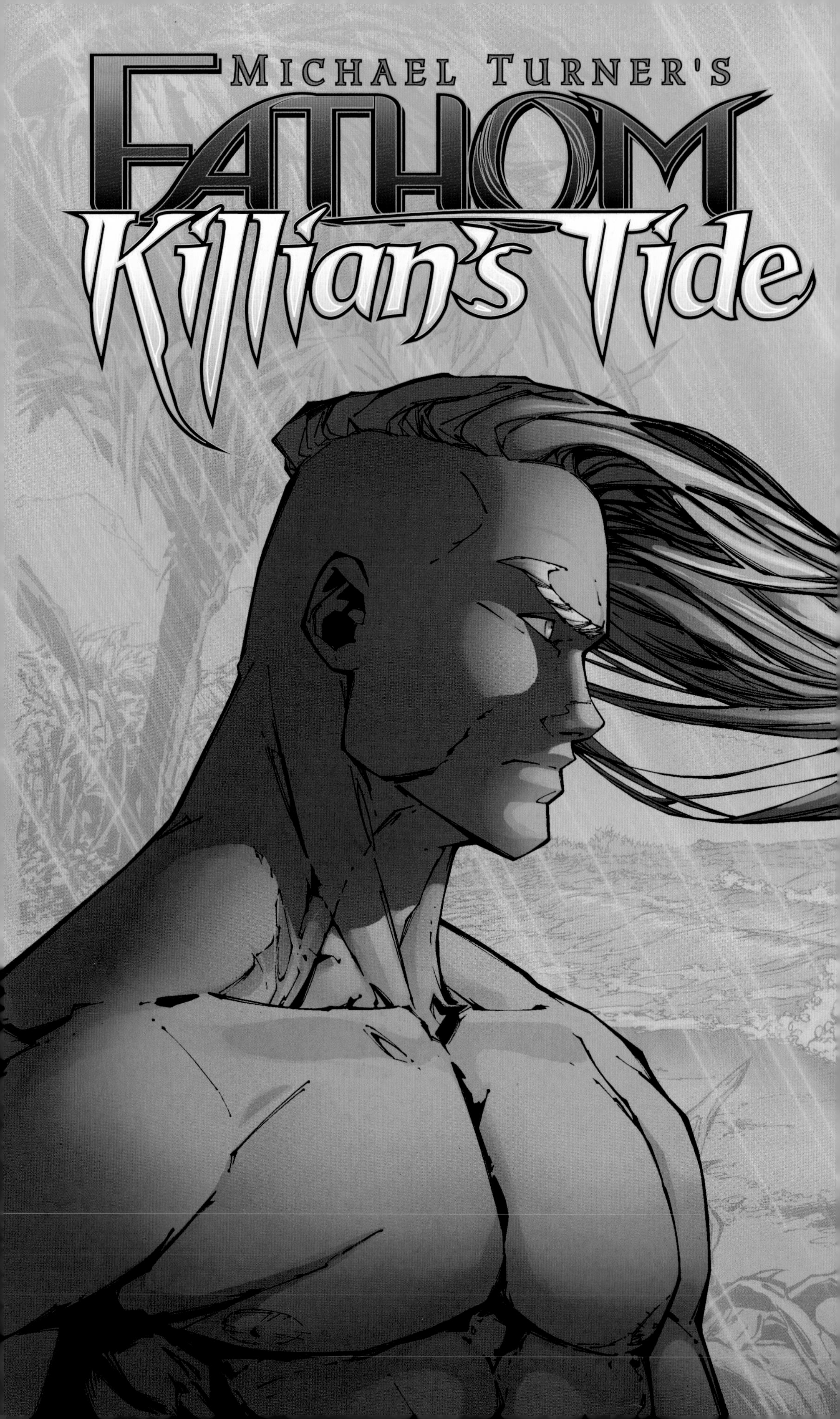
MICHAEL TURNER'S
FATHOM
Killian's Tide

STORY BY:
Michael Turner, Bill O'Neil
AND Talent Caldwell

SCRIPT BY:
Bill O'Neil

PENCILS BY:
Talent Caldwell

INKS BY:
Jonathan Sibal,
Eric Basaldua
AND Jason Gorder

COLORS BY:
Peter Steigerwald
AND Avalon Studios

LETTERING BY:
Robin Spehar AND
Dennis Heisler

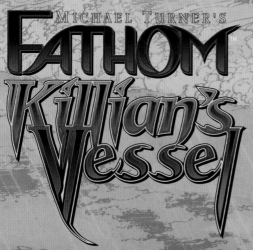

MICHAEL TURNER'S
FATHOM
Killian's Vessel

WRITTEN BY:
Vince Hernandez

PENCILS BY:
Ryan Odagawa

COLORS BY:
John Starr

LETTERING BY:
Josh Reed

FATHOM CREATED BY:
MICHAEL TURNER

MICHAEL TURNER'S FATHOM:™ KILLIAN'S TIDE
ISBN: 978-1-941511-00-8   FIRST PRINTING, 2017.
Collects material originally published as Michael Turner's Fathom: Killian's Tide Issues 1-4 and Michael Turner's Fathom: Killian's Vessel One-Shot

PUBLISHED BY ASPEN MLT, INC.
Office of Publication: 5701 W. Slauson Ave. Suite. 120, Culver City, CA 90230.

Address correspondence to:
FATHOM c/o Aspen MLT Inc.
5701 W. Slauson Ave. Suite. 120
Culver City, CA. 90230-6946
or fanmail@aspencomics.com

Visit us on the web at:
aspencomics.com
aspenstore.com
facebook.com/aspencomics
twitter.com/aspencomics

Fathom Killian's Tide Original Series Editors:
DAVID WOHL AND RENAE GEERLINGS

Fathom Killian's Vessel Original Series Editor:
FRANK MASTROMAURO

For this Edition:
SUPERVISING EDITOR: FRANK MASTROMAURO
EDITORS: VINCE HERNANDEZ, ANDREA SHEA AND GABE CARRASCO
COVER DESIGN: MARK ROSLAN
BOOK DESIGN AND PRODUCTION: GABE CARRASCO
LOGO DESIGN: PETER STEIGERWALD
COVER ILLUSTRATION: MICHAEL TURNER AND PETER STEIGERWALD

For Aspen:
FOUNDER: MICHAEL TURNER
CO-OWNER: PETER STEIGERWALD
CO-OWNER/PRESIDENT: FRANK MASTROMAURO
VICE PRESIDENT/EDITOR IN CHIEF: VINCE HERNANDEZ
VICE PRESIDENT/DESIGN AND PRODUCTION: MARK ROSLAN
EDITORIAL ASSISTANT: GABE CARRASCO
PRODUCTION ASSISTANT: CHAZ RIGGS
OFFICE COORDINATOR: MEGAN MADRIGAL
MARKETING INTERN: MEXI GREMILLION
ASPENSTORE.COM: CHRIS RUPP

Also Available from Aspen Comics:
A Tribute to Michael Turner — ISBN: 978-0-9774821-7-7
Aspen Universe: Revelations™ Volume 1 — ISBN: 978-1-941511-25-1
Bubblegun™ Volume 1: Heist Jinks — ISBN: 978-1-941511-15-2
Charismagic™ Volume 1 — ISBN: 978-0-9854473-7-3
Damsels In Excess™ Volume 1 — ISBN: 978-0-941511-32-9
Eternal Soulfire™ Volume 1 — ISBN: 978-1-941511-26-8
Executive Assistant: Iris™ Volume 1 — ISBN: 978-0-9823628-5-3
Executive Assistant: Iris™ Volume 2 — ISBN: 978-0-9854473-0-4
Executive Assistant: The Hitlist Agenda™ Volume 1 — ISBN: 978-0-9854473-1-1
Executive Assistant: Assassins™ Volume 1 — ISBN: 978-1-941511-09-1
Fathom™ Volume 1: The Definitive Edition — ISBN: 978-0-9774821-5-3
Fathom™ Volume 2: Into The Deep — ISBN: 978-1-6317369-2-6
Fathom™ Volume 3: Worlds at War — ISBN: 978-0-9774821-9-1
Fathom™ Volume 4: The Rig — ISBN: 978-1-941511-07-7
Fathom™ Volume 5: Cold Destiny — ISBN: 978-1-941511-14-5
Fathom Blue™ Volume 1 — ISBN: 978-1-941511-27-5
Fathom™: Dawn of War — ISBN: 978-1-941511-33-6
Fathom™: Kiani: Volume 1: Blade of Fire — ISBN: 978-0-9774821-8-4
Fathom™: Kiani: Volume 2: Blade of Fury — ISBN: 978-1-941511-06-0
Fathom™: Killian's Tide — ISBN: 978-1-941511-00-8
The Four Points™ Volume 1: Horsemen — ISBN: 978-1-941511-10-7

Homecoming™ Volume 1 — ISBN: 978-1-941511-18-3
Jirni™ Volume I: Shadows and Dust — ISBN: 978-0-9854473-8-0
Jirni™ Volume II: New Horizons — ISBN: 978-0-9823628-9-1
Lola XOXO™ Volume 1 — ISBN: 978-1-941511-03-9
Lola XOXO™: Wasteland Madam Volume 1 — ISBN: 978-1-941511-04-6
Shrugged™ Volume 1: A Little Perspective — ISBN: 978-0-9774821-6-0
Soulfire™ Volume 1: part 1 — ISBN: 978-0-9774821-2-2
Soulfire™ Volume 1: part 2 — ISBN: 978-0-9823628-1-5
Soulfire™ Volume 1: The Definitive Edition — ISBN: 978-0-9823628-6-0
Soulfire™ Volume 2: Dragon Fall — ISBN: 978-0-9854473-2-8
Soulfire™ Volume 3: Seeds of Chaos — ISBN: 978-1-941511-13-8
Soulfire™ Volume 4: Dark Grace — ISBN: 978-1-941511-22-0
Soulfire™ Volume 5: Pandemonium — ISBN: 978-1-941511-30-5
Soulfire™: Chaos Reign — ISBN: 978-0-9774821-4-6
Soulfire™: Dying of the Light — ISBN: 978-0-9774821-1-5
Soulfire™: Shadow Magic — ISBN: 978-0-9823628-7-7

Aspen Novels:
Seven To Die™ — ISBN: 978-1-941511-02-2
The Lost Spark™ — ISBN: 978-0-9854473-3-5
The Lost Spark™: Masks and Monsters — ISBN: 978-0-6925559-3-4

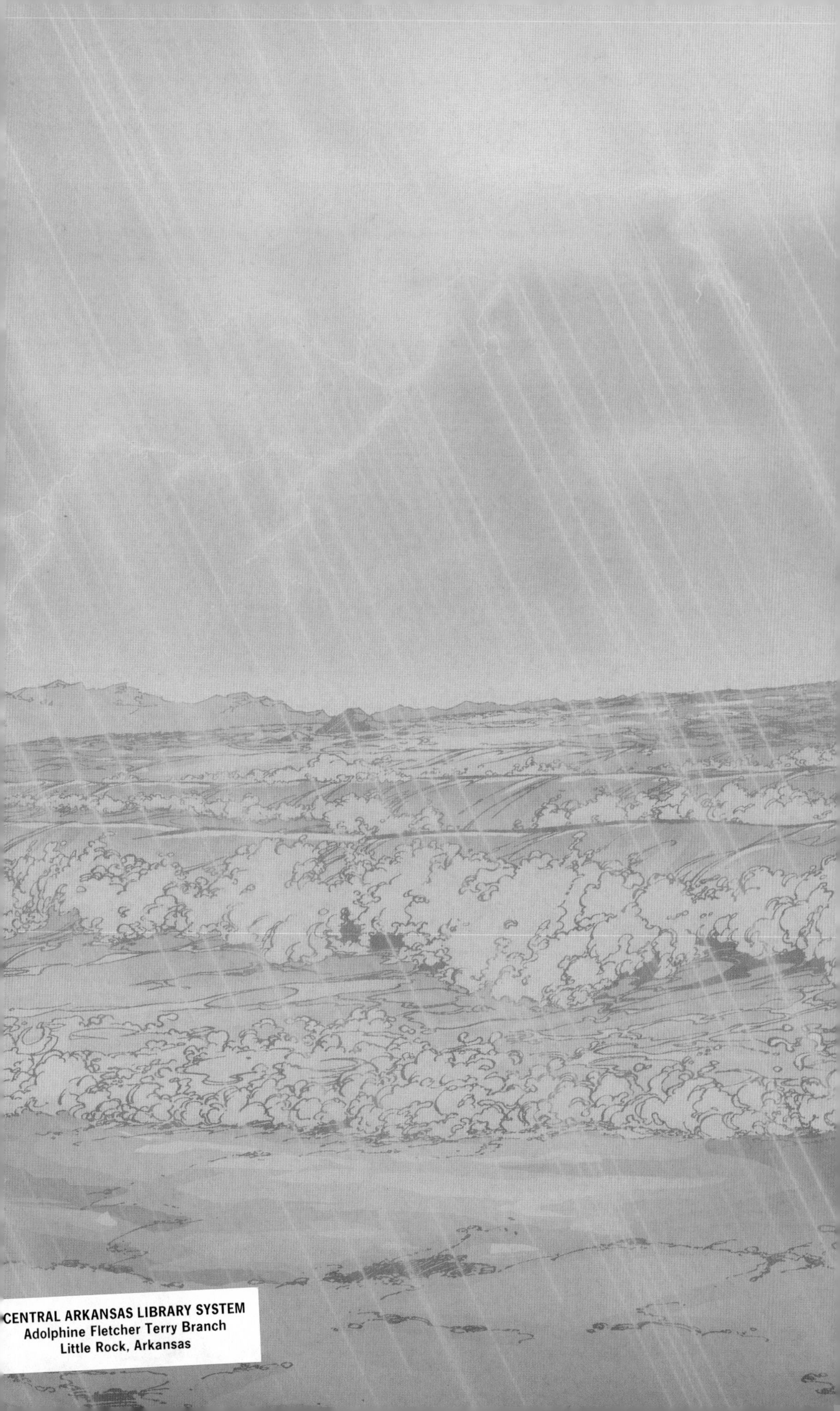

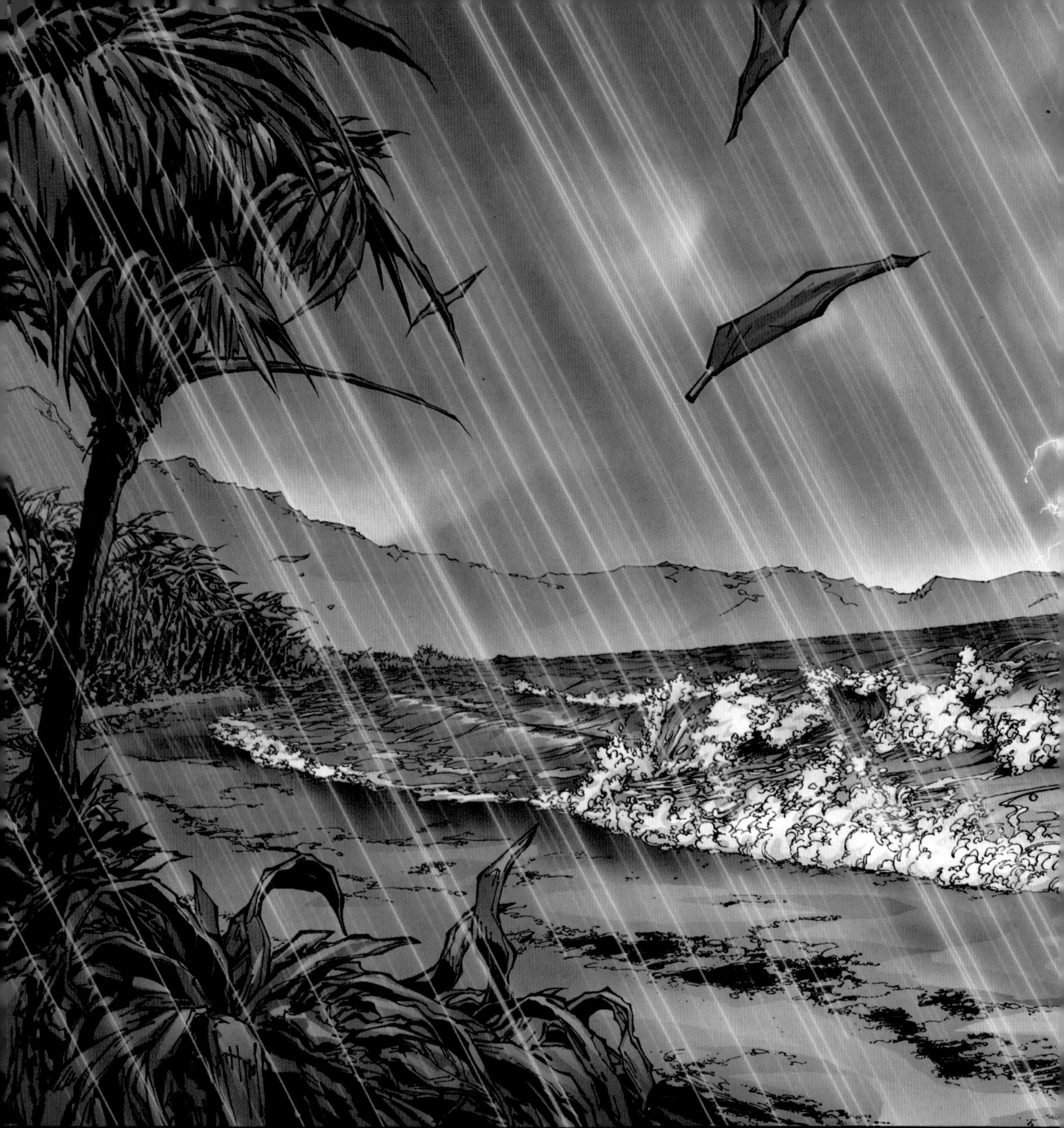

OCTOBER. 1952.

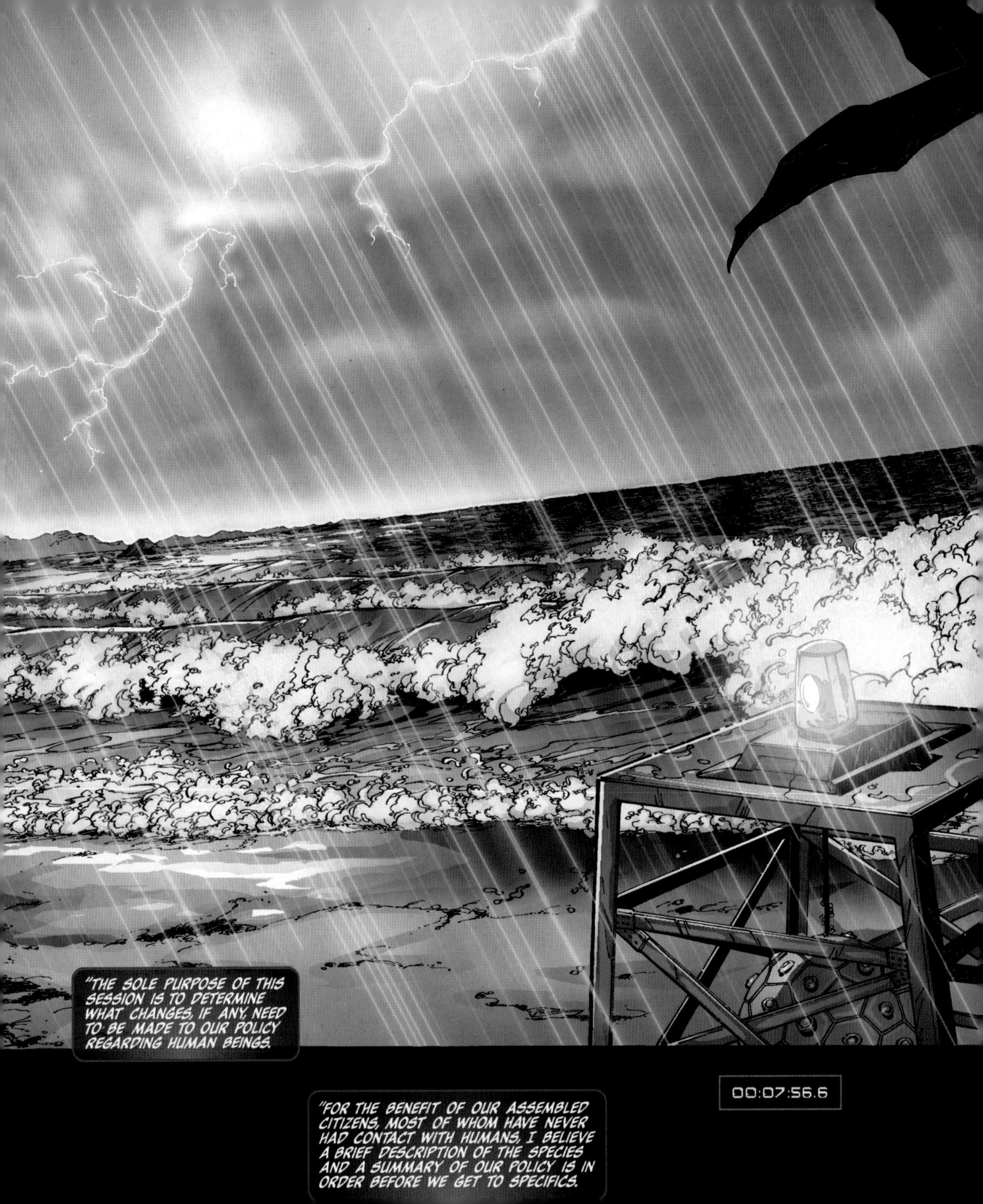
"THE SOLE PURPOSE OF THIS SESSION IS TO DETERMINE WHAT CHANGES, IF ANY, NEED TO BE MADE TO OUR POLICY REGARDING HUMAN BEINGS.
00:07:56.6
"FOR THE BENEFIT OF OUR ASSEMBLED CITIZENS, MOST OF WHOM HAVE NEVER HAD CONTACT WITH HUMANS, I BELIEVE A BRIEF DESCRIPTION OF THE SPECIES AND A SUMMARY OF OUR POLICY IS IN ORDER BEFORE WE GET TO SPECIFICS.

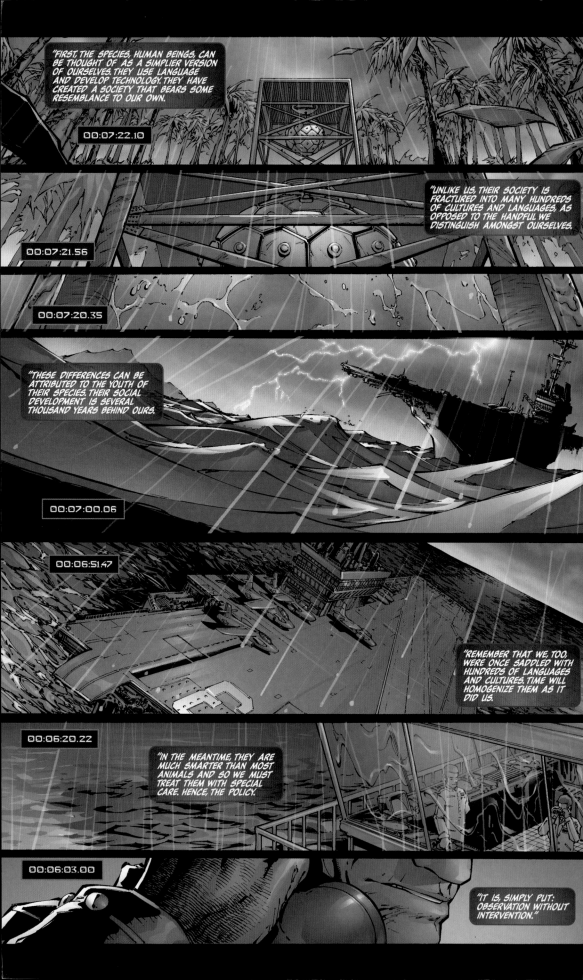

"FIRST, THE SPECIES, HUMAN BEINGS, CAN BE THOUGHT OF AS A SIMPLIER VERSION OF OURSELVES. THEY USE LANGUAGE AND DEVELOP TECHNOLOGY. THEY HAVE CREATED A SOCIETY THAT BEARS SOME RESEMBLANCE TO OUR OWN.

00:07:22.10

00:07:21.56

"UNLIKE US, THEIR SOCIETY IS FRACTURED INTO MANY HUNDREDS OF CULTURES AND LANGUAGES, AS OPPOSED TO THE HANDFUL WE DISTINGUISH AMONGST OURSELVES.

00:07:20.35

"THESE DIFFERENCES CAN BE ATTRIBUTED TO THE YOUTH OF THEIR SPECIES. THEIR SOCIAL DEVELOPMENT IS SEVERAL THOUSAND YEARS BEHIND OURS.

00:07:00.06

00:06:51.47

"REMEMBER THAT WE, TOO, WERE ONCE SADDLED WITH HUNDREDS OF LANGUAGES AND CULTURES. TIME WILL HOMOGENIZE THEM AS IT DID US.

00:06:20.22

"IN THE MEANTIME, THEY ARE MUCH SMARTER THAN MOST ANIMALS AND SO WE MUST TREAT THEM WITH SPECIAL CARE. HENCE, THE POLICY.

00:06:03.00

"IT IS, SIMPLY PUT: OBSERVATION WITHOUT INTERVENTION."

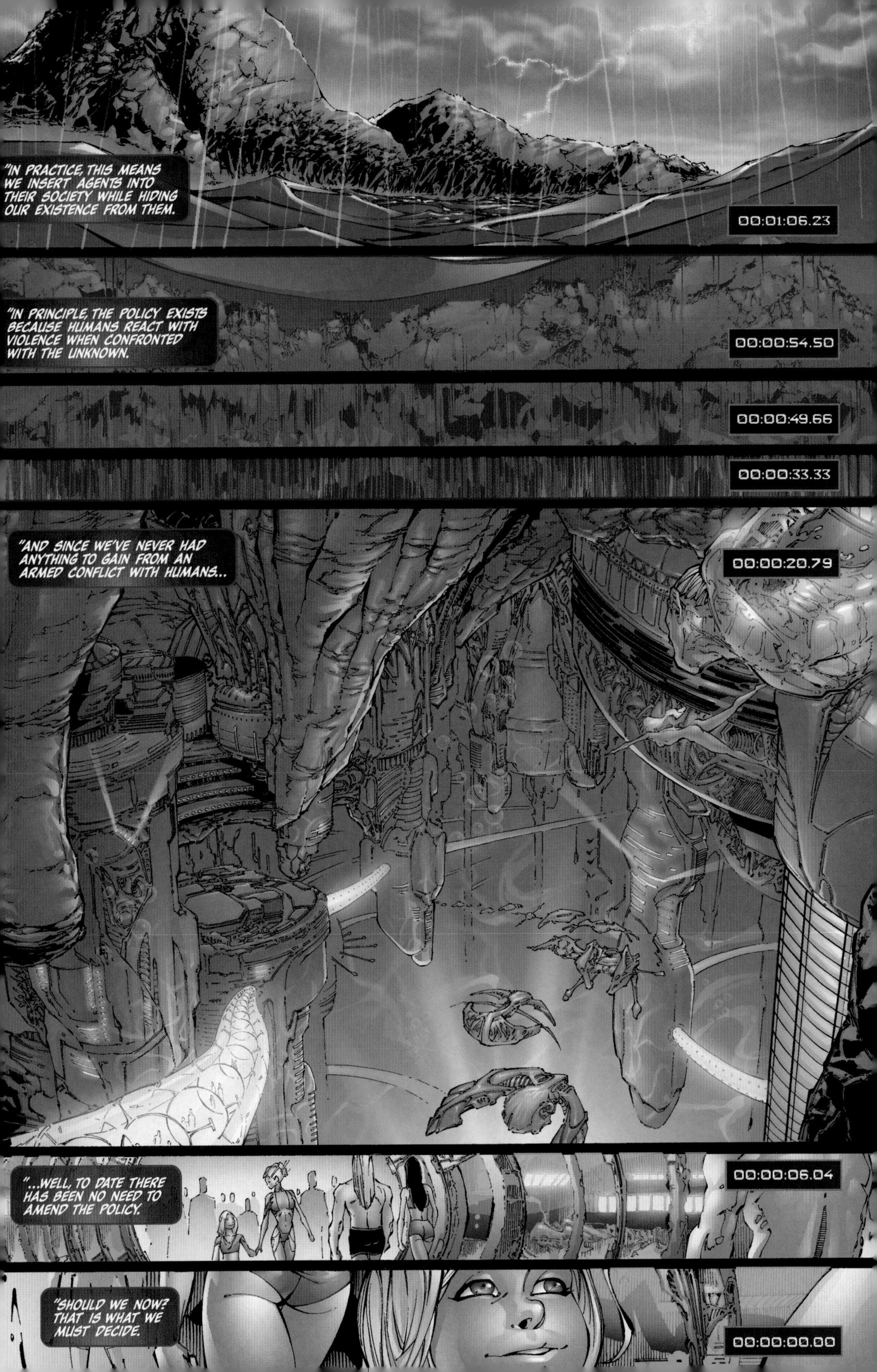
"IN PRACTICE, THIS MEANS WE INSERT AGENTS INTO THEIR SOCIETY WHILE HIDING OUR EXISTENCE FROM THEM.
00:01:06.23
"IN PRINCIPLE, THE POLICY EXISTS BECAUSE HUMANS REACT WITH VIOLENCE WHEN CONFRONTED WITH THE UNKNOWN.
00:00:54.50
00:00:49.66
00:00:33.33
"AND SINCE WE'VE NEVER HAD ANYTHING TO GAIN FROM AN ARMED CONFLICT WITH HUMANS...
00:00:20.79
"...WELL, TO DATE THERE HAS BEEN NO NEED TO AMEND THE POLICY.
00:00:06.04
"SHOULD WE NOW? THAT IS WHAT WE MUST DECIDE.
00:00:00.00

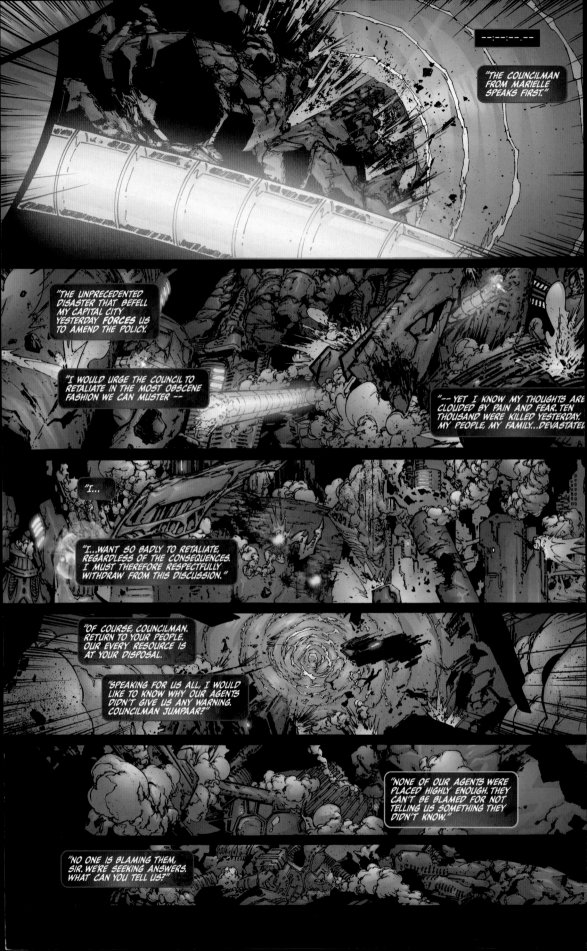

"THE COUNCILMAN FROM MARIELLE SPEAKS FIRST."

"THE UNPRECEDENTED DISASTER THAT BEFELL MY CAPITAL CITY YESTERDAY **FORCES** US TO AMEND THE POLICY.

"I WOULD URGE THE COUNCIL TO RETALIATE IN THE MOST OBSCENE FASHION WE CAN MUSTER --

"-- YET I KNOW MY THOUGHTS ARE CLOUDED BY PAIN AND FEAR. TEN THOUSAND WERE KILLED YESTERDAY. MY PEOPLE, MY FAMILY...DEVASTATED

"I...

"I...WANT SO BADLY TO RETALIATE, REGARDLESS OF THE CONSEQUENCES. I MUST THEREFORE RESPECTFULLY WITHDRAW FROM THIS DISCUSSION."

"OF COURSE, COUNCILMAN. RETURN TO YOUR PEOPLE. OUR EVERY RESOURCE IS AT YOUR DISPOSAL.

"SPEAKING FOR US ALL, I WOULD LIKE TO KNOW WHY OUR AGENTS DIDN'T GIVE US ANY WARNING, COUNCILMAN JUMPAAR?"

"NONE OF OUR AGENTS WERE PLACED HIGHLY ENOUGH. THEY CAN'T BE BLAMED FOR NOT TELLING US SOMETHING THEY DIDN'T KNOW."

"NO ONE IS BLAMING THEM, SIR. WE'RE SEEKING ANSWERS. WHAT CAN YOU TELL US?"

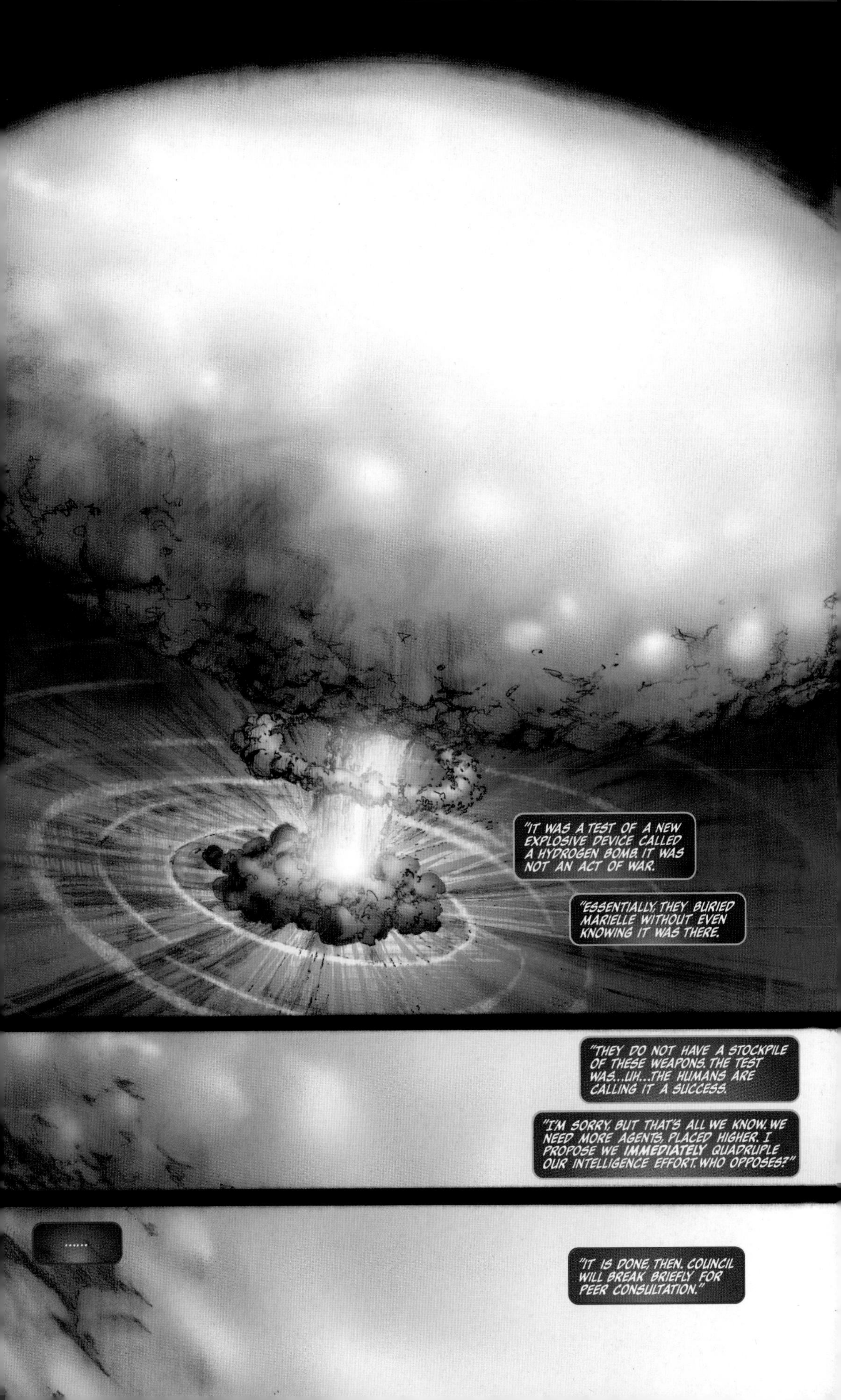
"IT WAS A TEST OF A NEW EXPLOSIVE DEVICE CALLED A HYDROGEN BOMB. IT WAS NOT AN ACT OF WAR.
"ESSENTIALLY, THEY BURIED MARIELLE WITHOUT EVEN KNOWING IT WAS THERE.
"THEY DO NOT HAVE A STOCKPILE OF THESE WEAPONS. THE TEST WAS...UH...THE HUMANS ARE CALLING IT A SUCCESS.
"I'M SORRY, BUT THAT'S ALL WE KNOW. WE NEED MORE AGENTS, PLACED HIGHER. I PROPOSE WE IMMEDIATELY QUADRUPLE OUR INTELLIGENCE EFFORT. WHO OPPOSES?"
......
"IT IS DONE, THEN. COUNCIL WILL BREAK BRIEFLY FOR PEER CONSULTATION."

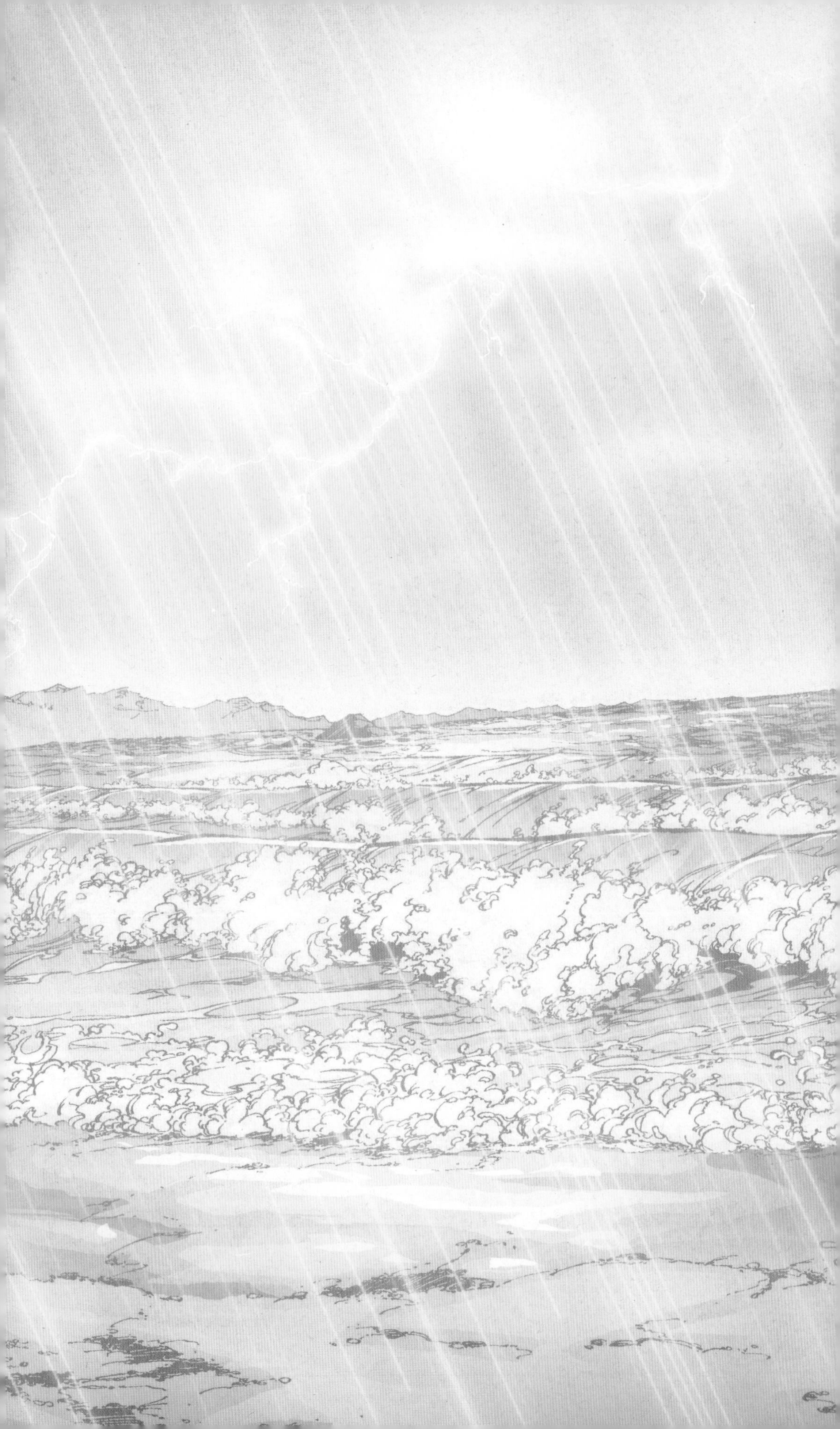

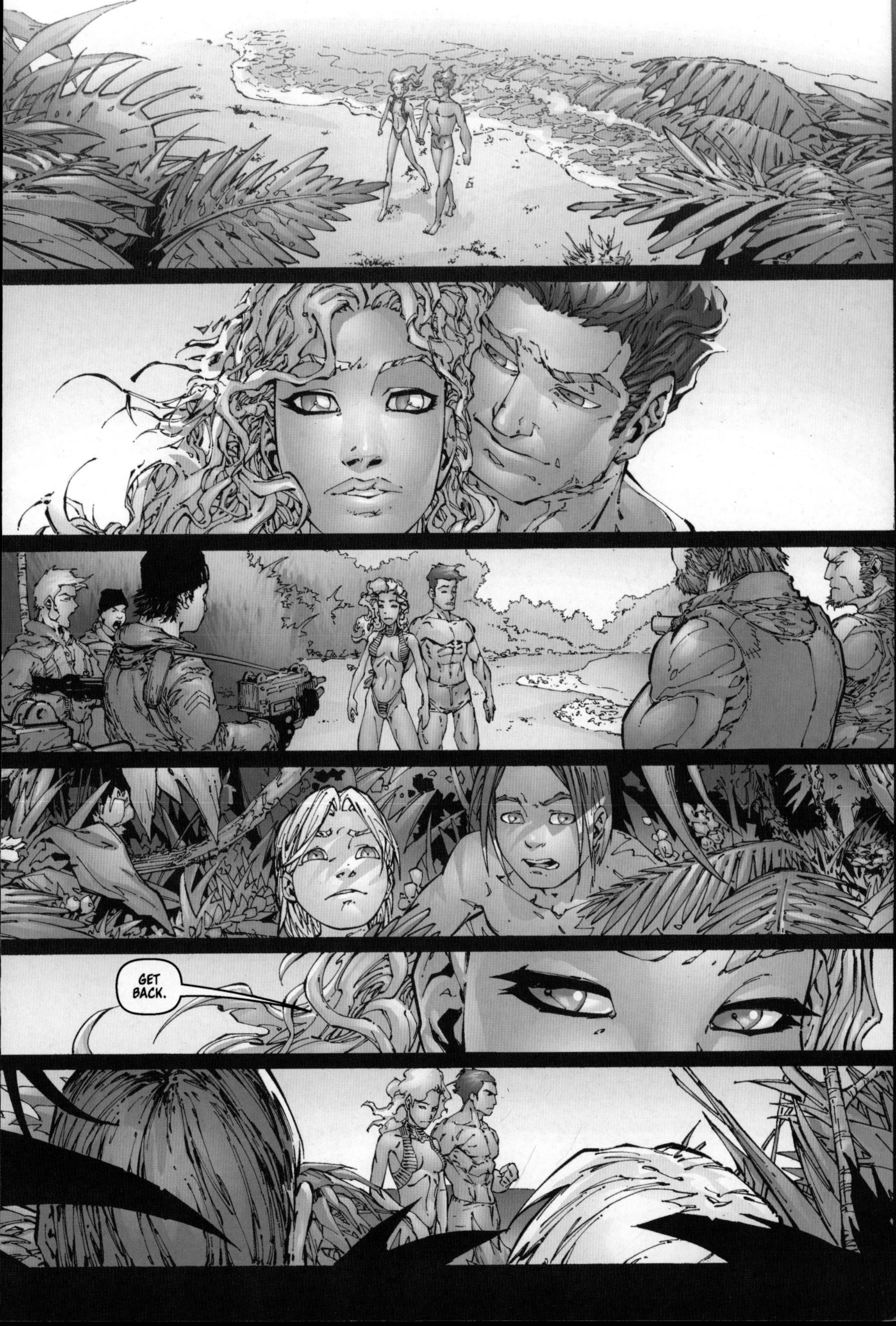
GET BACK.

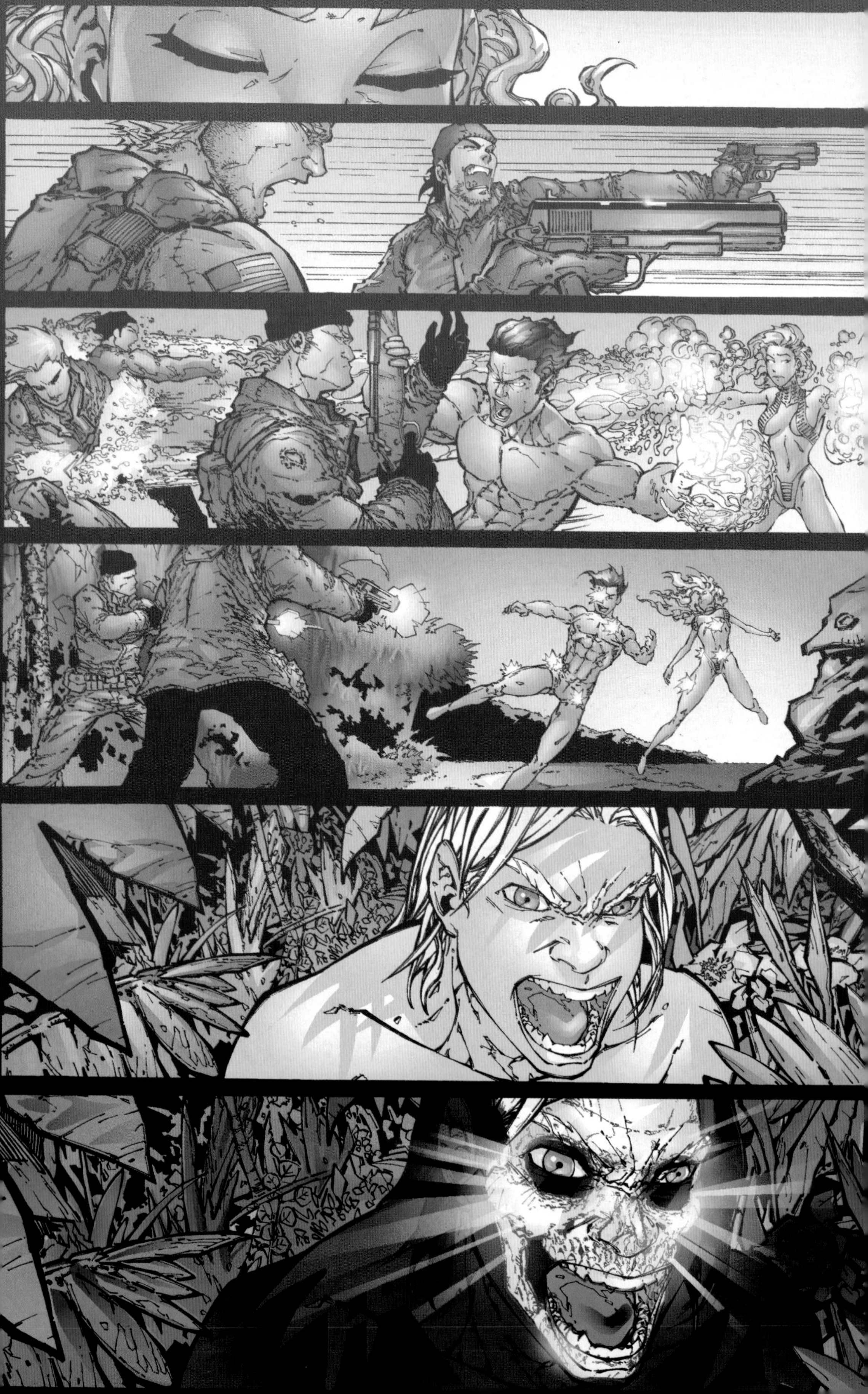

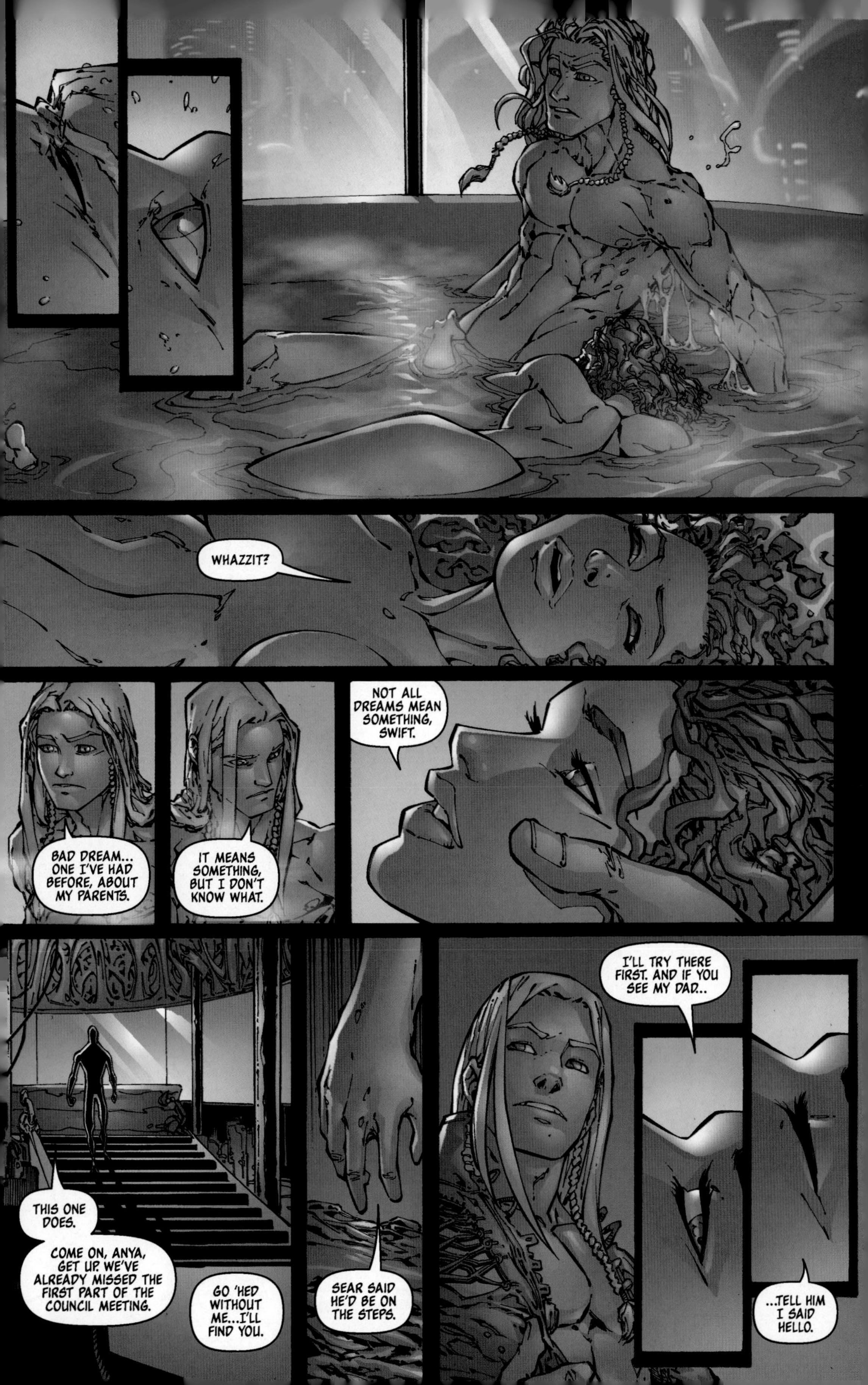
WHAZZIT?
BAD DREAM... ONE I'VE HAD BEFORE, ABOUT MY PARENTS.
IT MEANS SOMETHING, BUT I DON'T KNOW WHAT.
NOT ALL DREAMS MEAN SOMETHING, SWIFT.
THIS ONE DOES.
COME ON, ANYA, GET UP. WE'VE ALREADY MISSED THE FIRST PART OF THE COUNCIL MEETING.
GO 'HED WITHOUT ME...I'LL FIND YOU.
SEAR SAID HE'D BE ON THE STEPS.
I'LL TRY THERE FIRST. AND IF YOU SEE MY DAD...
...TELL HIM I SAID HELLO.

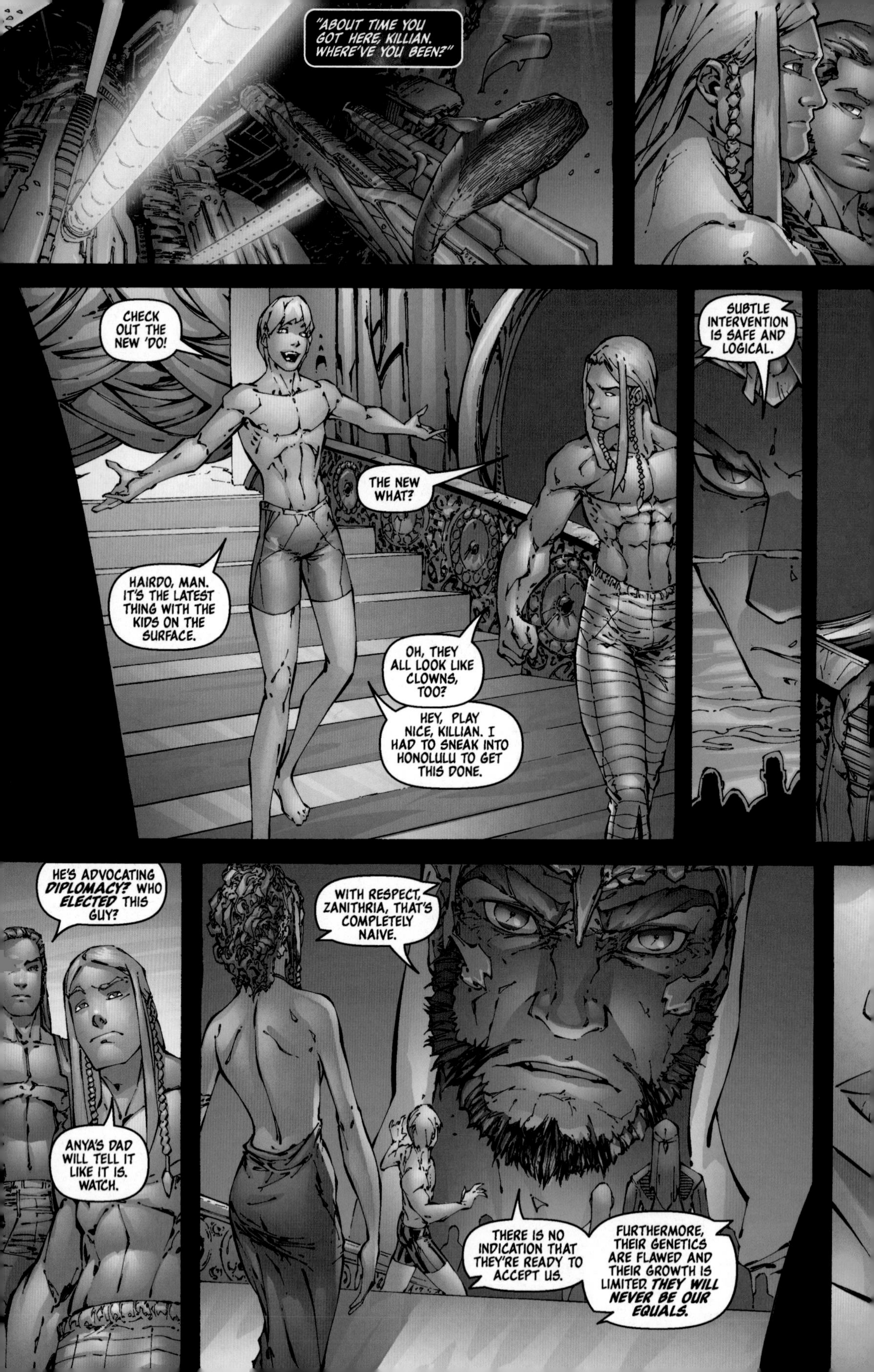
"ABOUT TIME YOU GOT HERE, KILLIAN. WHERE'VE YOU BEEN?"
CHECK OUT THE NEW 'DO!
THE NEW WHAT?
HAIRDO, MAN. IT'S THE LATEST THING WITH THE KIDS ON THE SURFACE.
OH, THEY ALL LOOK LIKE CLOWNS, TOO?
HEY, PLAY NICE, KILLIAN. I HAD TO SNEAK INTO HONOLULU TO GET THIS DONE.
SUBTLE INTERVENTION IS SAFE AND LOGICAL.
HE'S ADVOCATING DIPLOMACY? WHO ELECTED THIS GUY?
ANYA'S DAD WILL TELL IT LIKE IT IS. WATCH.
WITH RESPECT, ZANITHRIA, THAT'S COMPLETELY NAIVE.
THERE IS NO INDICATION THAT THEY'RE READY TO ACCEPT US.
FURTHERMORE, THEIR GENETICS ARE FLAWED AND THEIR GROWTH IS LIMITED. THEY WILL NEVER BE OUR EQUALS.

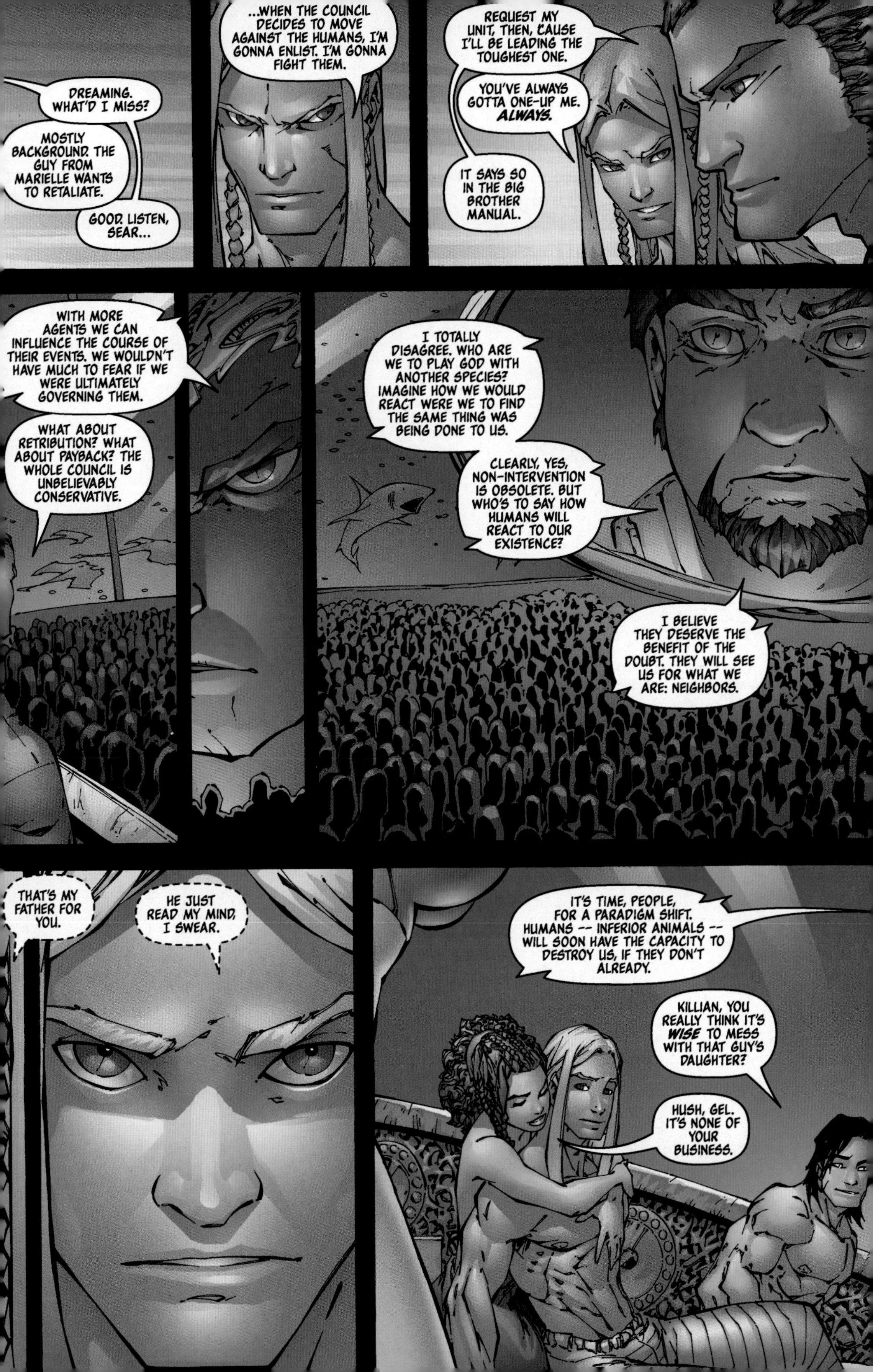
DREAMING. WHAT'D I MISS?
MOSTLY BACKGROUND. THE GUY FROM MARIELLE WANTS TO RETALIATE.
GOOD. LISTEN, SEAR...
...WHEN THE COUNCIL DECIDES TO MOVE AGAINST THE HUMANS, I'M GONNA ENLIST. I'M GONNA FIGHT THEM.
REQUEST MY UNIT, THEN, CAUSE I'LL BE LEADING THE TOUGHEST ONE.
YOU'VE ALWAYS GOTTA ONE-UP ME. ALWAYS.
IT SAYS SO IN THE BIG BROTHER MANUAL.
WITH MORE AGENTS WE CAN INFLUENCE THE COURSE OF THEIR EVENTS. WE WOULDN'T HAVE MUCH TO FEAR IF WE WERE ULTIMATELY GOVERNING THEM.
WHAT ABOUT RETRIBUTION? WHAT ABOUT PAYBACK? THE WHOLE COUNCIL IS UNBELIEVABLY CONSERVATIVE.
I TOTALLY DISAGREE. WHO ARE WE TO PLAY GOD WITH ANOTHER SPECIES? IMAGINE HOW WE WOULD REACT WERE WE TO FIND THE SAME THING WAS BEING DONE TO US.
CLEARLY, YES, NON-INTERVENTION IS OBSOLETE. BUT WHO'S TO SAY HOW HUMANS WILL REACT TO OUR EXISTENCE?
I BELIEVE THEY DESERVE THE BENEFIT OF THE DOUBT. THEY WILL SEE US FOR WHAT WE ARE: NEIGHBORS.
THAT'S MY FATHER FOR YOU.
HE JUST READ MY MIND, I SWEAR.
IT'S TIME, PEOPLE, FOR A PARADIGM SHIFT. HUMANS -- INFERIOR ANIMALS -- WILL SOON HAVE THE CAPACITY TO DESTROY US, IF THEY DON'T ALREADY.
KILLIAN, YOU REALLY THINK IT'S WISE TO MESS WITH THAT GUY'S DAUGHTER?
HUSH, GEL. IT'S NONE OF YOUR BUSINESS.

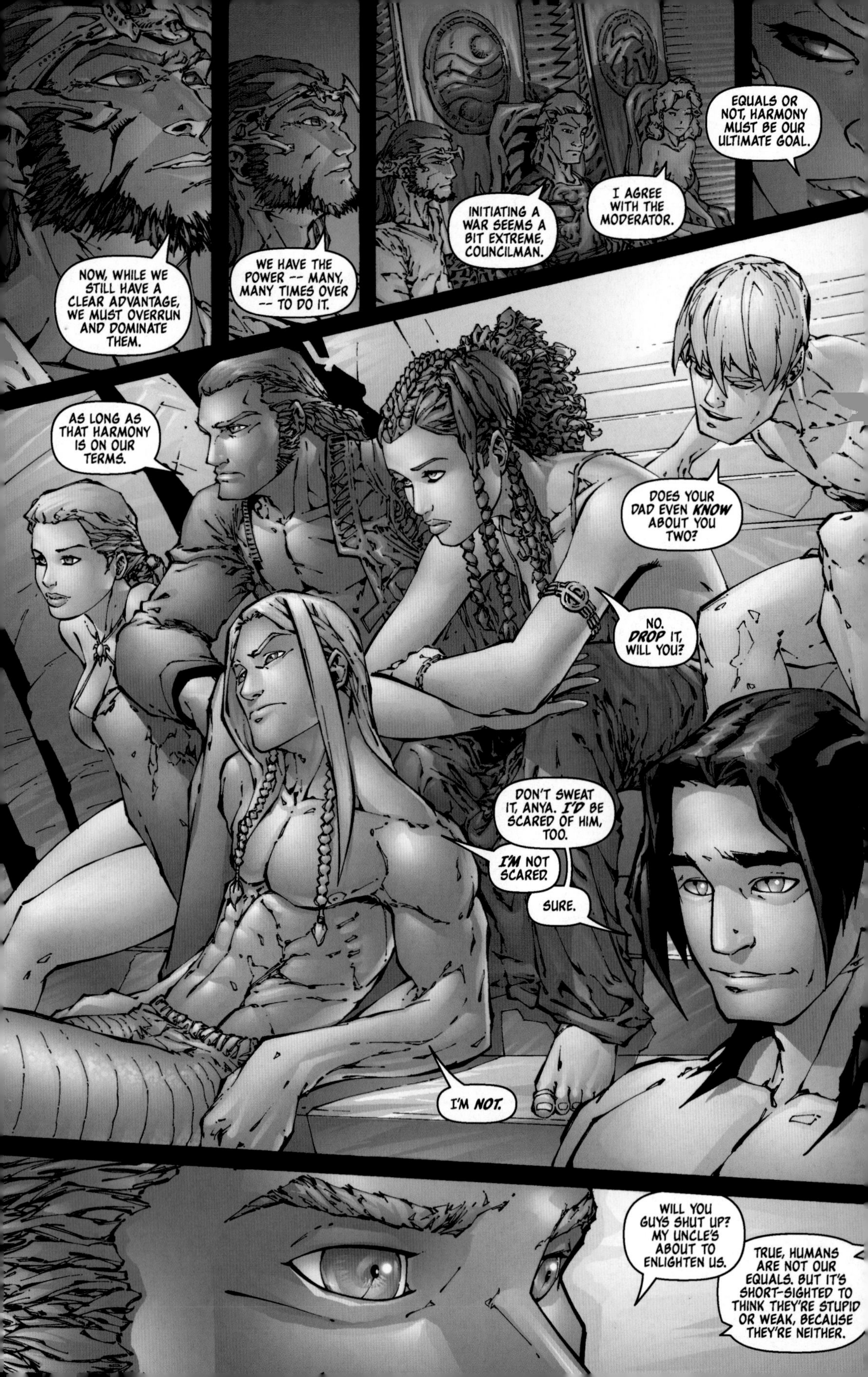
NOW, WHILE WE STILL HAVE A CLEAR ADVANTAGE, WE MUST OVERRUN AND DOMINATE THEM.
WE HAVE THE POWER -- MANY, MANY TIMES OVER -- TO DO IT.
INITIATING A WAR SEEMS A BIT EXTREME, COUNCILMAN.
I AGREE WITH THE MODERATOR.
EQUALS OR NOT, HARMONY MUST BE OUR ULTIMATE GOAL.
AS LONG AS THAT HARMONY IS ON OUR TERMS.
DOES YOUR DAD EVEN KNOW ABOUT YOU TWO?
NO. DROP IT, WILL YOU?
DON'T SWEAT IT, ANYA. I'D BE SCARED OF HIM, TOO.
I'M NOT SCARED.
SURE.
I'M NOT.
WILL YOU GUYS SHUT UP? MY UNCLE'S ABOUT TO ENLIGHTEN US.
TRUE, HUMANS ARE NOT OUR EQUALS. BUT IT'S SHORT-SIGHTED TO THINK THEY'RE STUPID OR WEAK, BECAUSE THEY'RE NEITHER.

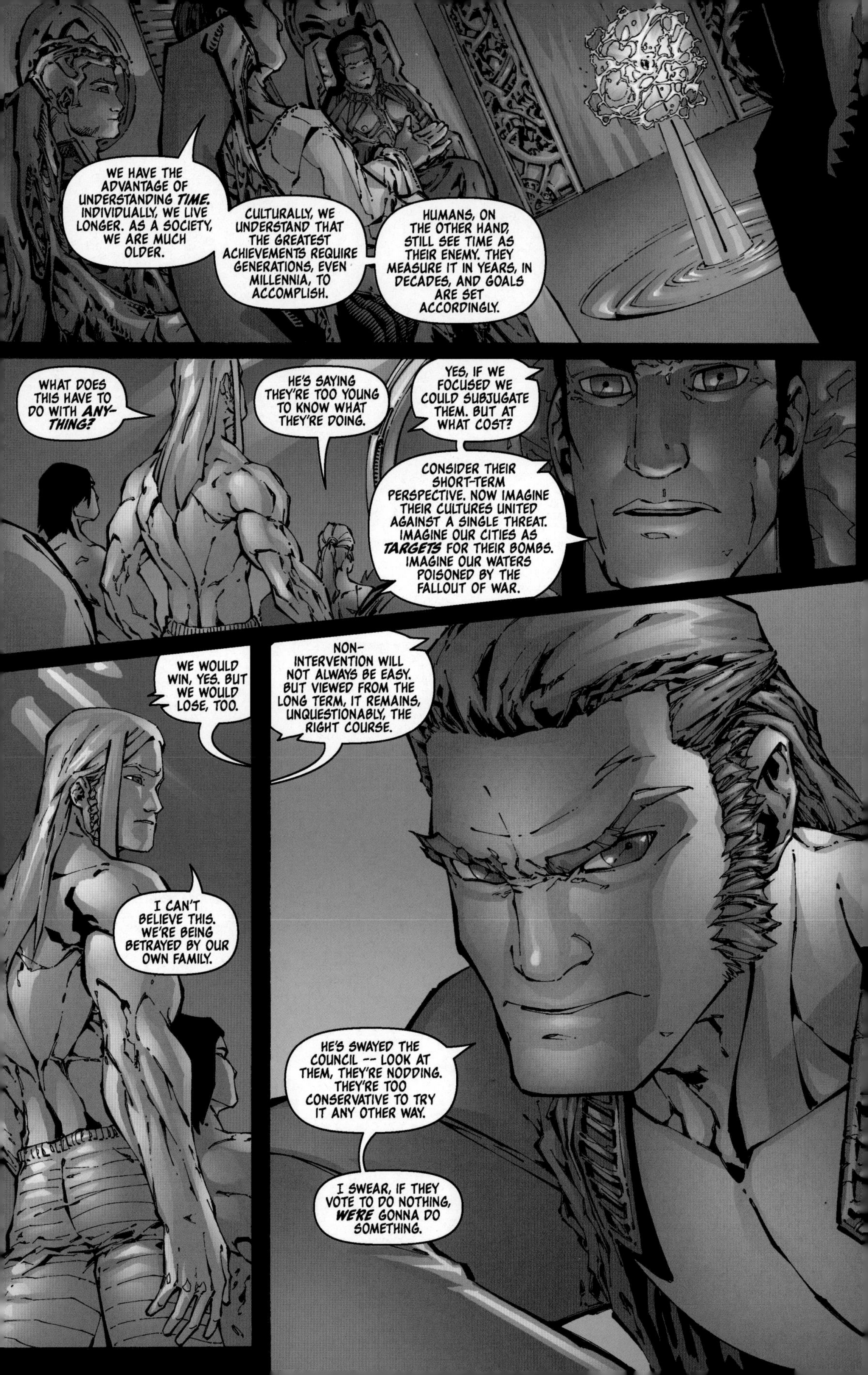
WE HAVE THE ADVANTAGE OF UNDERSTANDING *TIME.* INDIVIDUALLY, WE LIVE LONGER. AS A SOCIETY, WE ARE MUCH OLDER.
CULTURALLY, WE UNDERSTAND THAT THE GREATEST ACHIEVEMENTS REQUIRE GENERATIONS, EVEN MILLENNIA, TO ACCOMPLISH.
HUMANS, ON THE OTHER HAND, STILL SEE TIME AS THEIR ENEMY. THEY MEASURE IT IN YEARS, IN DECADES, AND GOALS ARE SET ACCORDINGLY.
WHAT DOES THIS HAVE TO DO WITH *ANY-THING?*
HE'S SAYING THEY'RE TOO YOUNG TO KNOW WHAT THEY'RE DOING.
YES, IF WE FOCUSED WE COULD SUBJUGATE THEM. BUT AT WHAT COST?
CONSIDER THEIR SHORT-TERM PERSPECTIVE. NOW IMAGINE THEIR CULTURES UNITED AGAINST A SINGLE THREAT. IMAGINE OUR CITIES AS *TARGETS* FOR THEIR BOMBS. IMAGINE OUR WATERS POISONED BY THE FALLOUT OF WAR.
WE WOULD WIN, YES. BUT WE WOULD LOSE, TOO.
NON-INTERVENTION WILL NOT ALWAYS BE EASY. BUT VIEWED FROM THE LONG TERM, IT REMAINS, UNQUESTIONABLY, THE RIGHT COURSE.
I CAN'T BELIEVE THIS. WE'RE BEING BETRAYED BY OUR OWN FAMILY.
HE'S SWAYED THE COUNCIL -- LOOK AT THEM, THEY'RE NODDING. THEY'RE TOO CONSERVATIVE TO TRY IT ANY OTHER WAY.
I SWEAR, IF THEY VOTE TO DO NOTHING, *WE'RE* GONNA DO SOMETHING.

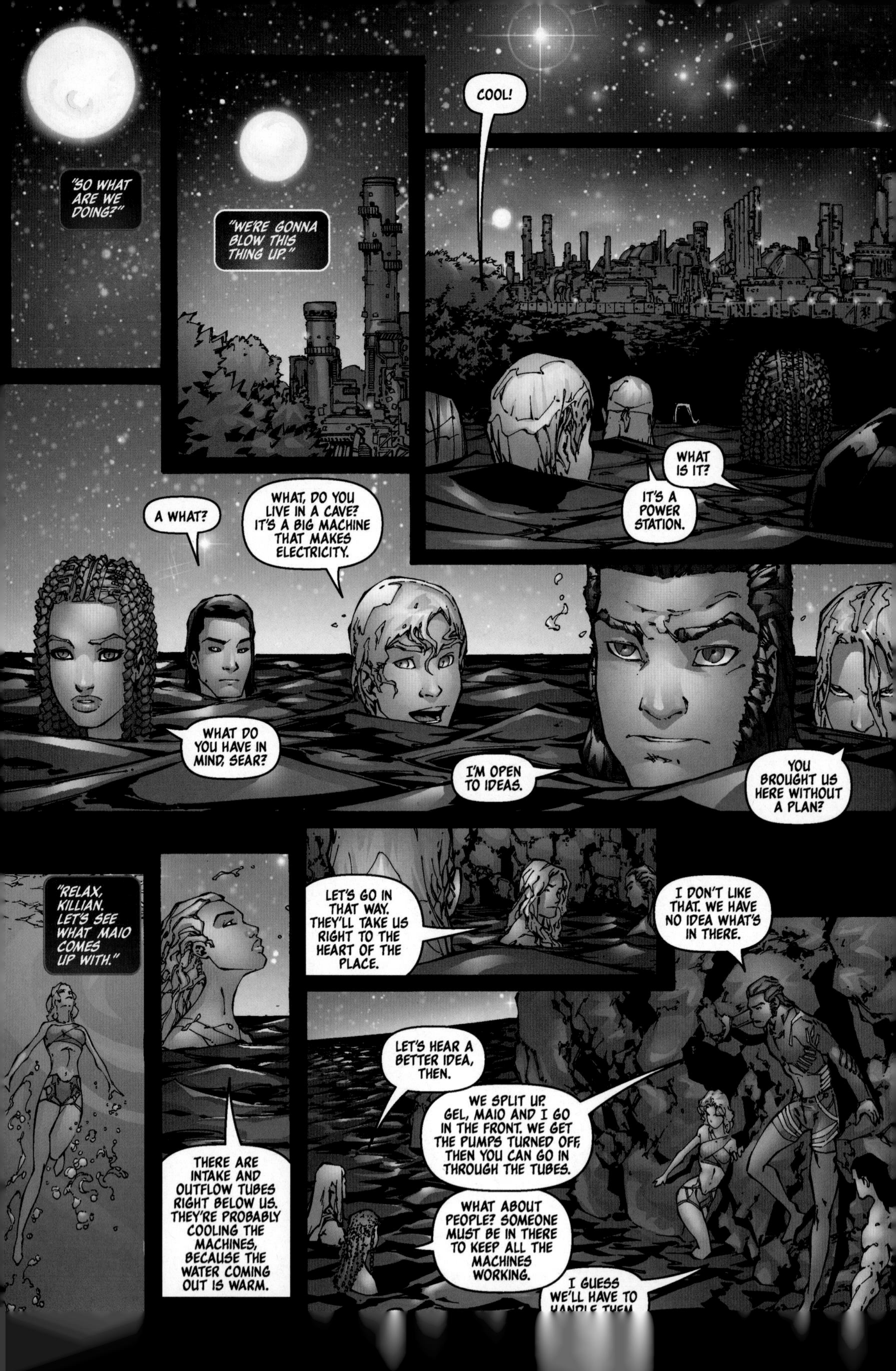
"SO WHAT ARE WE DOING?"
"WE'RE GONNA BLOW THIS THING UP."
COOL!
WHAT IS IT?
IT'S A POWER STATION.
A WHAT?
WHAT, DO YOU LIVE IN A CAVE? IT'S A BIG MACHINE THAT MAKES ELECTRICITY.
WHAT DO YOU HAVE IN MIND, SEAR?
I'M OPEN TO IDEAS.
YOU BROUGHT US HERE WITHOUT A PLAN?
"RELAX, KILLIAN. LET'S SEE WHAT MAIO COMES UP WITH."
THERE ARE INTAKE AND OUTFLOW TUBES RIGHT BELOW US. THEY'RE PROBABLY COOLING THE MACHINES, BECAUSE THE WATER COMING OUT IS WARM.
LET'S GO IN THAT WAY. THEY'LL TAKE US RIGHT TO THE HEART OF THE PLACE.
I DON'T LIKE THAT. WE HAVE NO IDEA WHAT'S IN THERE.
LET'S HEAR A BETTER IDEA, THEN.
WE SPLIT UP. GEL, MAIO AND I GO IN THE FRONT. WE GET THE PUMPS TURNED OFF, THEN YOU CAN GO IN THROUGH THE TUBES.
WHAT ABOUT PEOPLE? SOMEONE MUST BE IN THERE TO KEEP ALL THE MACHINES WORKING.
I GUESS WE'LL HAVE TO

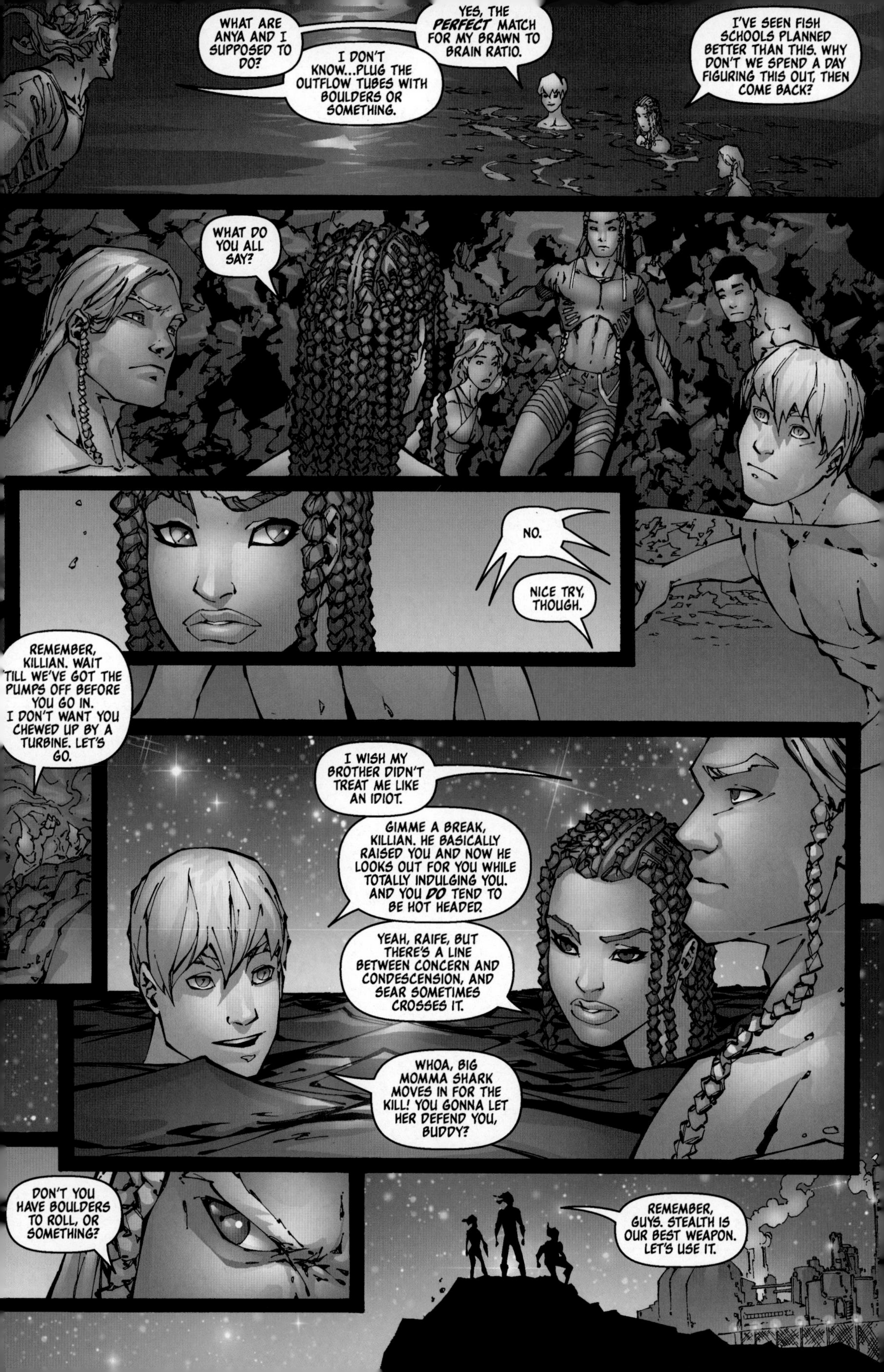
WHAT ARE ANYA AND I SUPPOSED TO DO?
I DON'T KNOW...PLUG THE OUTFLOW TUBES WITH BOULDERS OR SOMETHING.
YES, THE PERFECT MATCH FOR MY BRAWN TO BRAIN RATIO.
I'VE SEEN FISH SCHOOLS PLANNED BETTER THAN THIS. WHY DON'T WE SPEND A DAY FIGURING THIS OUT, THEN COME BACK?
WHAT DO YOU ALL SAY?
NO.
NICE TRY, THOUGH.
REMEMBER, KILLIAN. WAIT 'TILL WE'VE GOT THE PUMPS OFF BEFORE YOU GO IN. I DON'T WANT YOU CHEWED UP BY A TURBINE. LET'S GO.
I WISH MY BROTHER DIDN'T TREAT ME LIKE AN IDIOT.
GIMME A BREAK, KILLIAN. HE BASICALLY RAISED YOU AND NOW HE LOOKS OUT FOR YOU WHILE TOTALLY INDULGING YOU. AND YOU DO TEND TO BE HOT HEADED.
YEAH, RAIFE, BUT THERE'S A LINE BETWEEN CONCERN AND CONDESCENSION, AND SEAR SOMETIMES CROSSES IT.
WHOA, BIG MOMMA SHARK MOVES IN FOR THE KILL! YOU GONNA LET HER DEFEND YOU, BUDDY?
DON'T YOU HAVE BOULDERS TO ROLL, OR SOMETHING?
REMEMBER, GUYS. STEALTH IS OUR BEST WEAPON. LET'S USE IT.

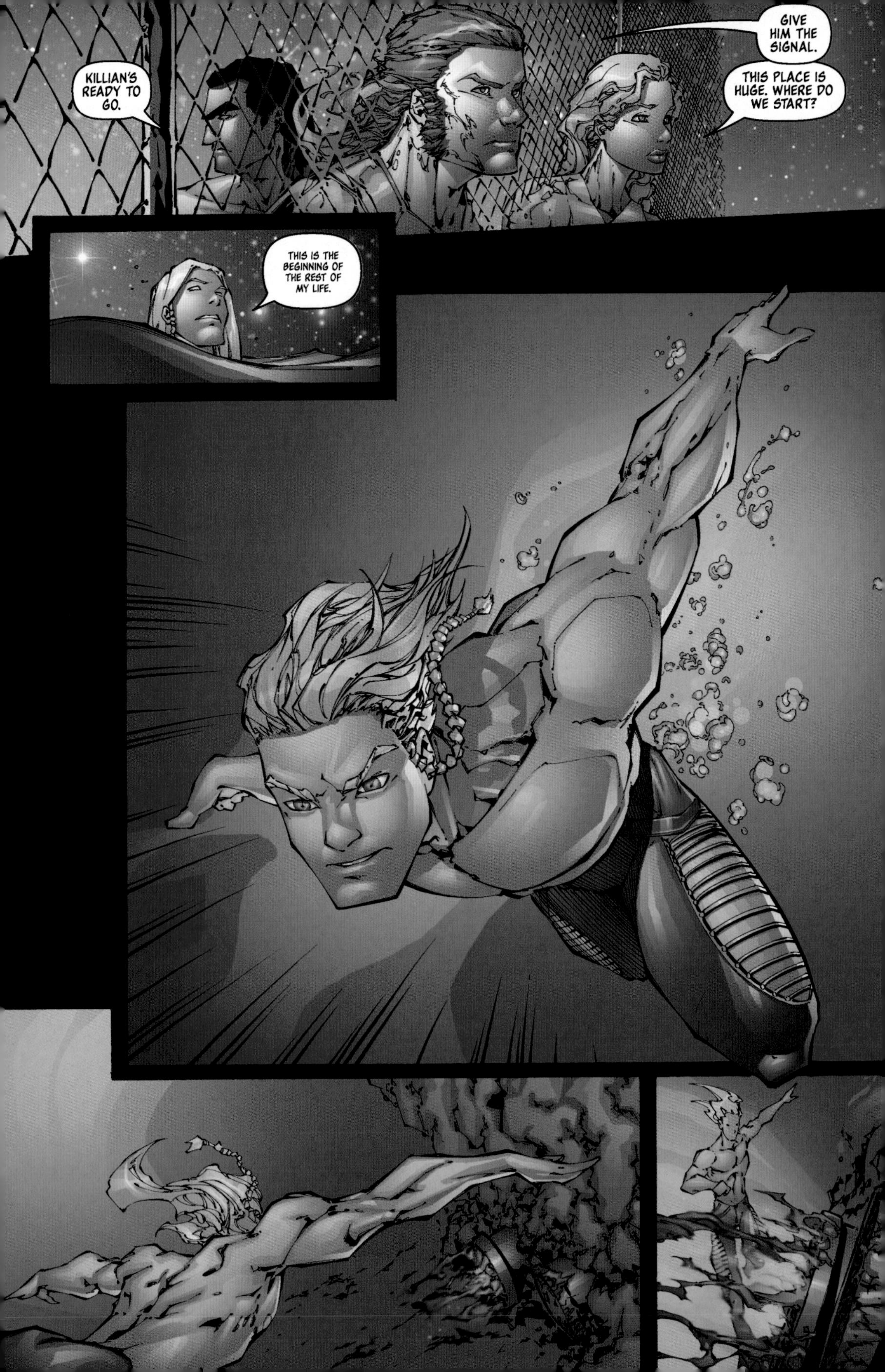
KILLIAN'S READY TO GO.
GIVE HIM THE SIGNAL.
THIS PLACE IS HUGE. WHERE DO WE START?
THIS IS THE BEGINNING OF THE REST OF MY LIFE.

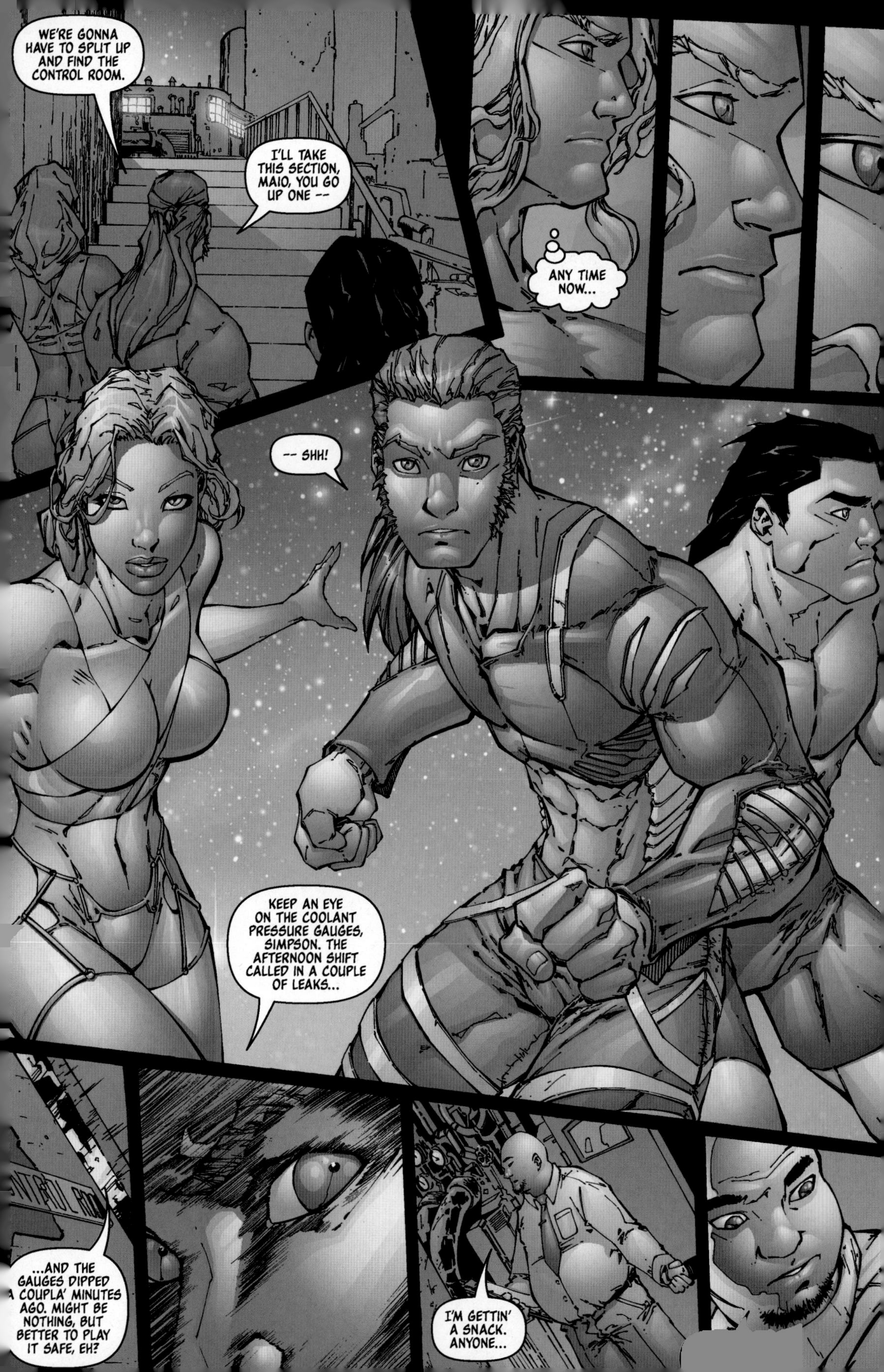
WE'RE GONNA HAVE TO SPLIT UP AND FIND THE CONTROL ROOM.
I'LL TAKE THIS SECTION, MAIO, YOU GO UP ONE --
ANY TIME NOW...
-- SHH!
KEEP AN EYE ON THE COOLANT PRESSURE GAUGES, SIMPSON. THE AFTERNOON SHIFT CALLED IN A COUPLE OF LEAKS...
...AND THE GAUGES DIPPED A COUPLA' MINUTES AGO. MIGHT BE NOTHING, BUT BETTER TO PLAY IT SAFE, EH?
I'M GETTIN' A SNACK. ANYONE...

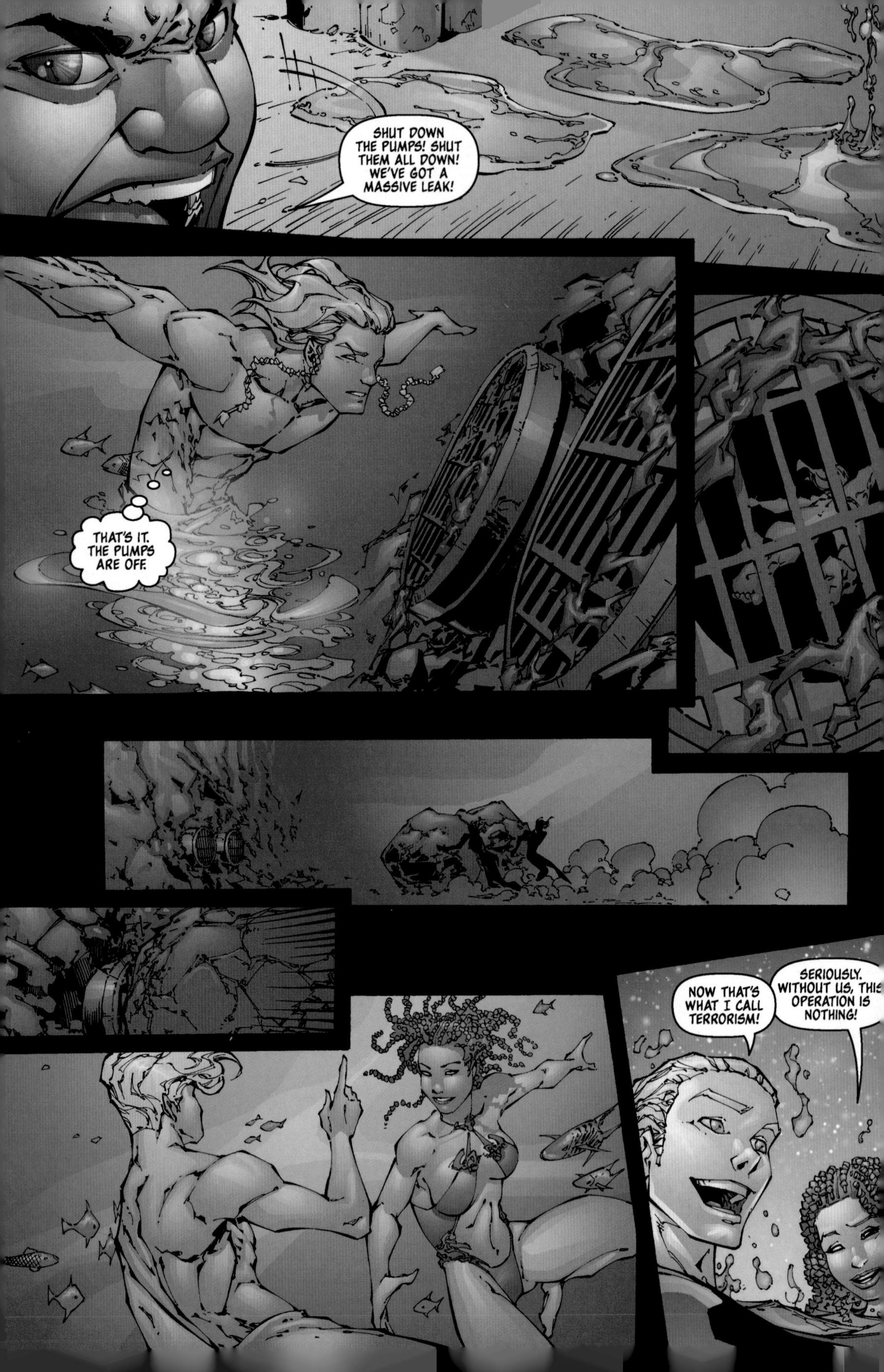
SHUT DOWN THE PUMPS! SHUT THEM ALL DOWN! WE'VE GOT A MASSIVE LEAK!
THAT'S IT. THE PUMPS ARE OFF.
NOW THAT'S WHAT I CALL TERRORISM!
SERIOUSLY. WITHOUT US, THIS OPERATION IS NOTHING!

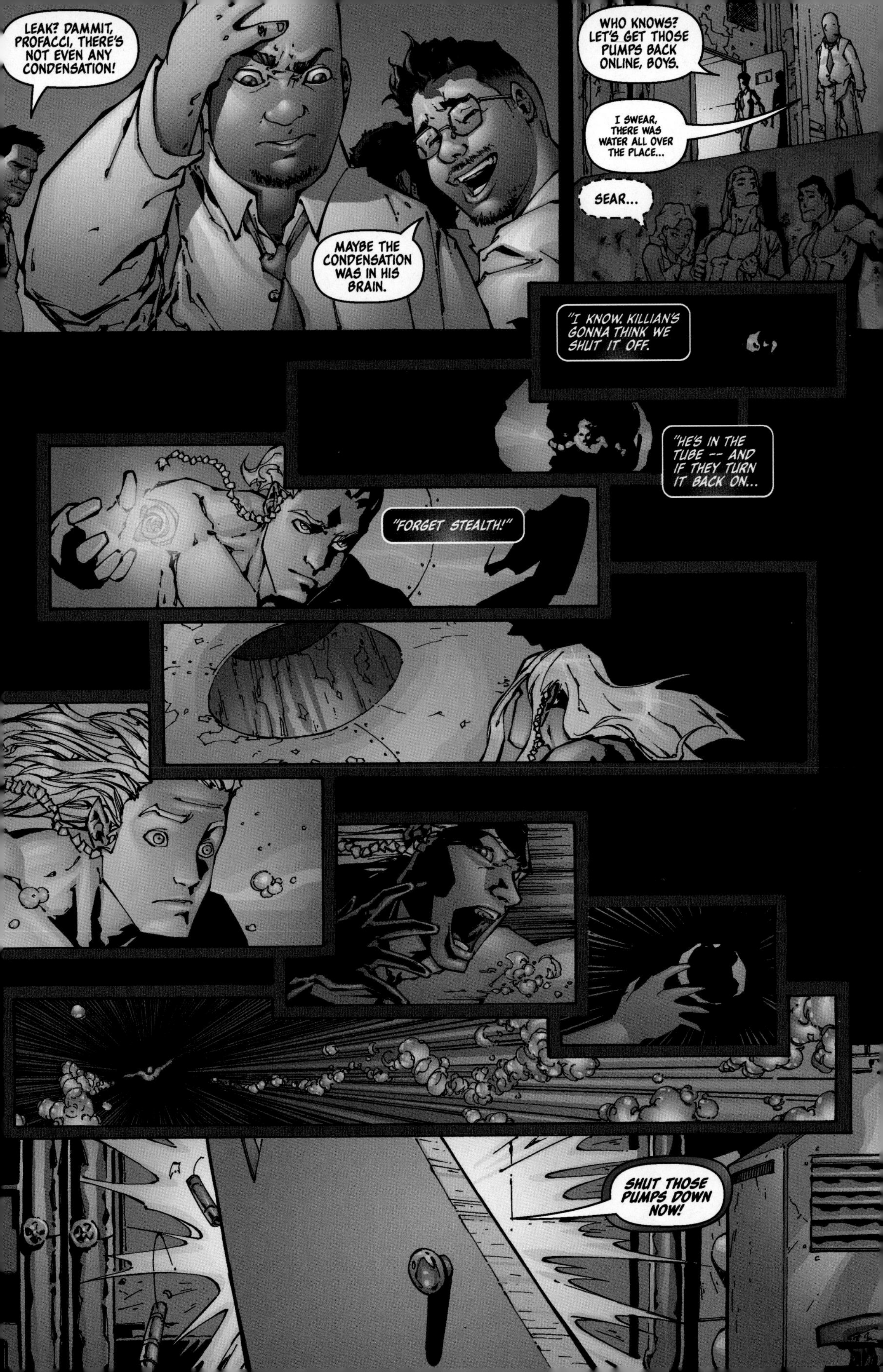
LEAK? DAMMIT, PROFACCI, THERE'S NOT EVEN ANY CONDENSATION!
MAYBE THE CONDENSATION WAS IN HIS BRAIN.
WHO KNOWS? LET'S GET THOSE PUMPS BACK ONLINE, BOYS.
I SWEAR, THERE WAS WATER ALL OVER THE PLACE...
SEAR...
"I KNOW. KILLIAN'S GONNA THINK WE SHUT IT OFF.
"HE'S IN THE TUBE -- AND IF THEY TURN IT BACK ON...
"FORGET STEALTH!"
SHUT THOSE PUMPS DOWN NOW!

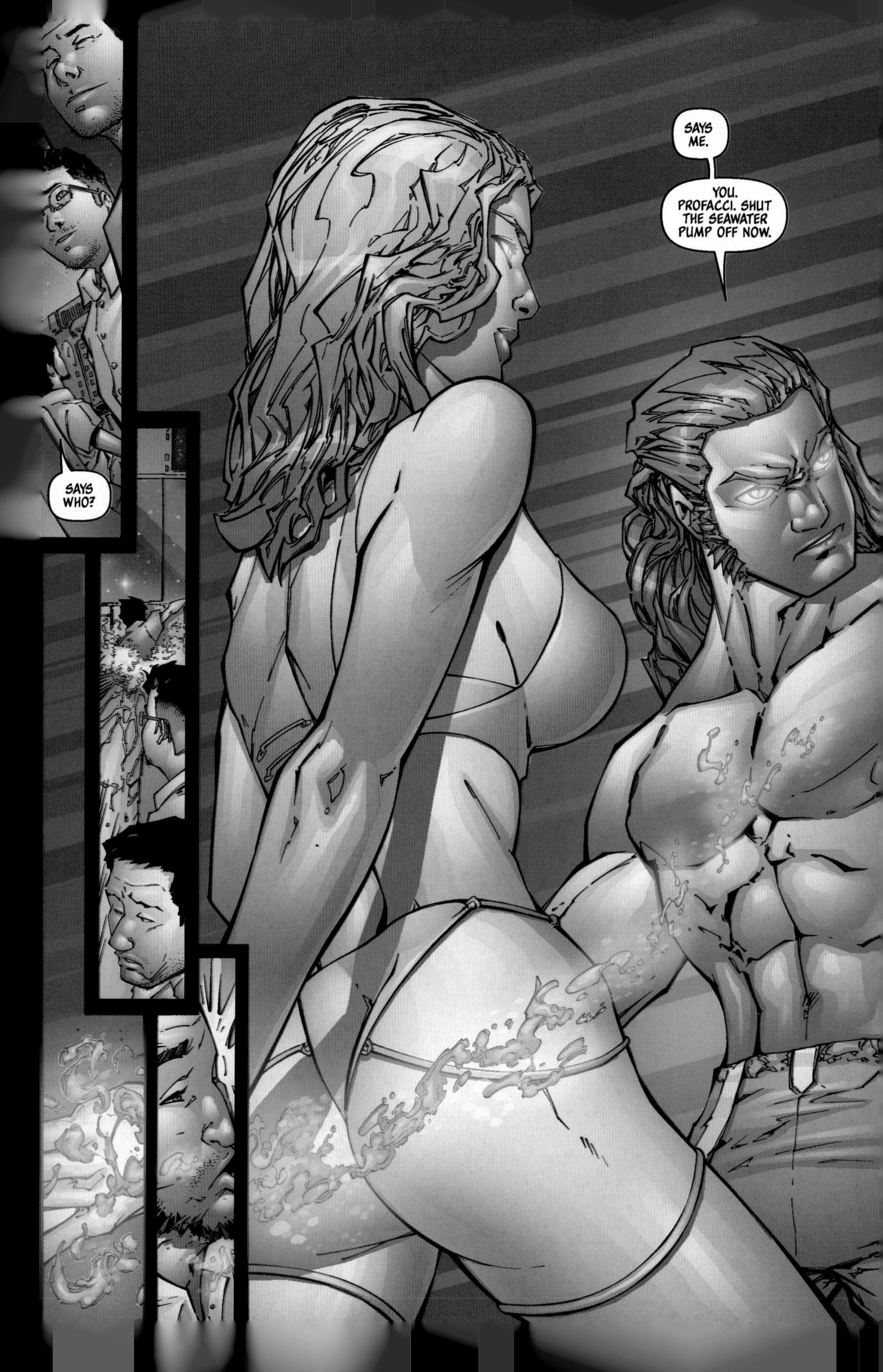
SAYS WHO?
SAYS ME.
YOU. PROFACCI. SHUT THE SEAWATER PUMP OFF NOW.

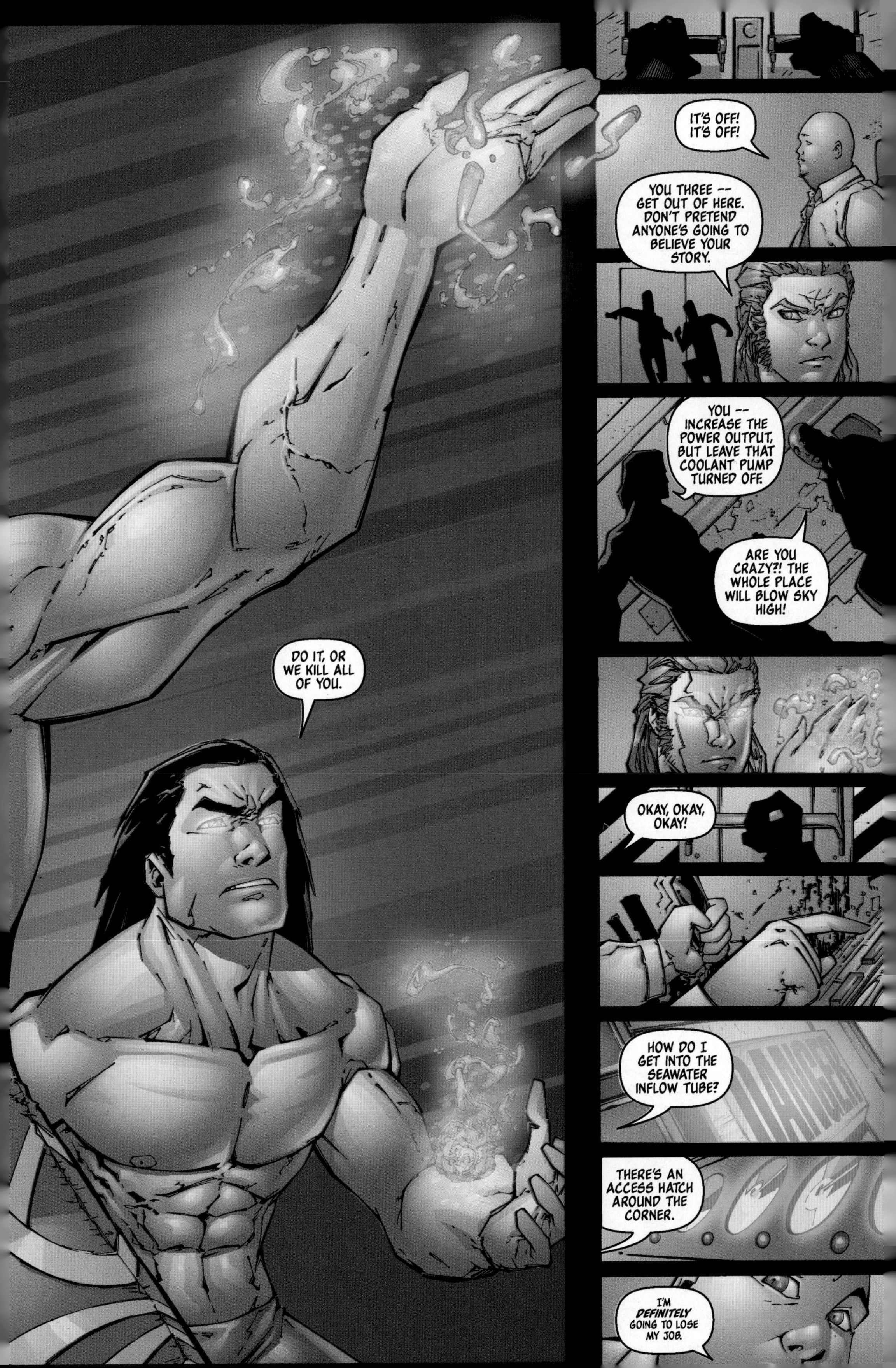
IT'S OFF! IT'S OFF!
YOU THREE -- GET OUT OF HERE. DON'T PRETEND ANYONE'S GOING TO BELIEVE YOUR STORY.
YOU -- INCREASE THE POWER OUTPUT, BUT LEAVE THAT COOLANT PUMP TURNED OFF.
ARE YOU CRAZY?! THE WHOLE PLACE WILL BLOW SKY HIGH!
DO IT, OR WE KILL ALL OF YOU.
OKAY, OKAY, OKAY!
HOW DO I GET INTO THE SEAWATER INFLOW TUBE?
THERE'S AN ACCESS HATCH AROUND THE CORNER.
I'M DEFINITELY GOING TO LOSE MY JOB.

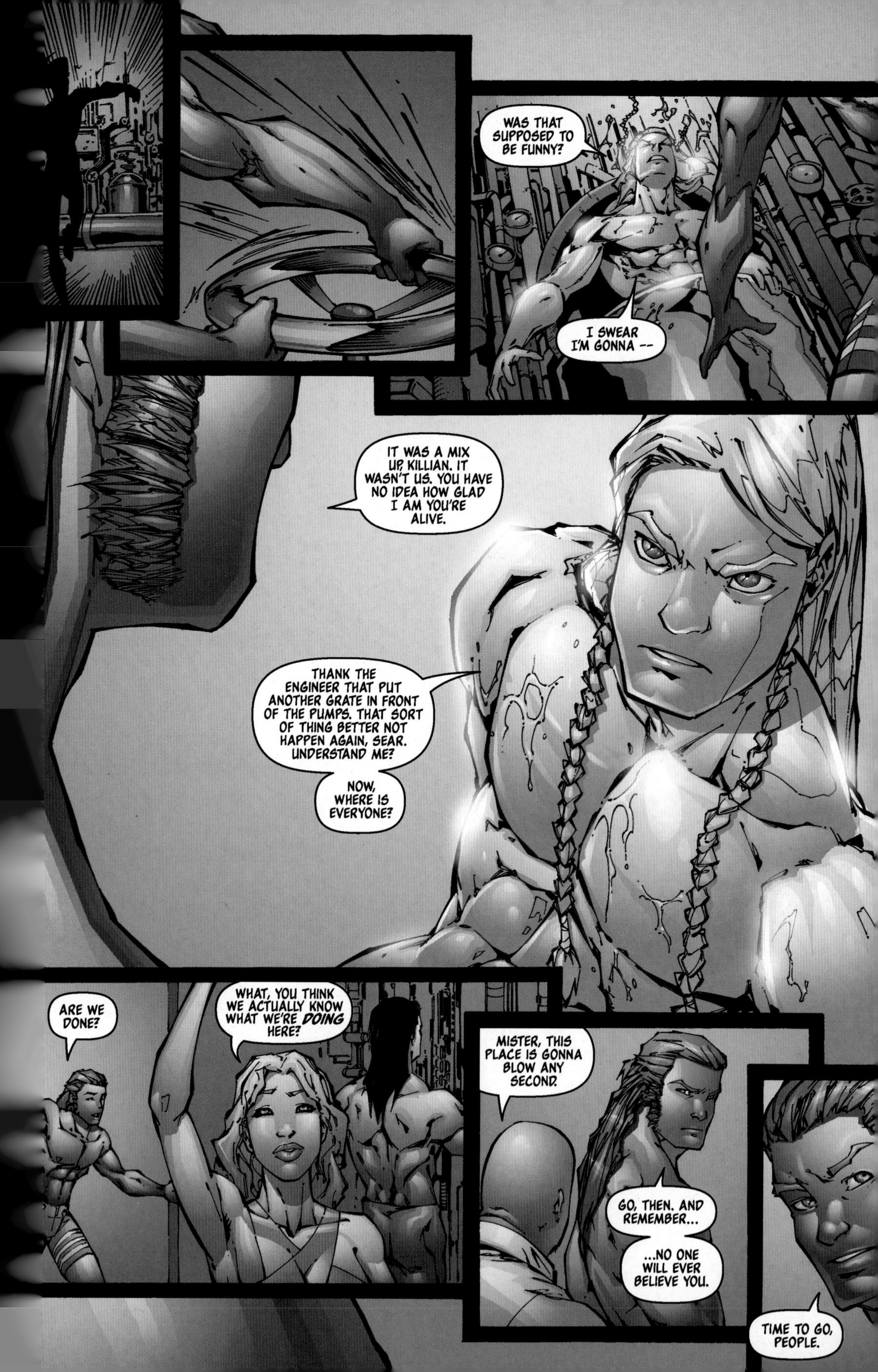
WAS THAT SUPPOSED TO BE FUNNY?
I SWEAR I'M GONNA --
IT WAS A MIX UP, KILLIAN. IT WASN'T US. YOU HAVE NO IDEA HOW GLAD I AM YOU'RE ALIVE.
THANK THE ENGINEER THAT PUT ANOTHER GRATE IN FRONT OF THE PUMPS. THAT SORT OF THING BETTER NOT HAPPEN AGAIN, SEAR. UNDERSTAND ME?
NOW, WHERE IS EVERYONE?
ARE WE DONE?
WHAT, YOU THINK WE ACTUALLY KNOW WHAT WE'RE *DOING* HERE?
MISTER, THIS PLACE IS GONNA BLOW ANY SECOND.
GO, THEN. AND REMEMBER...
...NO ONE WILL EVER BELIEVE YOU.
TIME TO GO, PEOPLE.

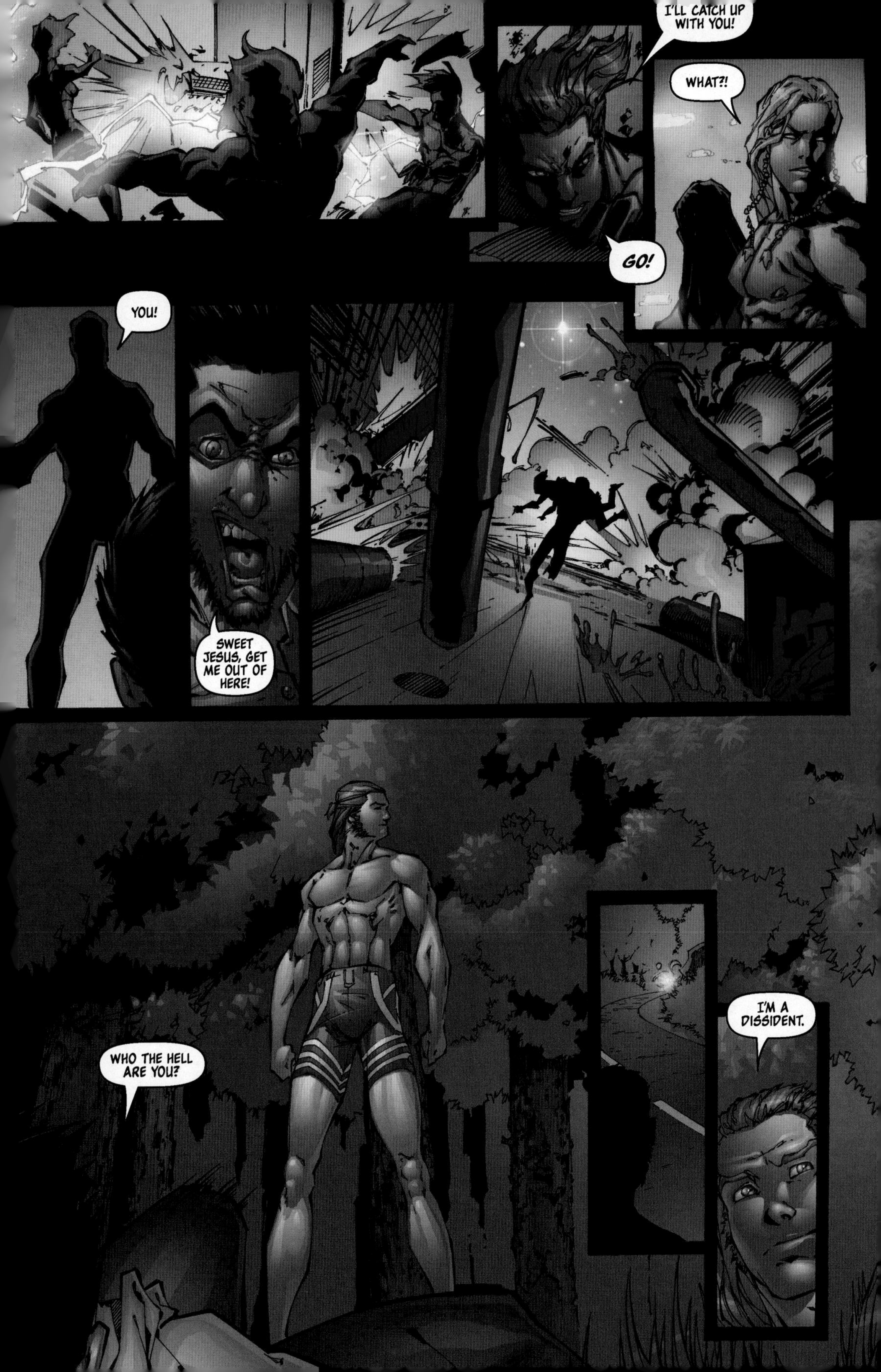
I'LL CATCH UP WITH YOU!
GO!
WHAT?!
YOU!
SWEET JESUS, GET ME OUT OF HERE!
WHO THE HELL ARE YOU?
I'M A DISSIDENT.

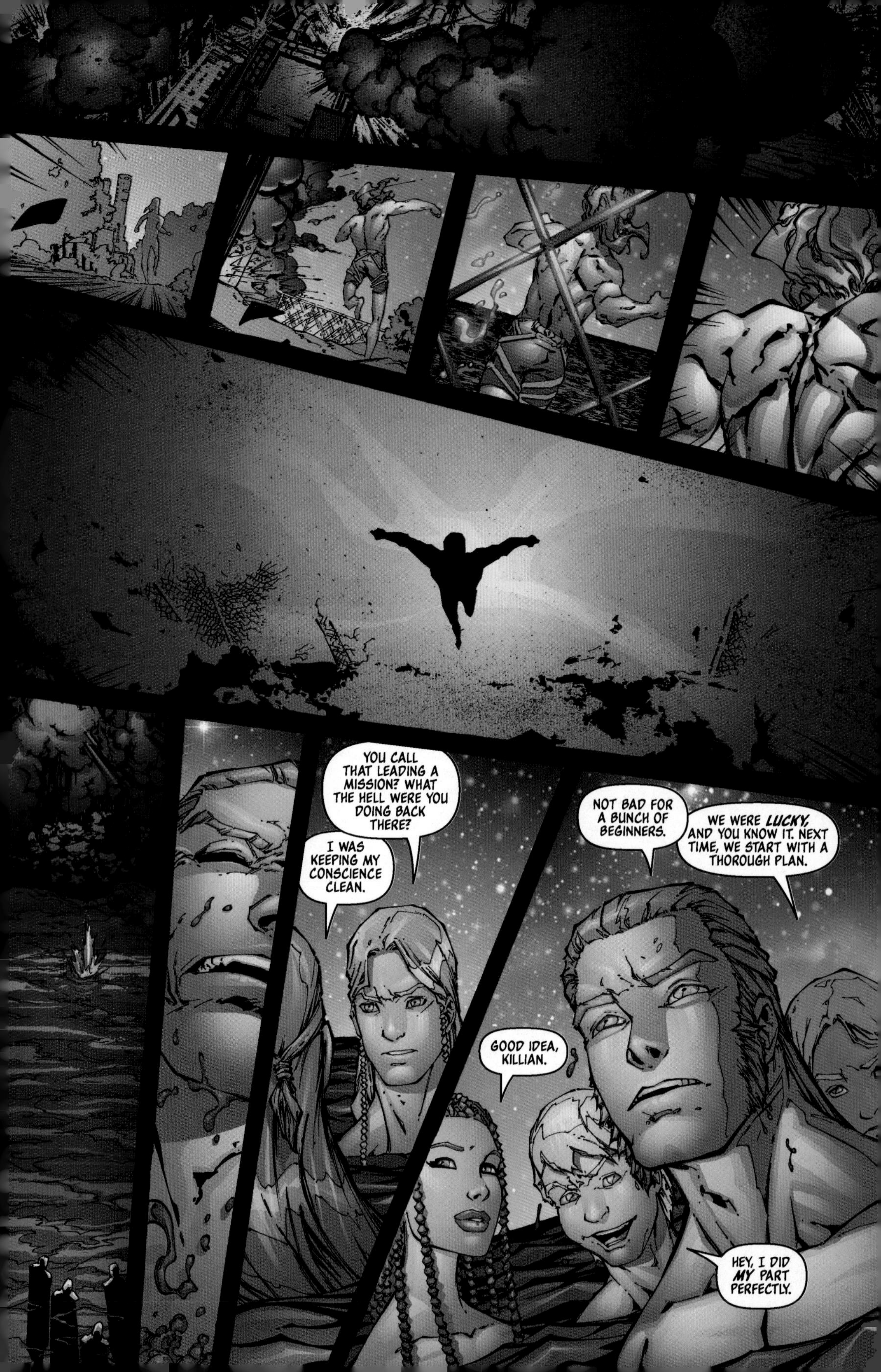
YOU CALL THAT LEADING A MISSION? WHAT THE HELL WERE YOU DOING BACK THERE?
I WAS KEEPING MY CONSCIENCE CLEAN.
NOT BAD FOR A BUNCH OF BEGINNERS.
WE WERE LUCKY, AND YOU KNOW IT. NEXT TIME, WE START WITH A THOROUGH PLAN.
GOOD IDEA, KILLIAN.
HEY, I DID MY PART PERFECTLY.

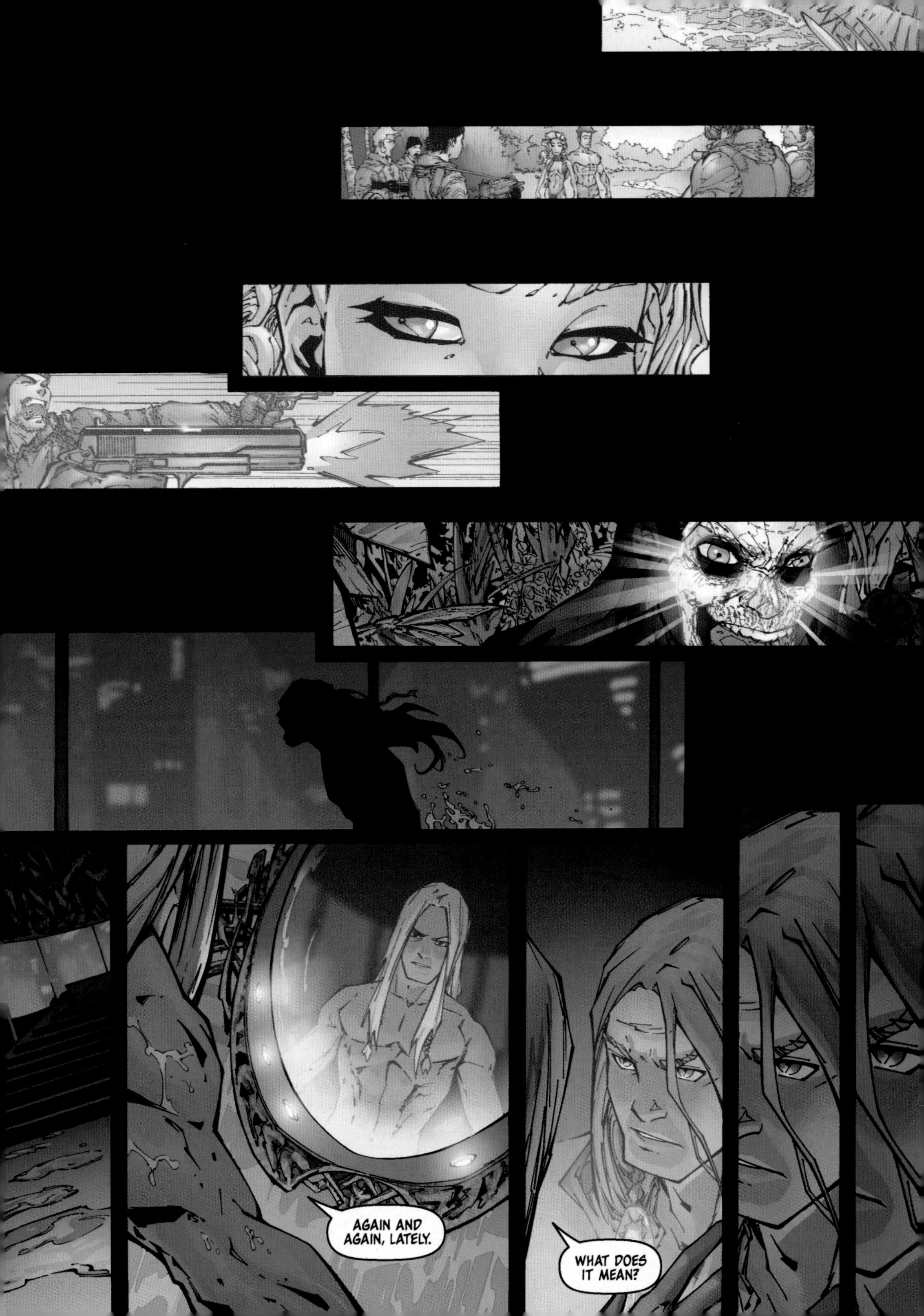
AGAIN AND AGAIN, LATELY.
WHAT DOES IT MEAN?

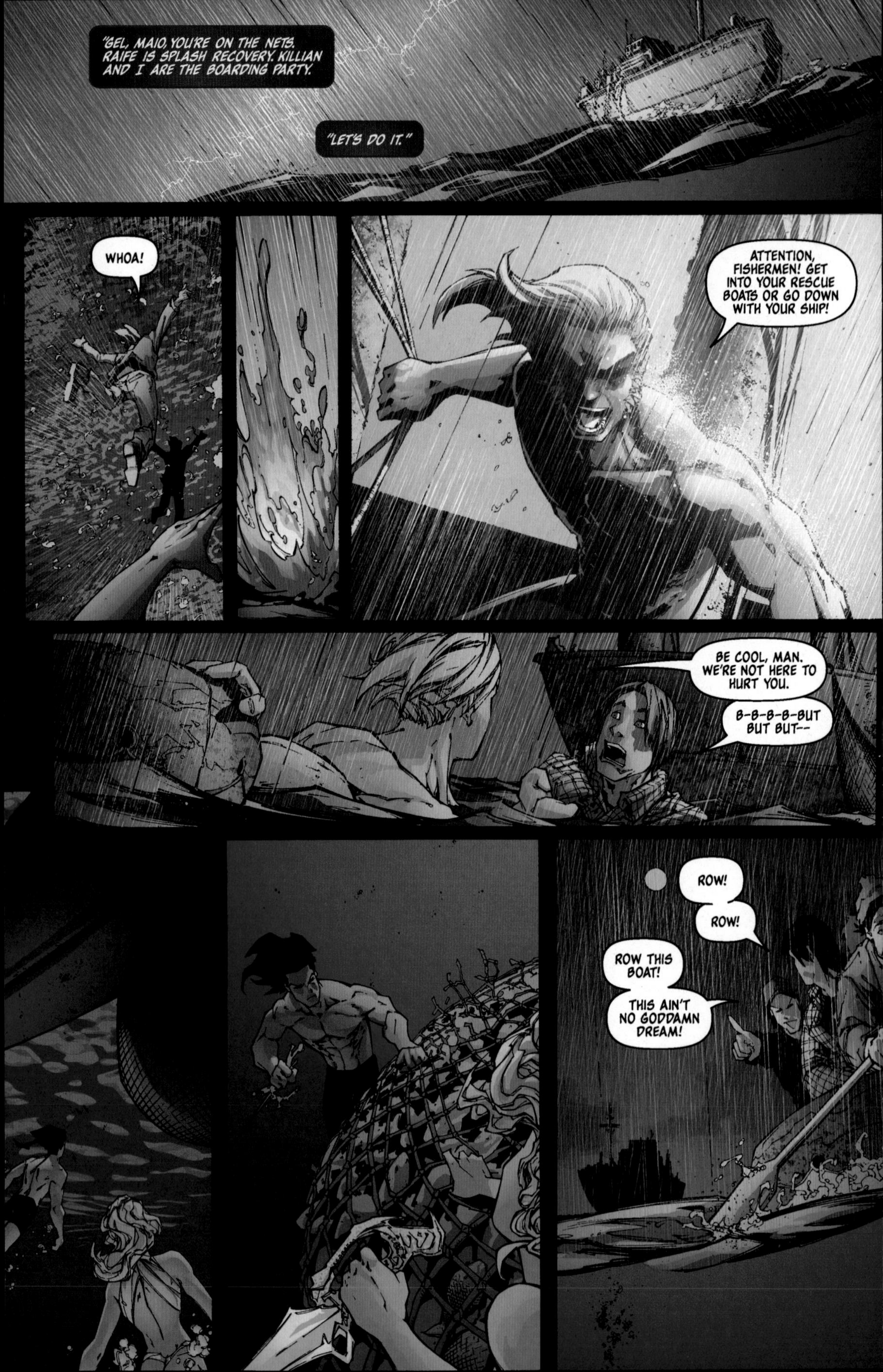
"GEL, MAIO, YOU'RE ON THE NETS. RAIFE IS SPLASH RECOVERY. KILLIAN AND I ARE THE BOARDING PARTY.
"LET'S DO IT."
WHOA!
ATTENTION, FISHERMEN! GET INTO YOUR RESCUE BOATS OR GO DOWN WITH YOUR SHIP!
BE COOL, MAN. WE'RE NOT HERE TO HURT YOU.
B-B-B-B-BUT BUT BUT--
ROW!
ROW!
ROW THIS BOAT!
THIS AIN'T NO GODDAMN DREAM!

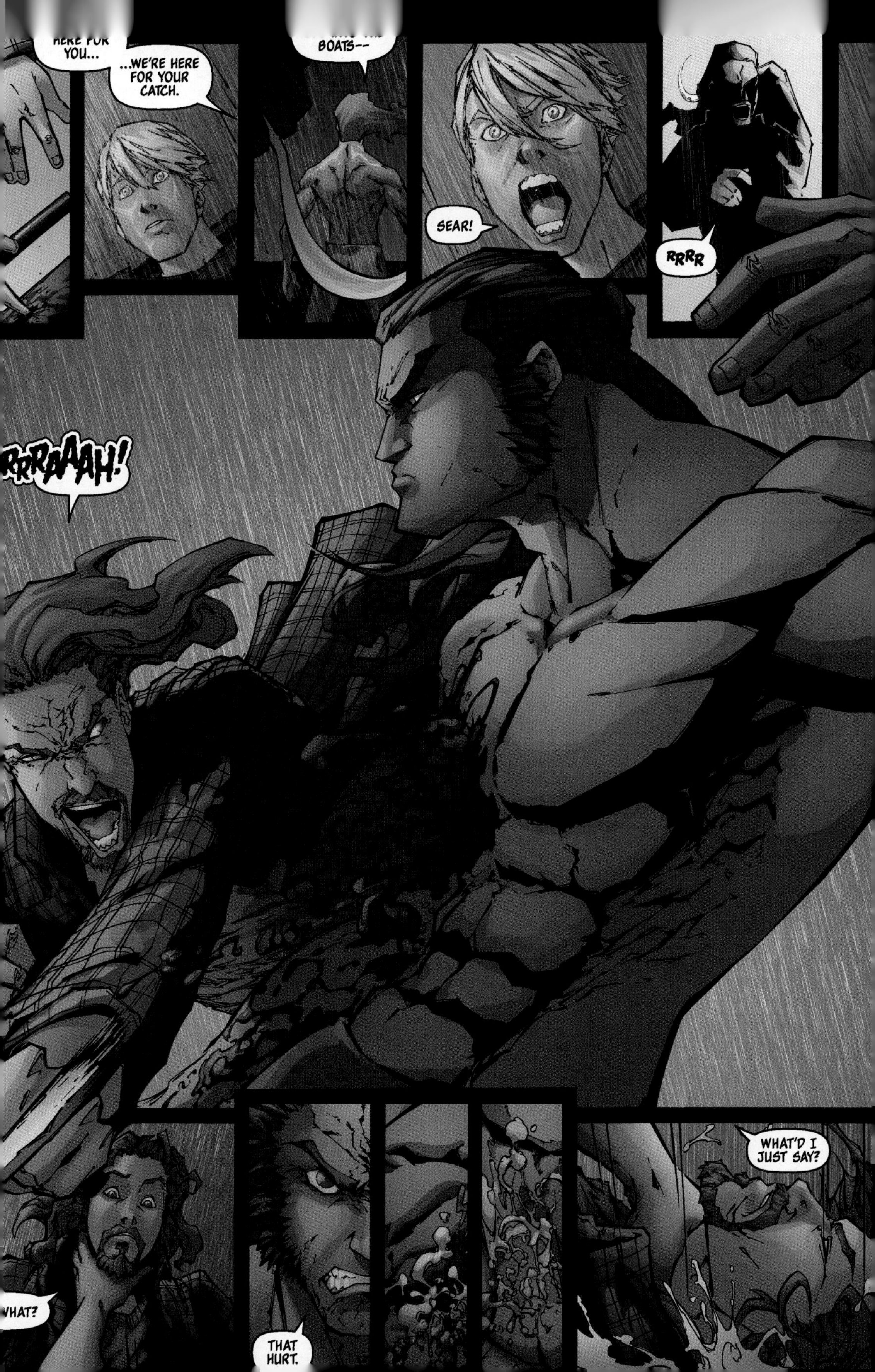
HERE FOR YOU...
...WE'RE HERE FOR YOUR CATCH.
BOATS--
SEAR!
RRRR
RRRRAAAH!
WHAT?
THAT HURT.
WHAT'D I JUST SAY?

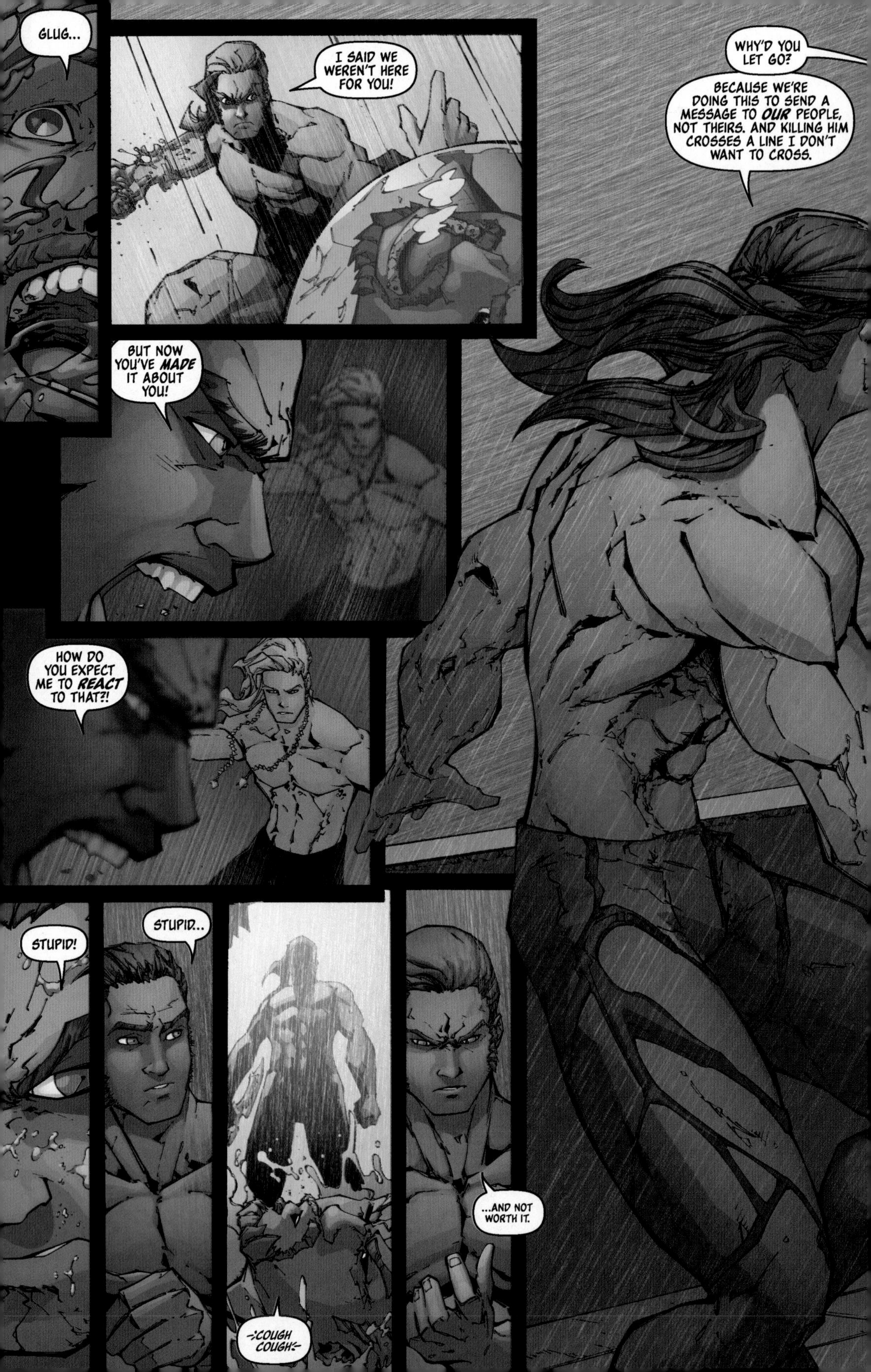
GLUG...
I SAID WE WEREN'T HERE FOR YOU!
BUT NOW YOU'VE MADE IT ABOUT YOU!
HOW DO YOU EXPECT ME TO REACT TO THAT?!
WHY'D YOU LET GO?
BECAUSE WE'RE DOING THIS TO SEND A MESSAGE TO OUR PEOPLE, NOT THEIRS. AND KILLING HIM CROSSES A LINE I DON'T WANT TO CROSS.
STUPID!
STUPID..
COUGH COUGH
...AND NOT WORTH IT.

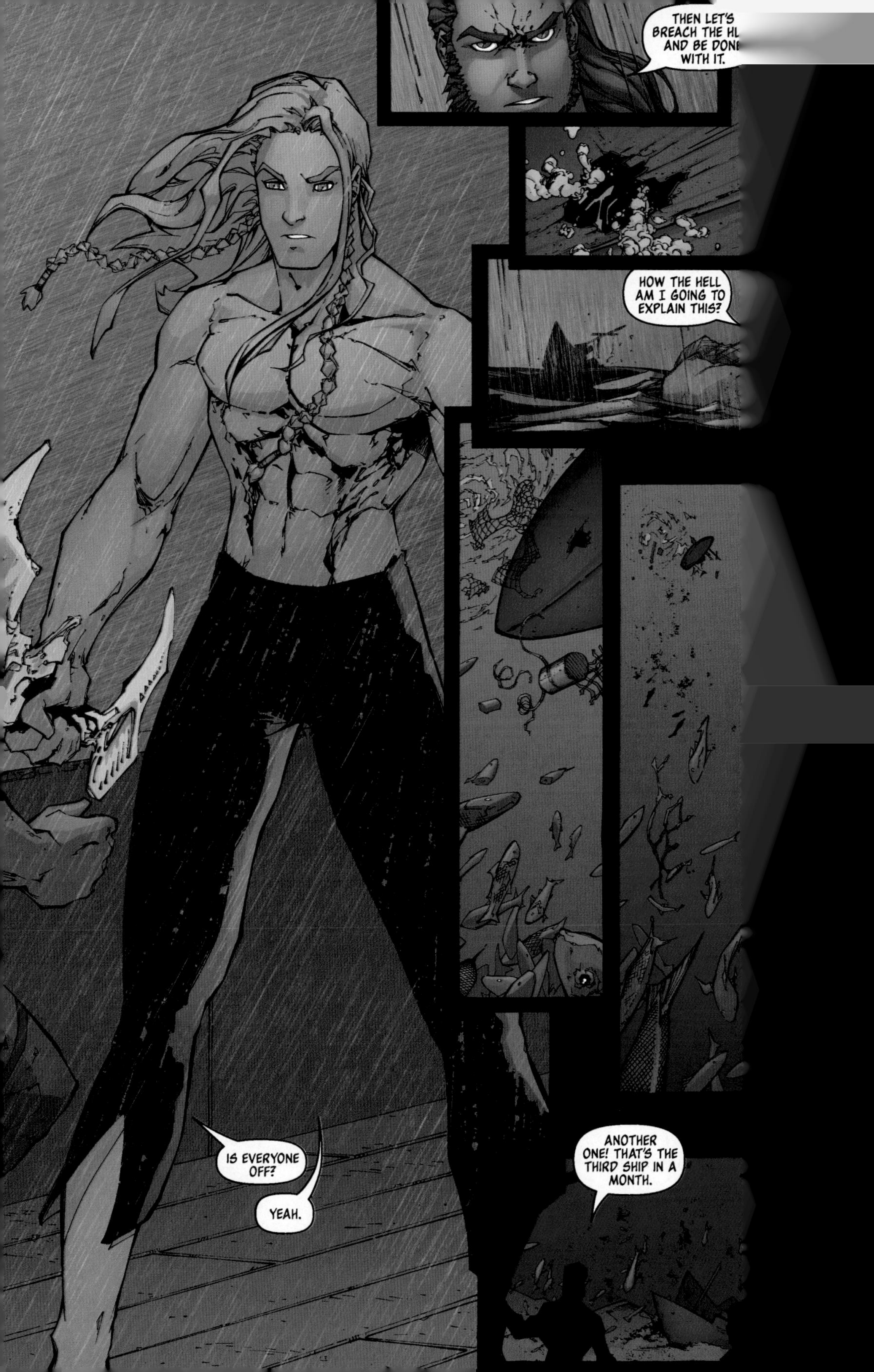
IS EVERYONE OFF?
YEAH.
THEN LET'S BREACH THE H AND BE DON WITH IT.
HOW THE HELL AM I GOING TO EXPLAIN THIS?
ANOTHER ONE! THAT'S THE THIRD SHIP IN A MONTH.

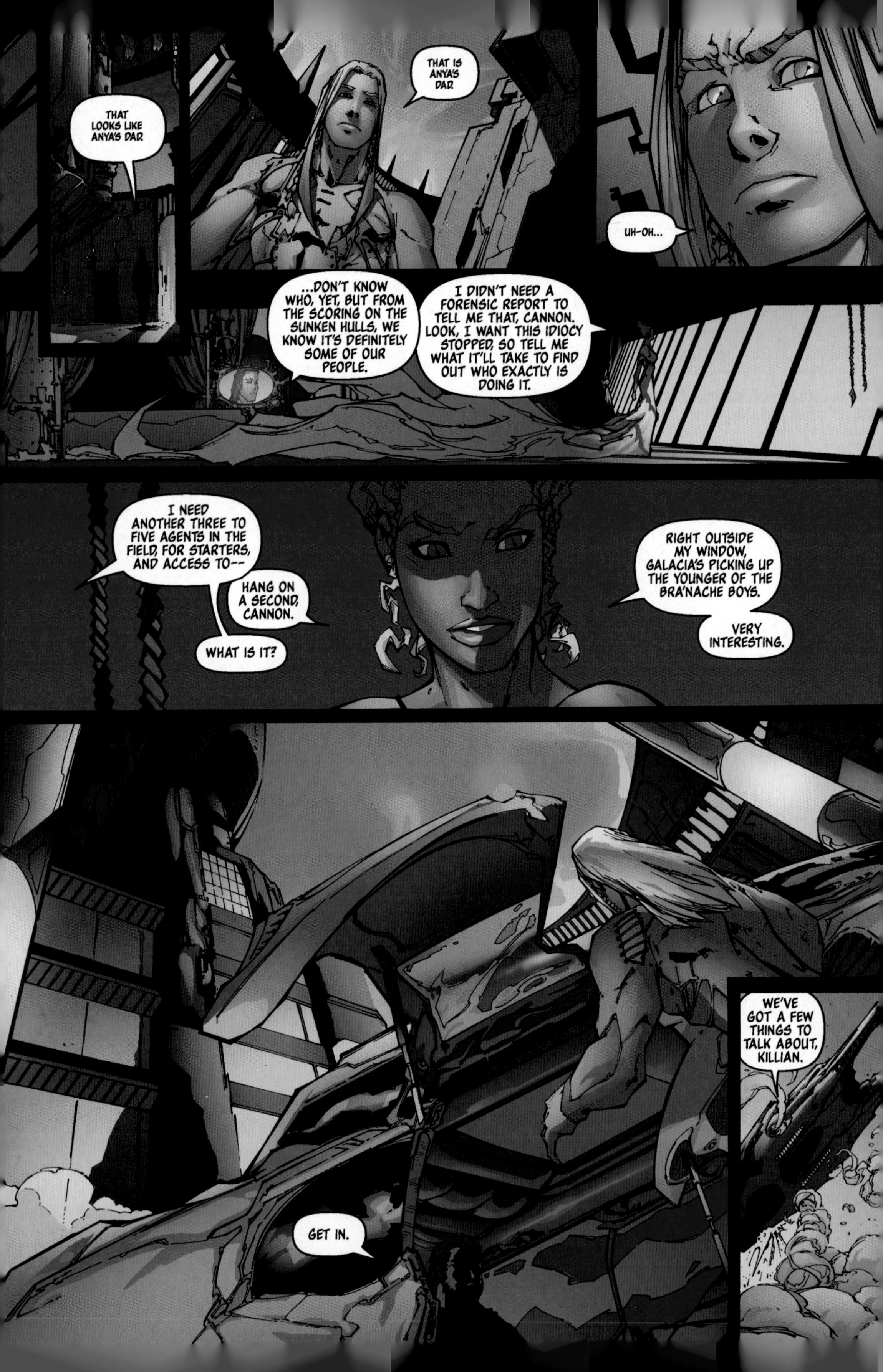
THAT LOOKS LIKE ANYA'S DAD.
THAT IS ANYA'S DAD.
UH-OH...
...DON'T KNOW WHO, YET, BUT FROM THE SCORING ON THE SUNKEN HULLS, WE KNOW IT'S DEFINITELY SOME OF OUR PEOPLE.
I DIDN'T NEED A FORENSIC REPORT TO TELL ME THAT, CANNON. LOOK, I WANT THIS IDIOCY STOPPED, SO TELL ME WHAT IT'LL TAKE TO FIND OUT WHO EXACTLY IS DOING IT.
I NEED ANOTHER THREE TO FIVE AGENTS IN THE FIELD, FOR STARTERS, AND ACCESS TO--
HANG ON A SECOND, CANNON.
WHAT IS IT?
RIGHT OUTSIDE MY WINDOW, GALACIA'S PICKING UP THE YOUNGER OF THE BRA'NACHE BOYS.
VERY INTERESTING.
WE'VE GOT A FEW THINGS TO TALK ABOUT, KILLIAN.
GET IN.

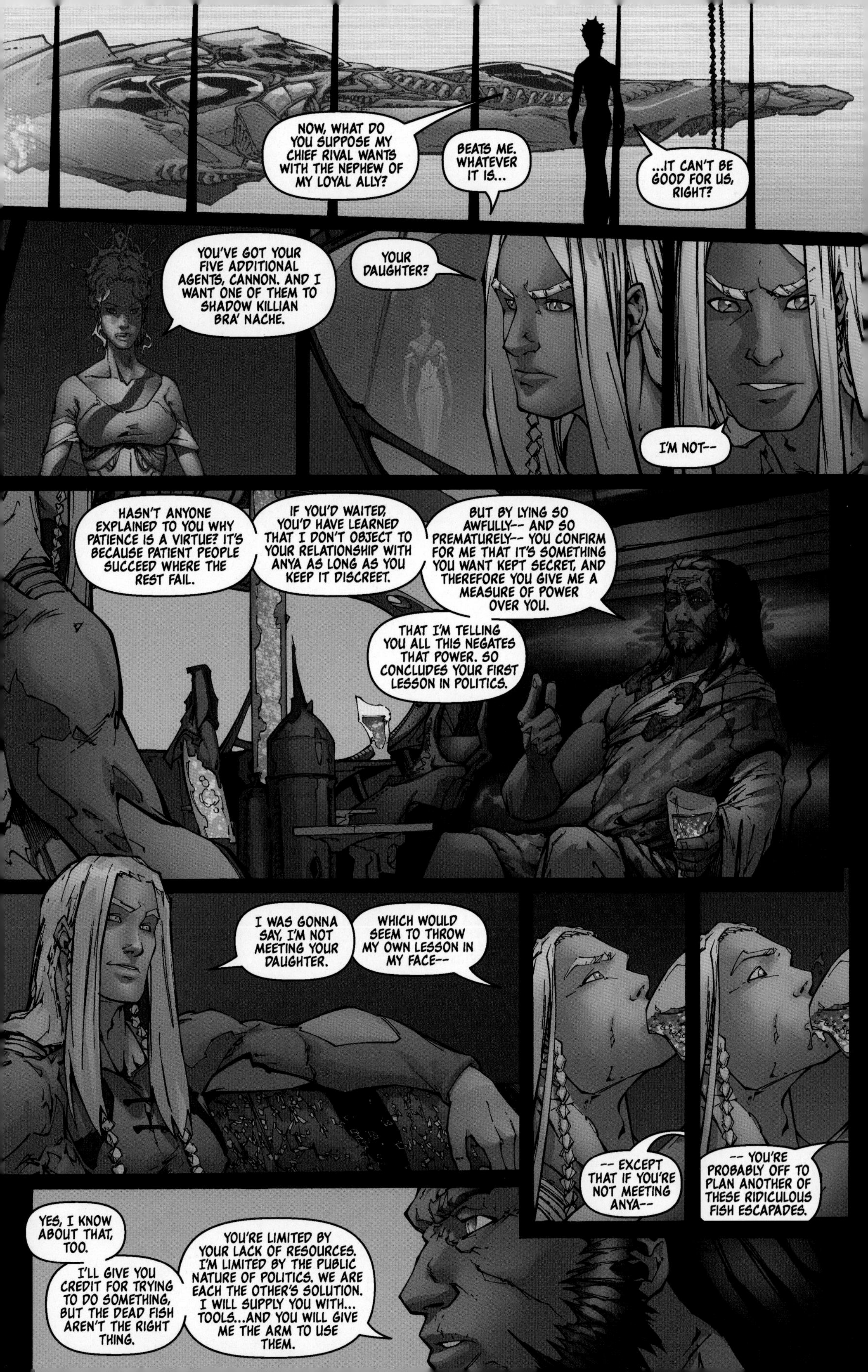

NOW, WHAT DO YOU SUPPOSE MY CHIEF RIVAL WANTS WITH THE NEPHEW OF MY LOYAL ALLY?
BEATS ME. WHATEVER IT IS...
...IT CAN'T BE GOOD FOR US, RIGHT?
YOU'VE GOT YOUR FIVE ADDITIONAL AGENTS, CANNON. AND I WANT ONE OF THEM TO SHADOW KILLIAN BRA' NACHE.
YOUR DAUGHTER?
I'M NOT--
HASN'T ANYONE EXPLAINED TO YOU WHY PATIENCE IS A VIRTUE? IT'S BECAUSE PATIENT PEOPLE SUCCEED WHERE THE REST FAIL.
IF YOU'D WAITED, YOU'D HAVE LEARNED THAT I DON'T OBJECT TO YOUR RELATIONSHIP WITH ANYA AS LONG AS YOU KEEP IT DISCREET.
BUT BY LYING SO AWFULLY-- AND SO PREMATURELY-- YOU CONFIRM FOR ME THAT IT'S SOMETHING YOU WANT KEPT SECRET, AND THEREFORE YOU GIVE ME A MEASURE OF POWER OVER YOU.
THAT I'M TELLING YOU ALL THIS NEGATES THAT POWER. SO CONCLUDES YOUR FIRST LESSON IN POLITICS.
I WAS GONNA SAY, I'M NOT MEETING YOUR DAUGHTER.
WHICH WOULD SEEM TO THROW MY OWN LESSON IN MY FACE--
-- EXCEPT THAT IF YOU'RE NOT MEETING ANYA--
-- YOU'RE PROBABLY OFF TO PLAN ANOTHER OF THESE RIDICULOUS FISH ESCAPADES.
YES, I KNOW ABOUT THAT, TOO.
I'LL GIVE YOU CREDIT FOR TRYING TO DO SOMETHING, BUT THE DEAD FISH AREN'T THE RIGHT THING.
YOU'RE LIMITED BY YOUR LACK OF RESOURCES. I'M LIMITED BY THE PUBLIC NATURE OF POLITICS. WE ARE EACH THE OTHER'S SOLUTION. I WILL SUPPLY YOU WITH... TOOLS...AND YOU WILL GIVE ME THE ARM TO USE THEM.

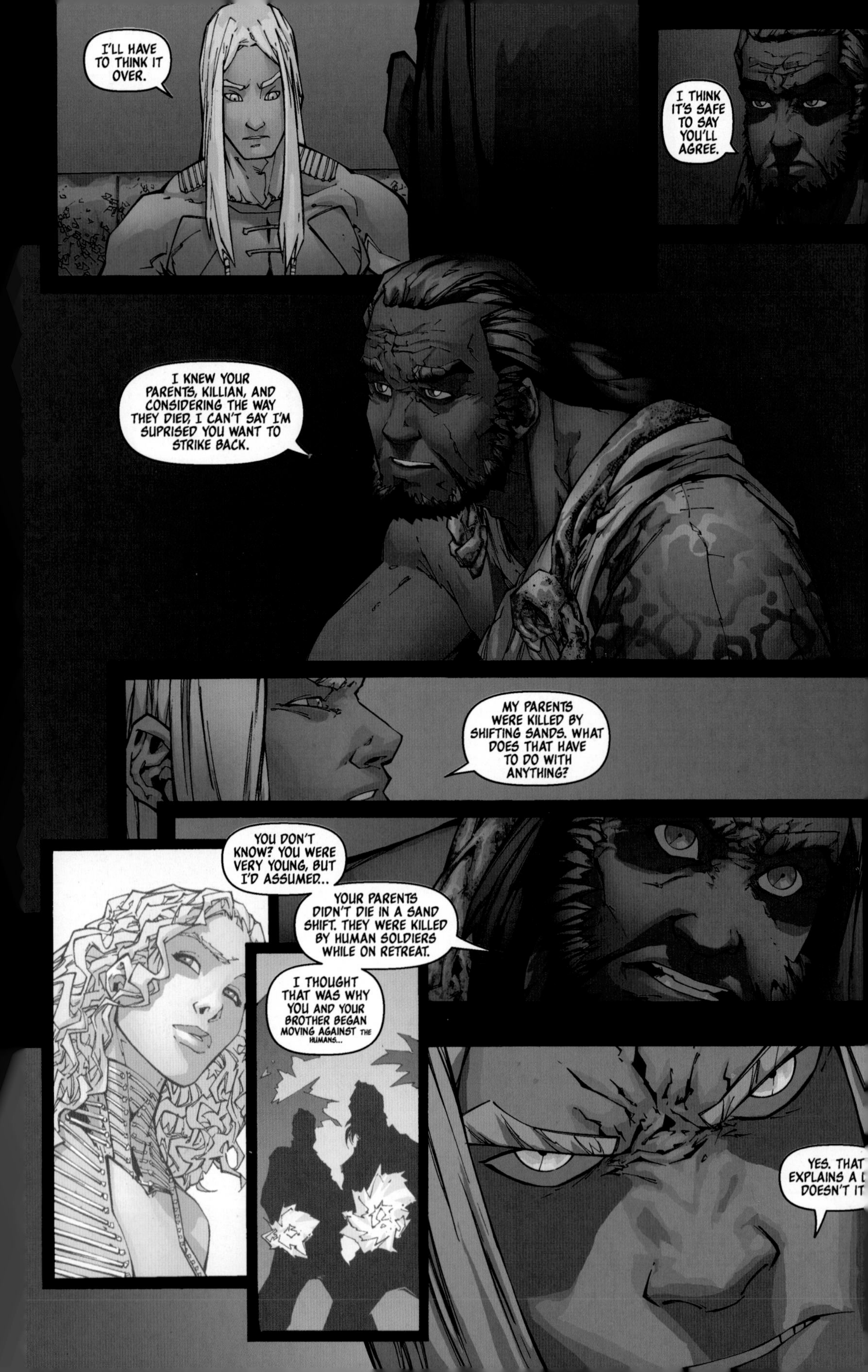

I'LL HAVE TO THINK IT OVER.
I THINK IT'S SAFE TO SAY YOU'LL AGREE.
I KNEW YOUR PARENTS, KILLIAN, AND CONSIDERING THE WAY THEY DIED, I CAN'T SAY I'M SUPRISED YOU WANT TO STRIKE BACK.
MY PARENTS WERE KILLED BY SHIFTING SANDS. WHAT DOES THAT HAVE TO DO WITH ANYTHING?
YOU DON'T KNOW? YOU WERE VERY YOUNG, BUT I'D ASSUMED...
YOUR PARENTS DIDN'T DIE IN A SAND SHIFT. THEY WERE KILLED BY HUMAN SOLDIERS WHILE ON RETREAT.
I THOUGHT THAT WAS WHY YOU AND YOUR BROTHER BEGAN MOVING AGAINST THE HUMANS...
YES. THAT EXPLAINS A
DOESN'T IT

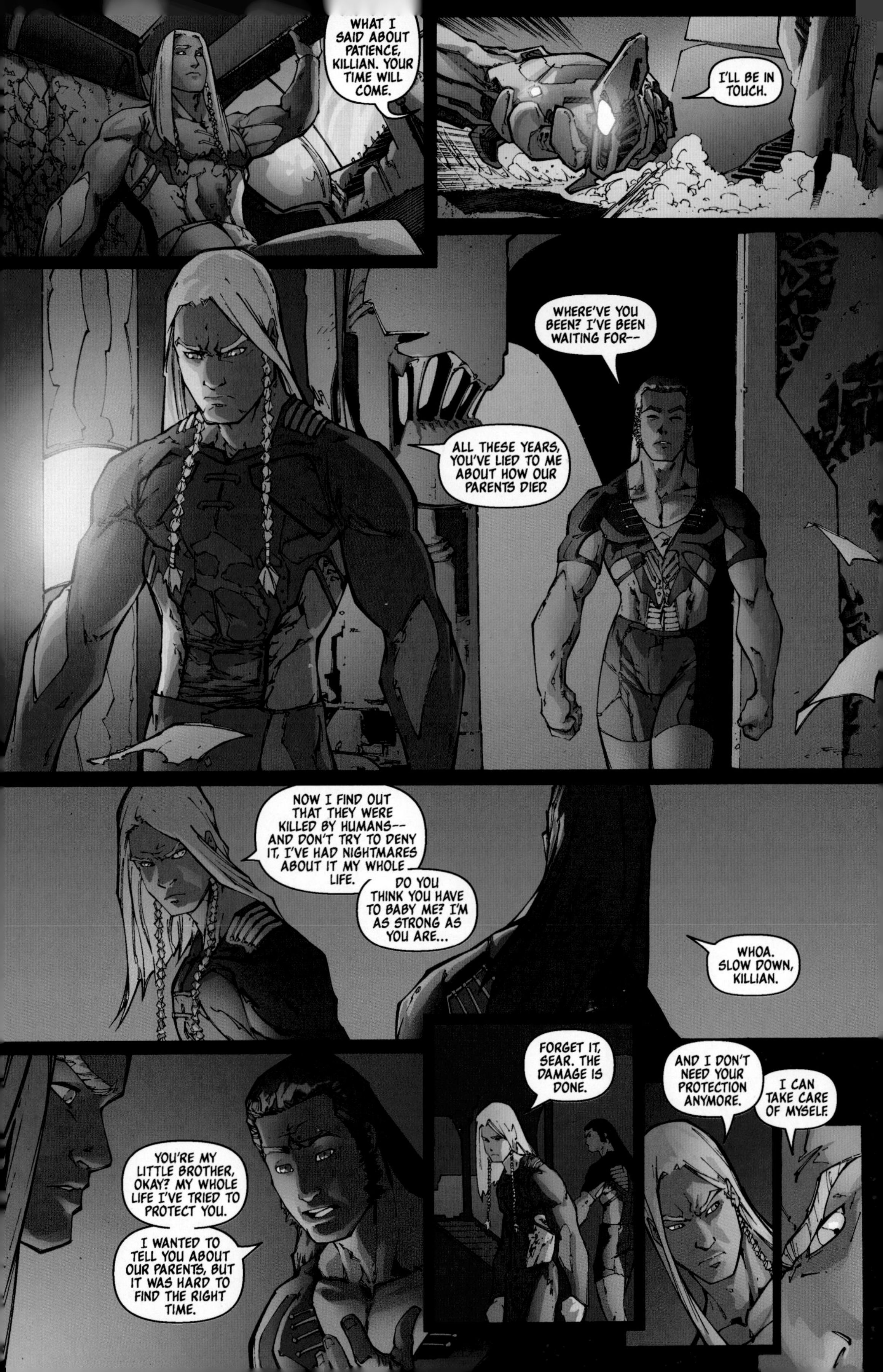
WHAT I SAID ABOUT PATIENCE, KILLIAN. YOUR TIME WILL COME.
I'LL BE IN TOUCH.
WHERE'VE YOU BEEN? I'VE BEEN WAITING FOR--
ALL THESE YEARS, YOU'VE LIED TO ME ABOUT HOW OUR PARENTS DIED.
NOW I FIND OUT THAT THEY WERE KILLED BY HUMANS-- AND DON'T TRY TO DENY IT, I'VE HAD NIGHTMARES ABOUT IT MY WHOLE LIFE.
DO YOU THINK YOU HAVE TO BABY ME? I'M AS STRONG AS YOU ARE...
WHOA. SLOW DOWN, KILLIAN.
YOU'RE MY LITTLE BROTHER, OKAY? MY WHOLE LIFE I'VE TRIED TO PROTECT YOU.
I WANTED TO TELL YOU ABOUT OUR PARENTS, BUT IT WAS HARD TO FIND THE RIGHT TIME.
FORGET IT, SEAR. THE DAMAGE IS DONE.
AND I DON'T NEED YOUR PROTECTION ANYMORE.
I CAN TAKE CARE OF MYSELF.

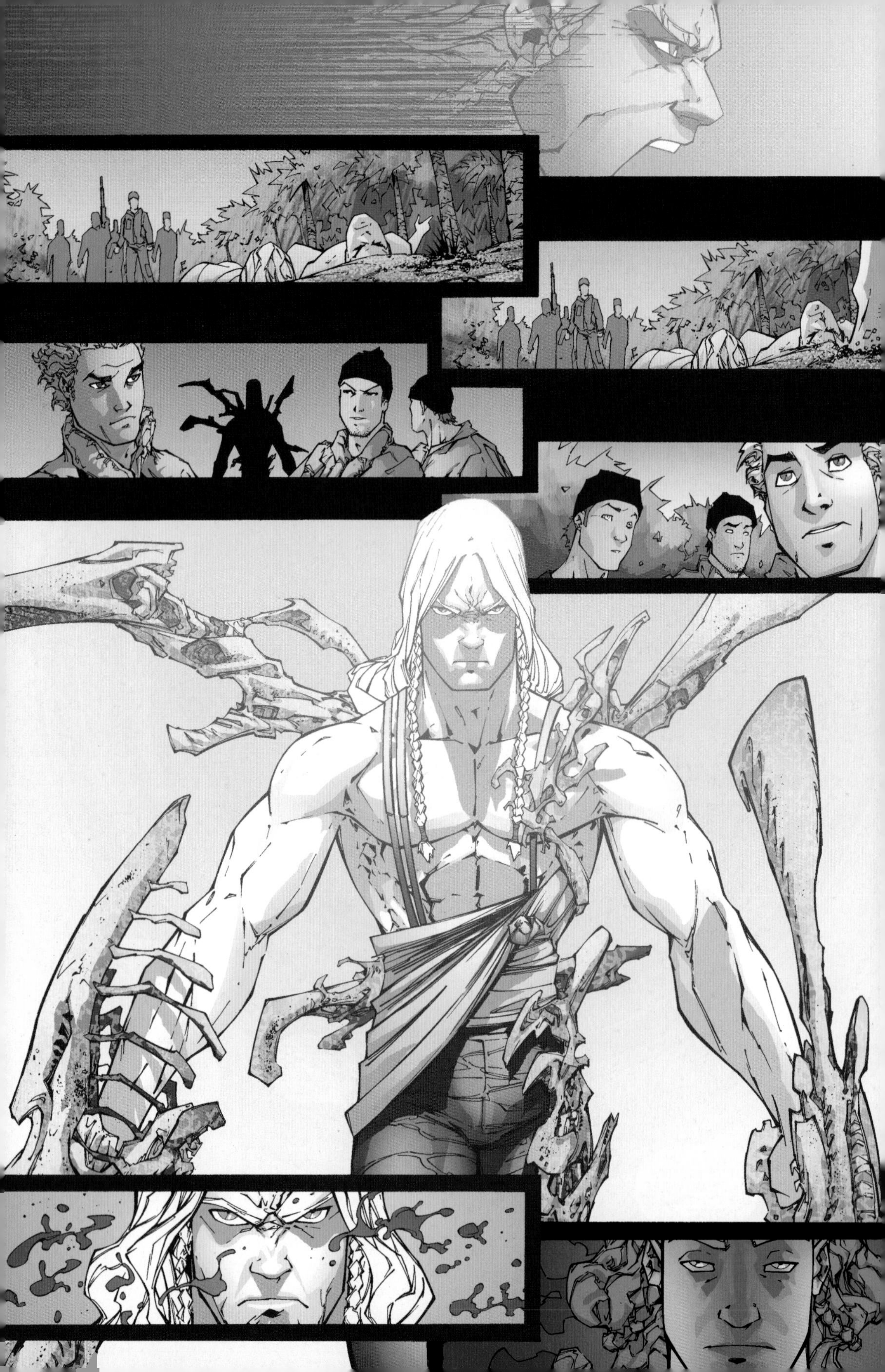

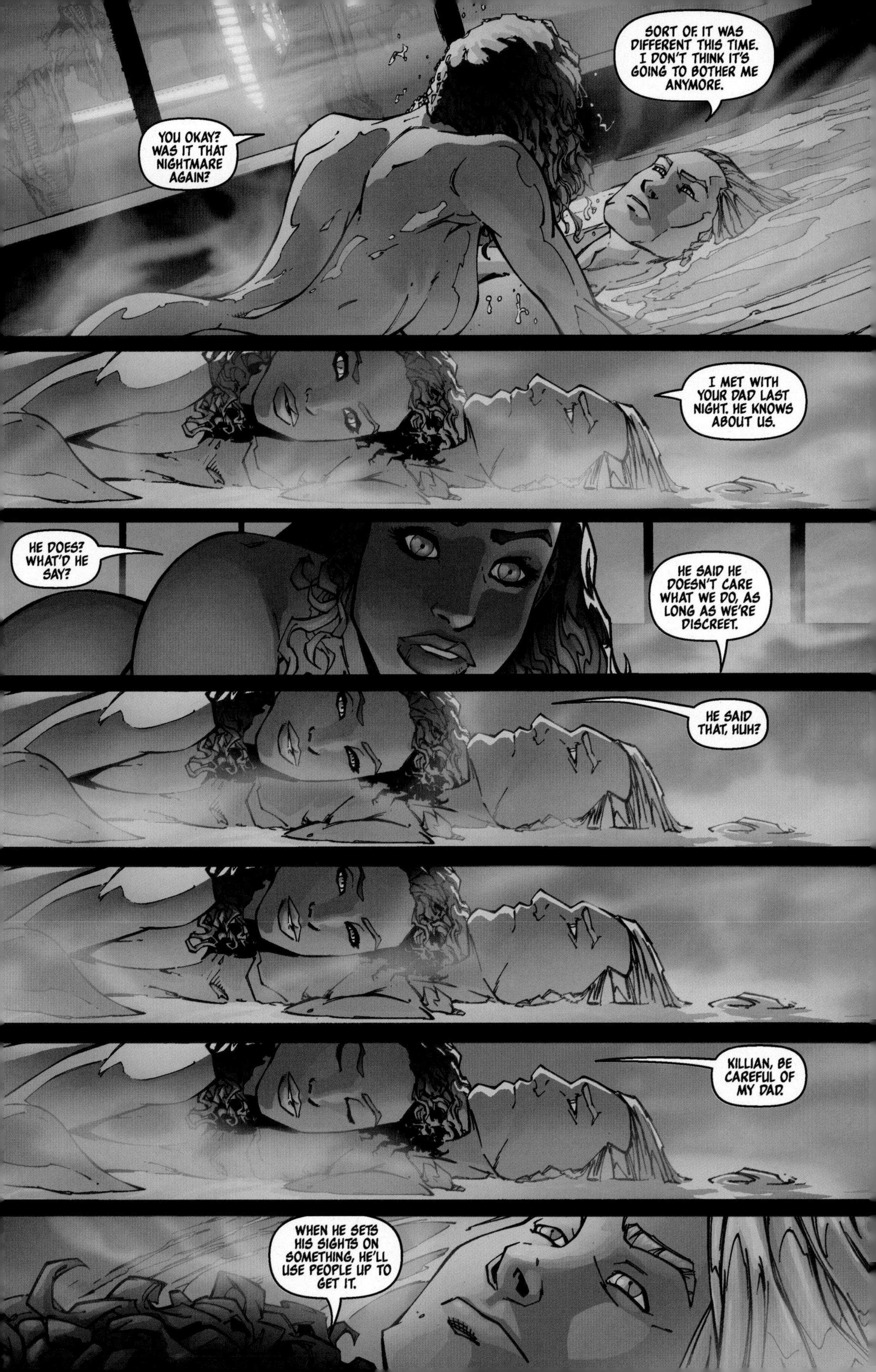
YOU OKAY? WAS IT THAT NIGHTMARE AGAIN?
SORT OF. IT WAS DIFFERENT THIS TIME. I DON'T THINK IT'S GOING TO BOTHER ME ANYMORE.
I MET WITH YOUR DAD LAST NIGHT. HE KNOWS ABOUT US.
HE DOES? WHAT'D HE SAY?
HE SAID HE DOESN'T CARE WHAT WE DO, AS LONG AS WE'RE DISCREET.
HE SAID THAT, HUH?
KILLIAN, BE CAREFUL OF MY DAD.
WHEN HE SETS HIS SIGHTS ON SOMETHING, HE'LL USE PEOPLE UP TO GET IT.

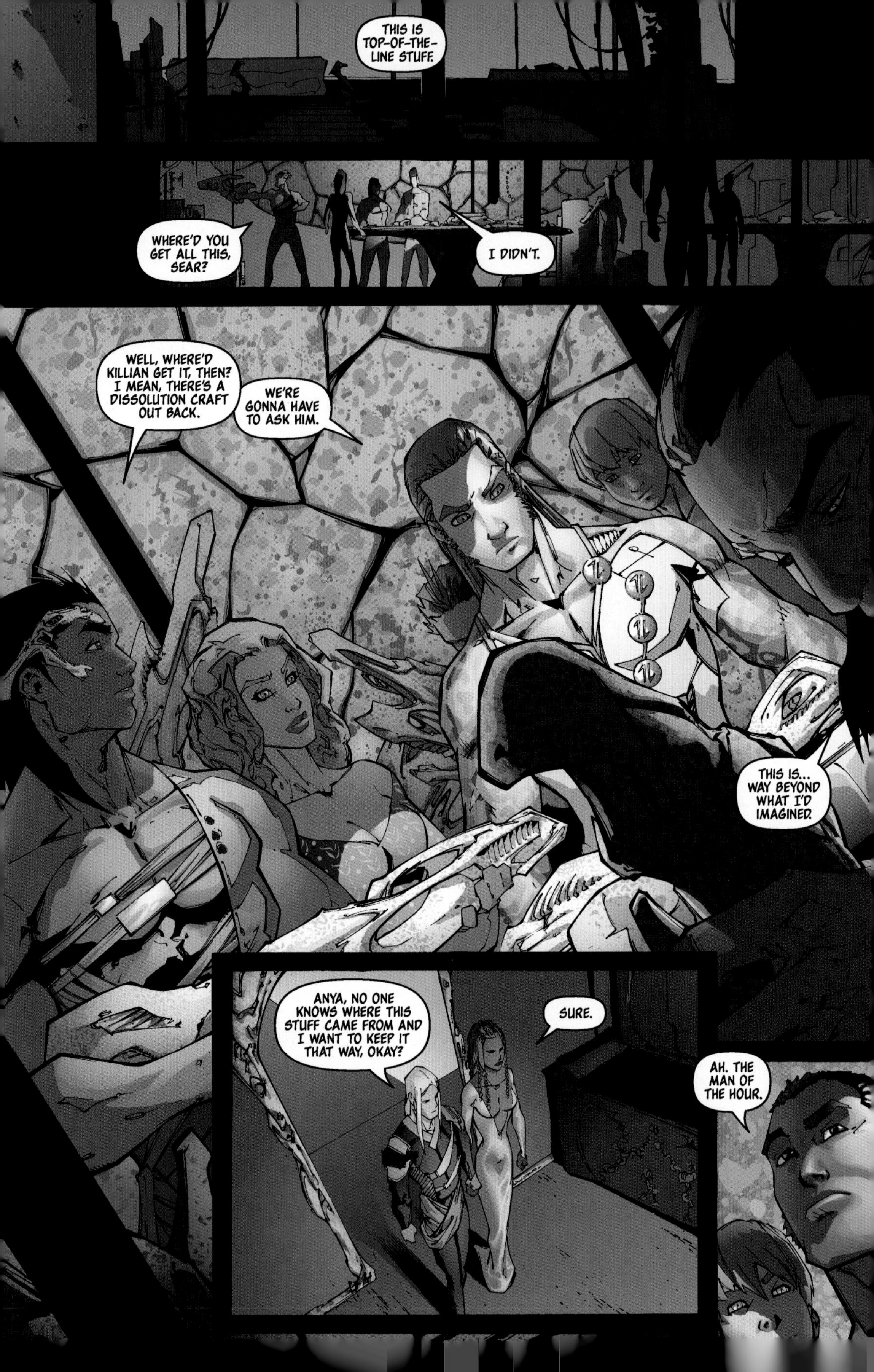
THIS IS TOP-OF-THE-LINE STUFF.
WHERE'D YOU GET ALL THIS, SEAR?
I DIDN'T.
WELL, WHERE'D KILLIAN GET IT, THEN? I MEAN, THERE'S A DISSOLUTION CRAFT OUT BACK.
WE'RE GONNA HAVE TO ASK HIM.
THIS IS... WAY BEYOND WHAT I'D IMAGINED.
ANYA, NO ONE KNOWS WHERE THIS STUFF CAME FROM AND I WANT TO KEEP IT THAT WAY, OKAY?
SURE.
AH. THE MAN OF THE HOUR.

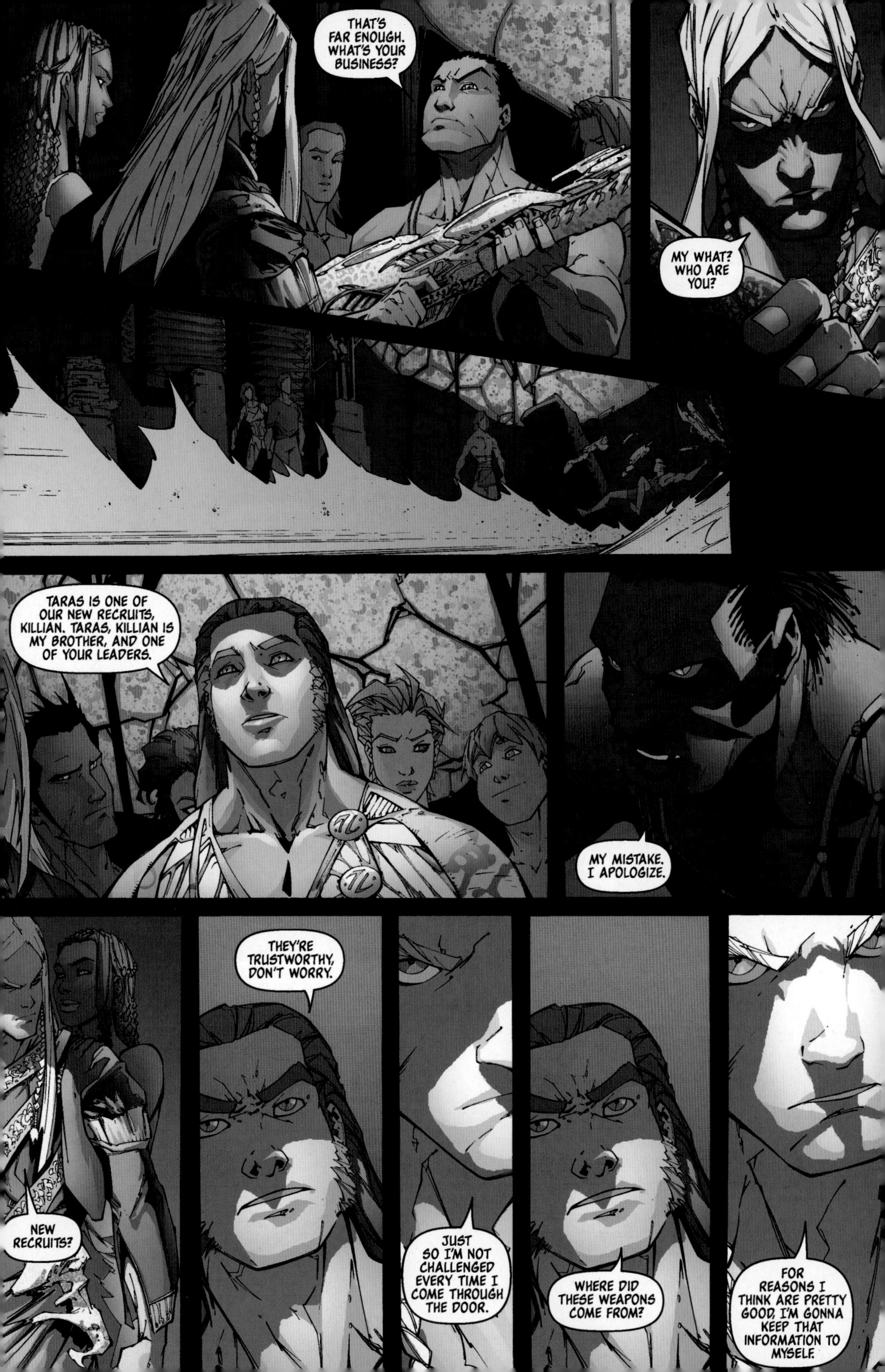
THAT'S FAR ENOUGH. WHAT'S YOUR BUSINESS?
MY WHAT? WHO ARE YOU?
TARAS IS ONE OF OUR NEW RECRUITS, KILLIAN. TARAS, KILLIAN IS MY BROTHER, AND ONE OF YOUR LEADERS.
MY MISTAKE. I APOLOGIZE.
NEW RECRUITS?
THEY'RE TRUSTWORTHY, DON'T WORRY.
JUST SO I'M NOT CHALLENGED EVERY TIME I COME THROUGH THE DOOR.
WHERE DID THESE WEAPONS COME FROM?
FOR REASONS I THINK ARE PRETTY GOOD, I'M GONNA KEEP THAT INFORMATION TO MYSELF.

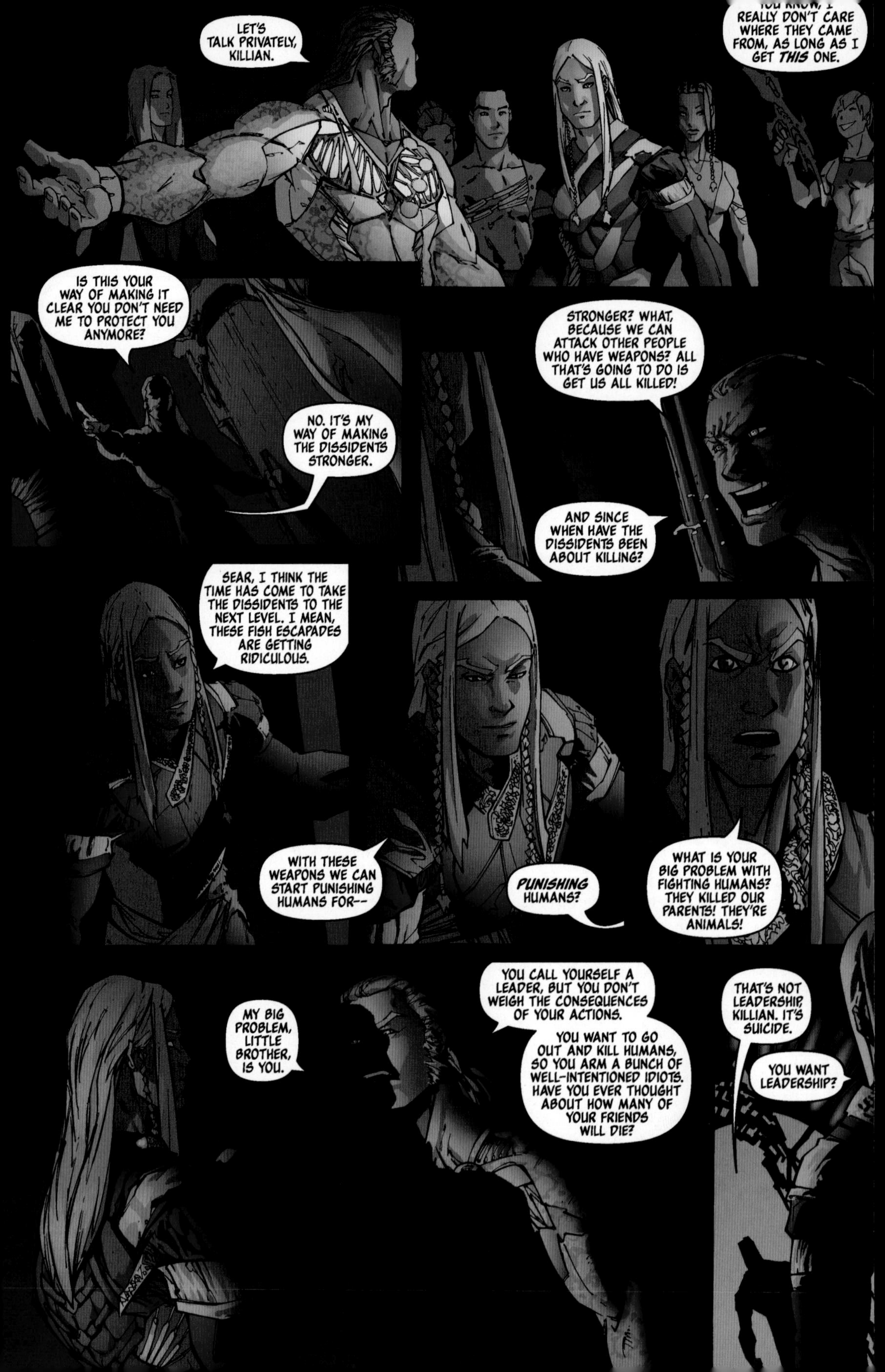

LET'S TALK PRIVATELY, KILLIAN.
REALLY DON'T CARE WHERE THEY CAME FROM, AS LONG AS I GET *THIS* ONE.
IS THIS YOUR WAY OF MAKING IT CLEAR YOU DON'T NEED ME TO PROTECT YOU ANYMORE?
NO. IT'S MY WAY OF MAKING THE DISSIDENTS STRONGER.
STRONGER? WHAT, BECAUSE WE CAN ATTACK OTHER PEOPLE WHO HAVE WEAPONS? ALL THAT'S GOING TO DO IS GET US ALL KILLED!
AND SINCE WHEN HAVE THE DISSIDENTS BEEN ABOUT KILLING?
SEAR, I THINK THE TIME HAS COME TO TAKE THE DISSIDENTS TO THE NEXT LEVEL. I MEAN, THESE FISH ESCAPADES ARE GETTING RIDICULOUS.
WITH THESE WEAPONS WE CAN START PUNISHING HUMANS FOR--
PUNISHING HUMANS?
WHAT IS YOUR BIG PROBLEM WITH FIGHTING HUMANS? THEY KILLED OUR PARENTS! THEY'RE ANIMALS!
MY BIG PROBLEM, LITTLE BROTHER, IS YOU.
YOU CALL YOURSELF A LEADER, BUT YOU DON'T WEIGH THE CONSEQUENCES OF YOUR ACTIONS.
YOU WANT TO GO OUT AND KILL HUMANS, SO YOU ARM A BUNCH OF WELL-INTENTIONED IDIOTS. HAVE YOU EVER THOUGHT ABOUT HOW MANY OF YOUR FRIENDS WILL DIE?
THAT'S NOT LEADERSHIP, KILLIAN. IT'S SUICIDE.
YOU WANT LEADERSHIP?

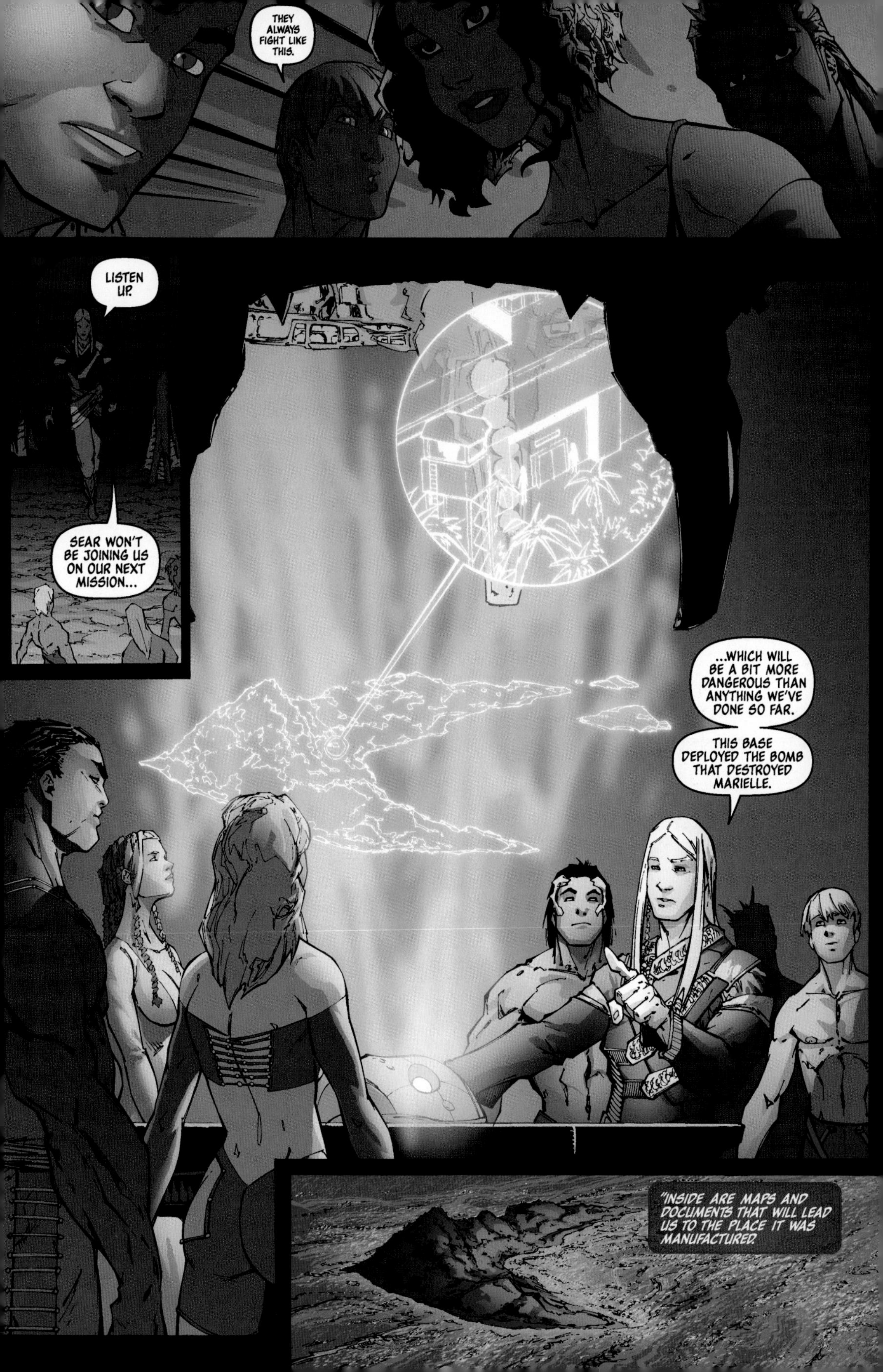
THEY ALWAYS FIGHT LIKE THIS.
LISTEN UP.
SEAR WON'T BE JOINING US ON OUR NEXT MISSION...
...WHICH WILL BE A BIT MORE DANGEROUS THAN ANYTHING WE'VE DONE SO FAR.
THIS BASE DEPLOYED THE BOMB THAT DESTROYED MARIELLE.
"INSIDE ARE MAPS AND DOCUMENTS THAT WILL LEAD US TO THE PLACE IT WAS MANUFACTURED.

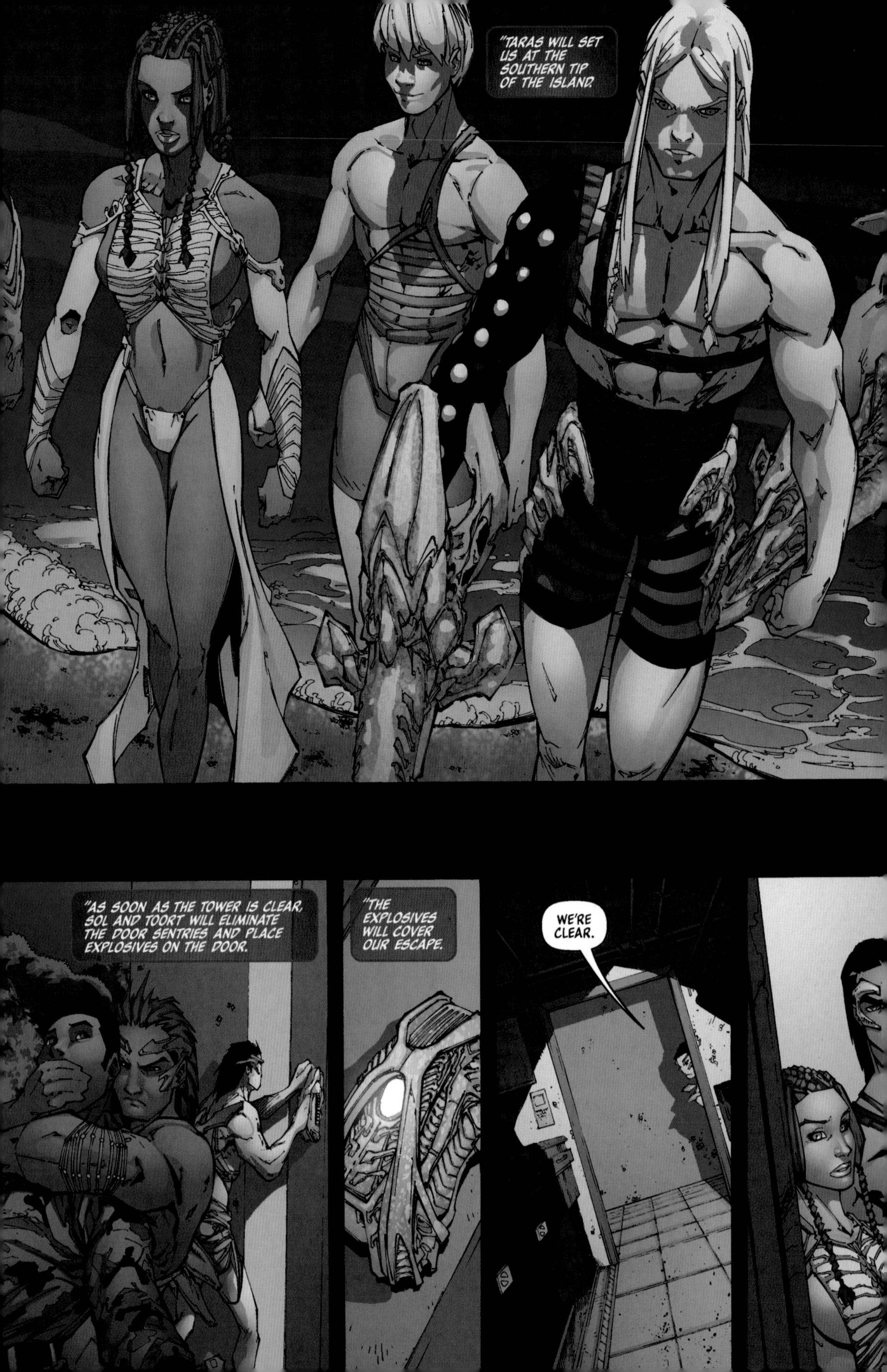
"TARAS WILL SET US AT THE SOUTHERN TIP OF THE ISLAND.
"AS SOON AS THE TOWER IS CLEAR, SOL AND TOORT WILL ELIMINATE THE DOOR SENTRIES AND PLACE EXPLOSIVES ON THE DOOR.
"THE EXPLOSIVES WILL COVER OUR ESCAPE.
WE'RE CLEAR.

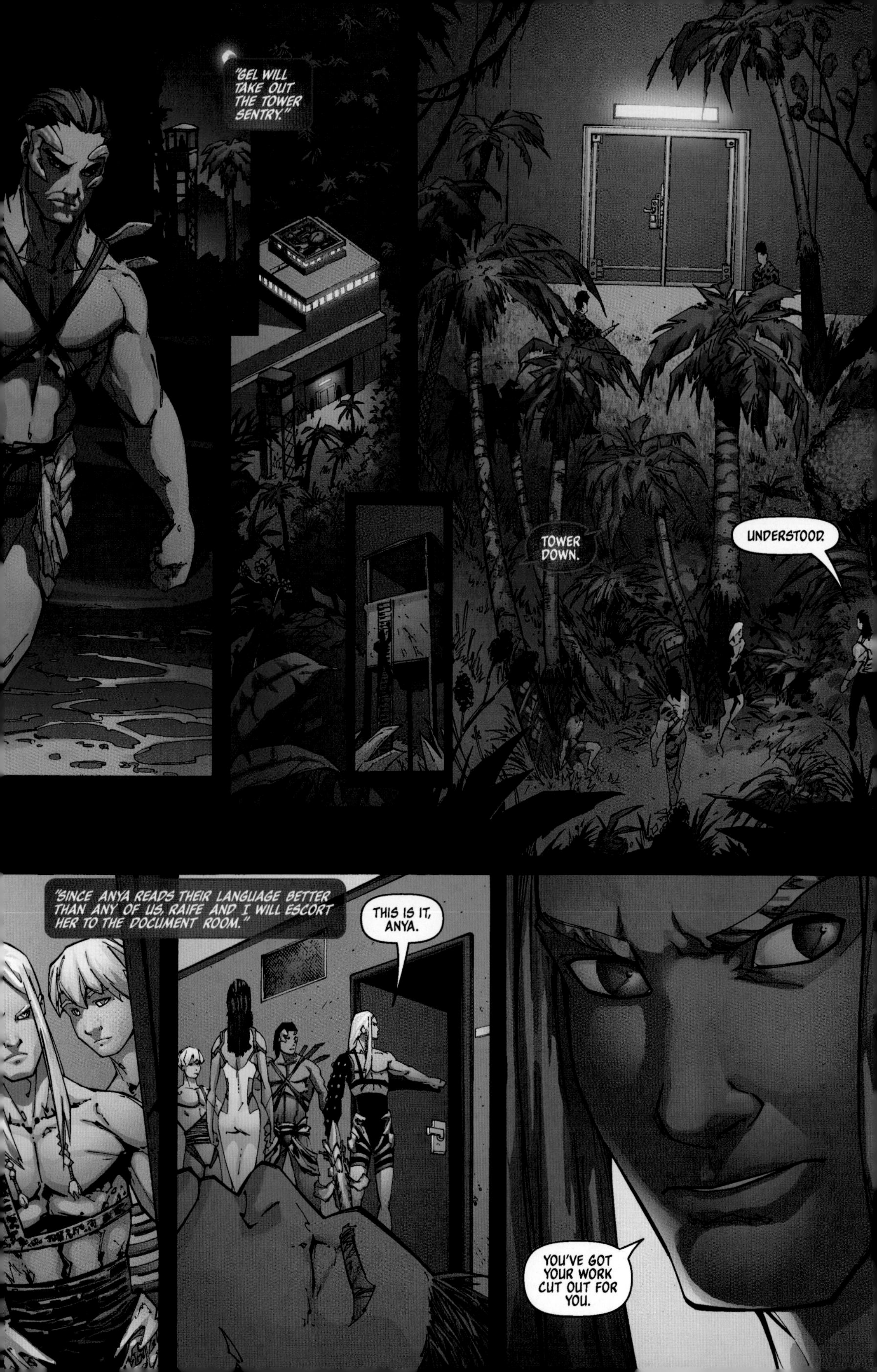
"GEL WILL TAKE OUT THE TOWER SENTRY."
TOWER DOWN.
UNDERSTOOD.
"SINCE ANYA READS THEIR LANGUAGE BETTER THAN ANY OF US, RAIFE AND I WILL ESCORT HER TO THE DOCUMENT ROOM."
THIS IS IT, ANYA.
YOU'VE GOT YOUR WORK CUT OUT FOR YOU.

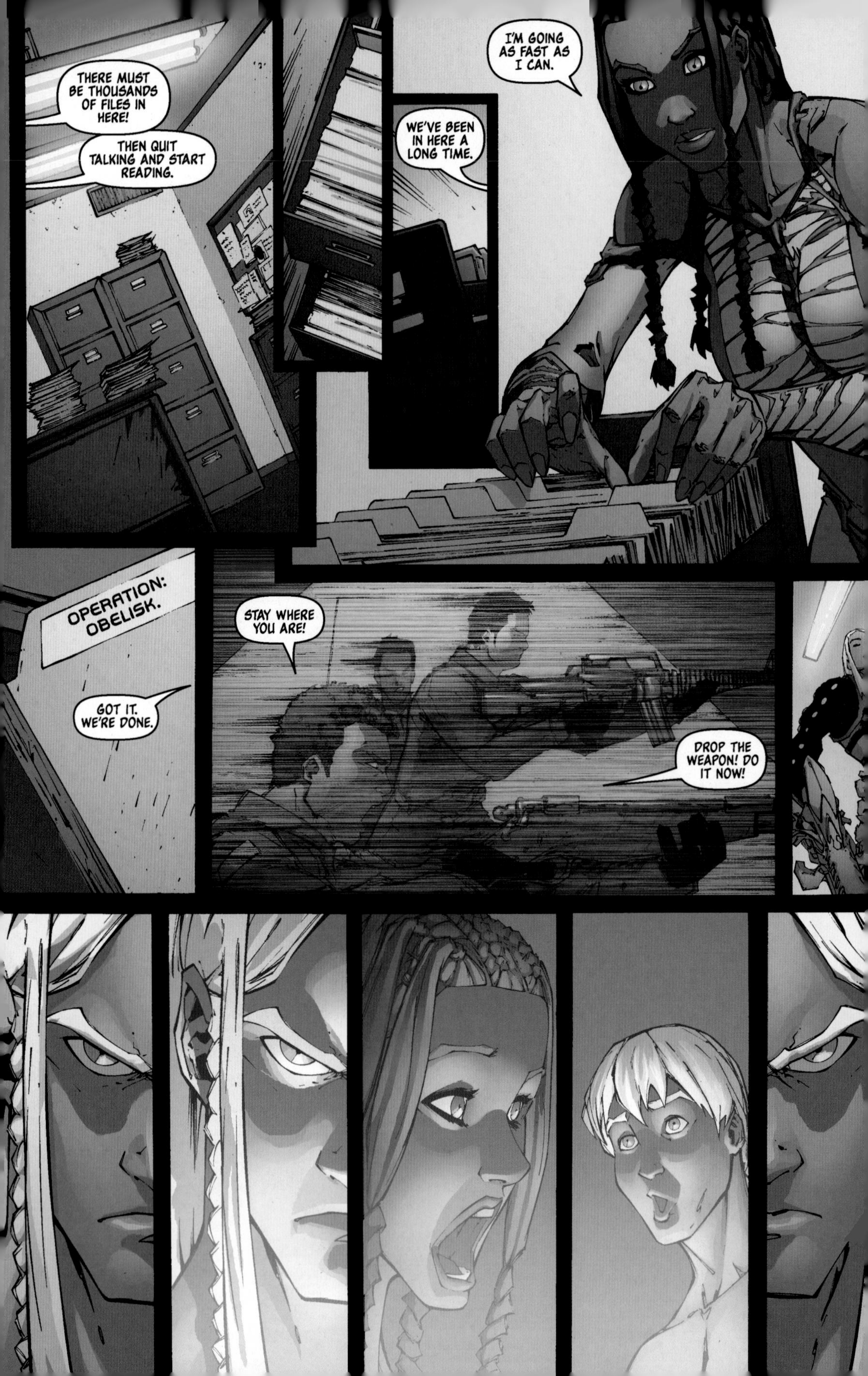
THERE MUST BE THOUSANDS OF FILES IN HERE!
THEN QUIT TALKING AND START READING.
I'M GOING AS FAST AS I CAN.
WE'VE BEEN IN HERE A LONG TIME.
OPERATION: OBELISK.
GOT IT. WE'RE DONE.
STAY WHERE YOU ARE!
DROP THE WEAPON! DO IT NOW!

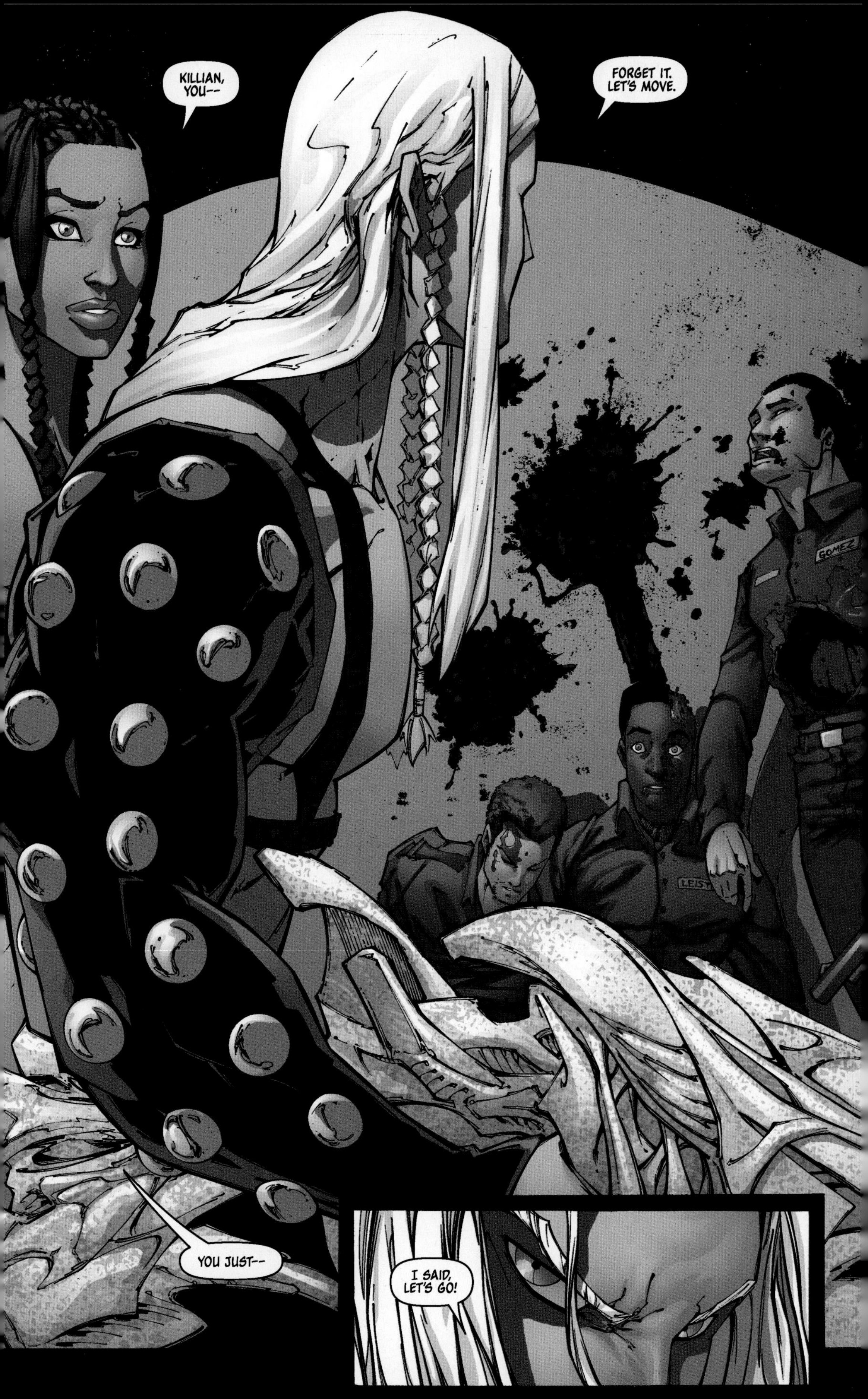
KILLIAN, YOU--
FORGET IT. LET'S MOVE.
GOMEZ
YOU JUST--
I SAID, LET'S GO!

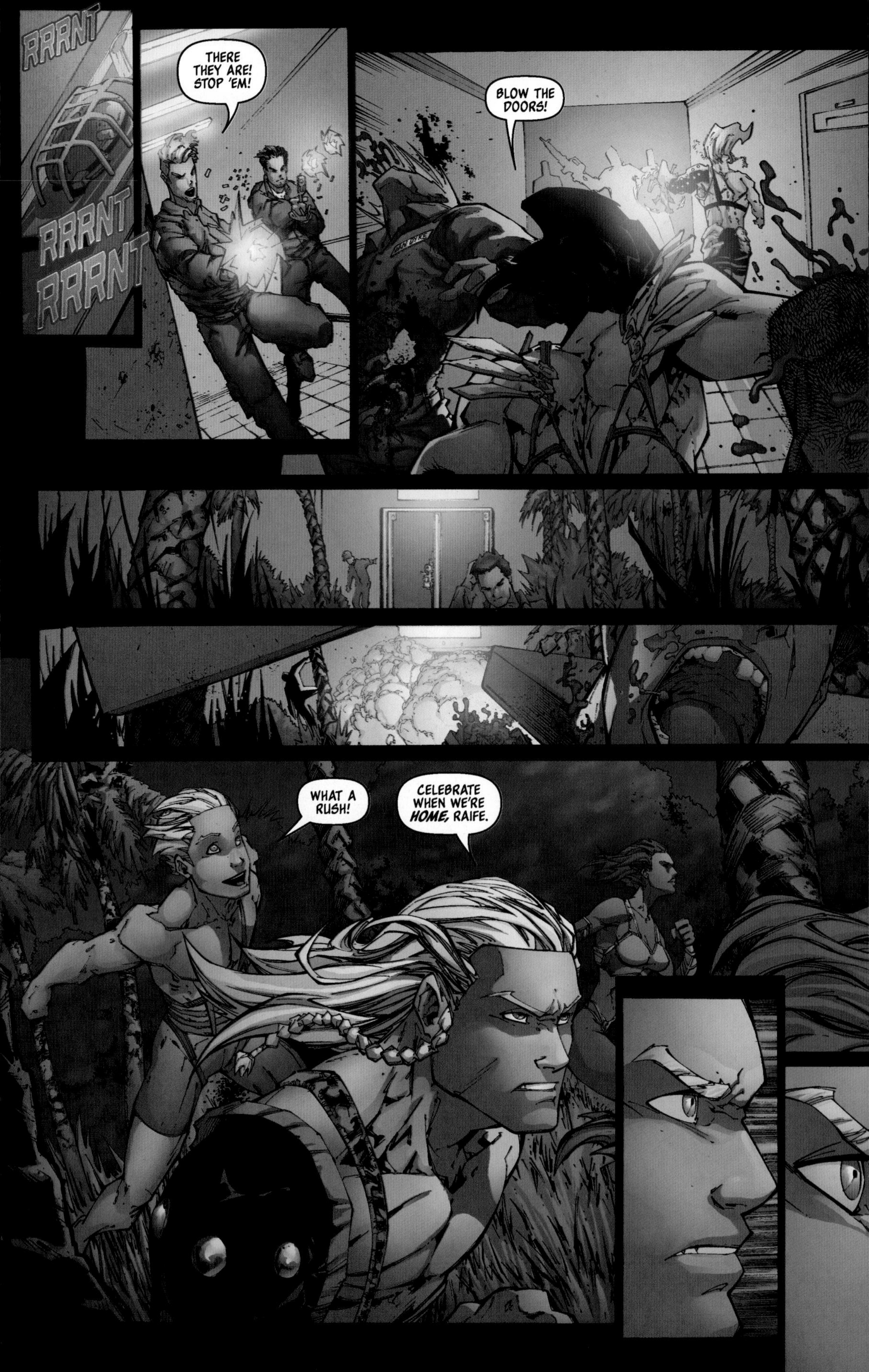
RRRNT
THERE THEY ARE! STOP 'EM!
RRRNT RRRNT
BLOW THE DOORS!
WHAT A RUSH!
CELEBRATE WHEN WE'RE *HOME,* RAIFE.

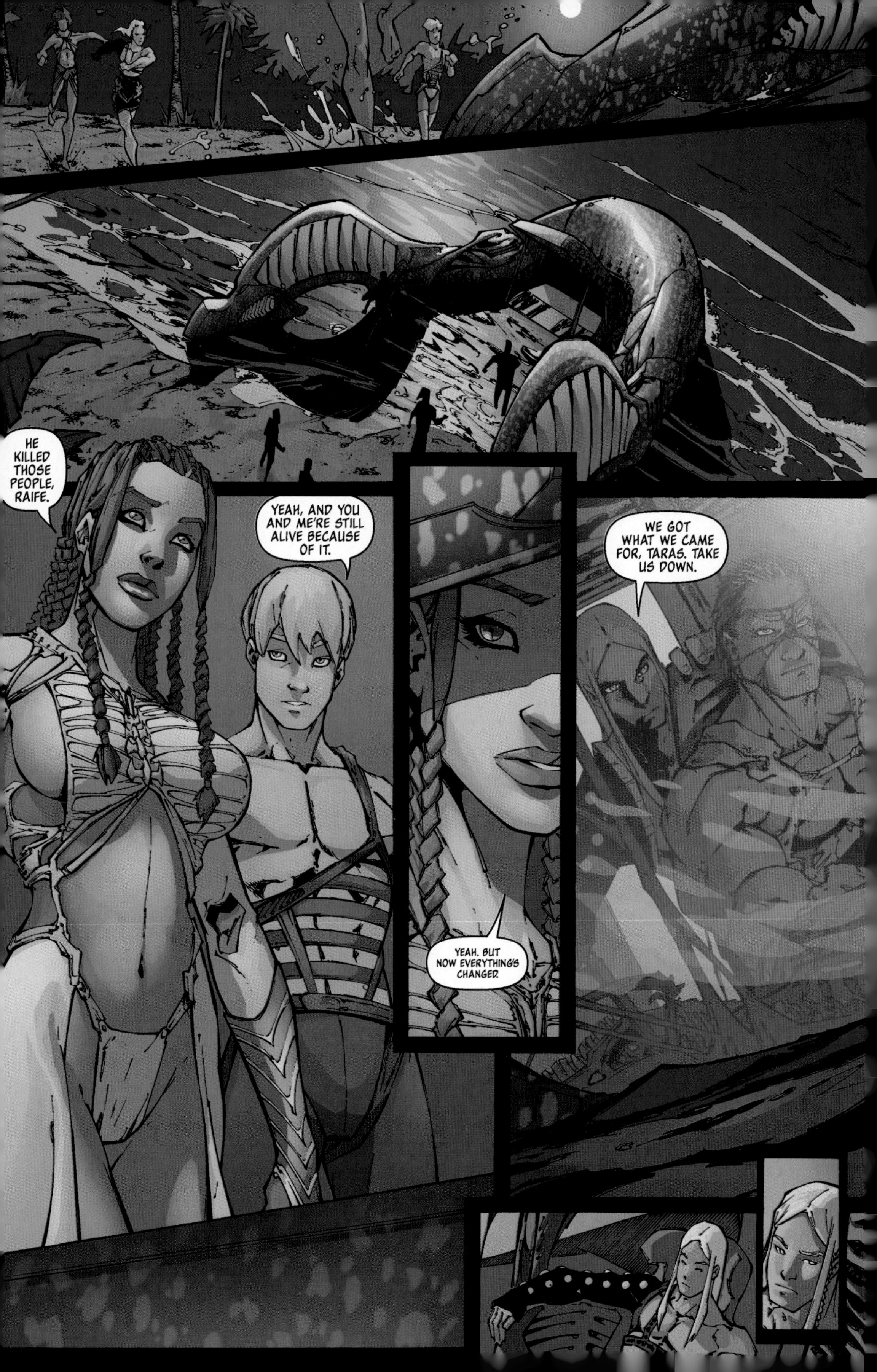
HE KILLED THOSE PEOPLE, RAIFE.
YEAH, AND YOU AND ME'RE STILL ALIVE BECAUSE OF IT.
YEAH. BUT NOW EVERYTHING'S CHANGED.
WE GOT WHAT WE CAME FOR, TARAS. TAKE US DOWN.

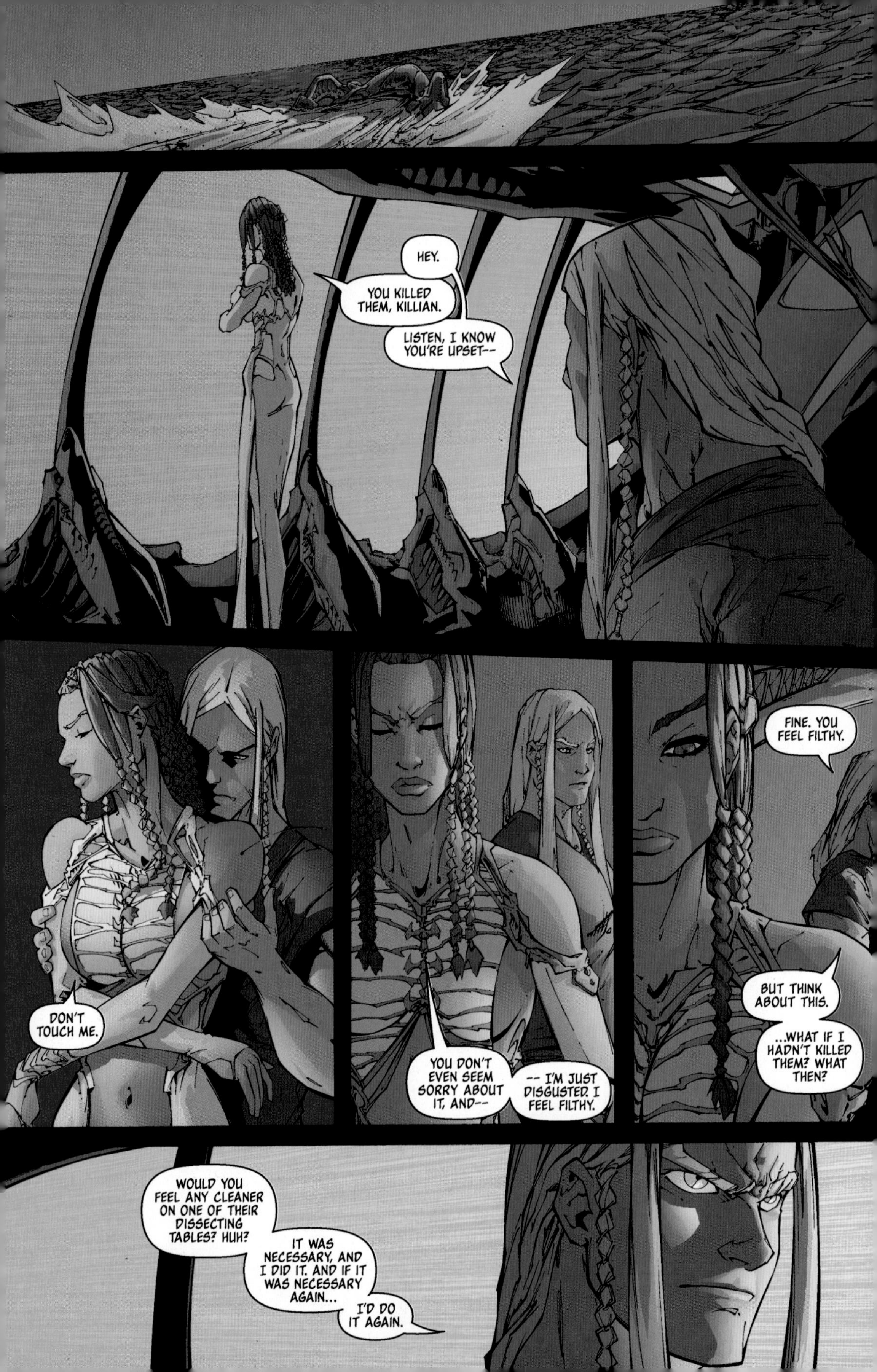
HEY.
YOU KILLED THEM, KILLIAN.
LISTEN, I KNOW YOU'RE UPSET--
DON'T TOUCH ME.
YOU DON'T EVEN SEEM SORRY ABOUT IT, AND--
-- I'M JUST DISGUSTED. I FEEL FILTHY.
FINE. YOU FEEL FILTHY.
BUT THINK ABOUT THIS.
...WHAT IF I HADN'T KILLED THEM? WHAT THEN?
WOULD YOU FEEL ANY CLEANER ON ONE OF THEIR DISSECTING TABLES? HUH?
IT WAS NECESSARY, AND I DID IT. AND IF IT WAS NECESSARY AGAIN...
I'D DO IT AGAIN.

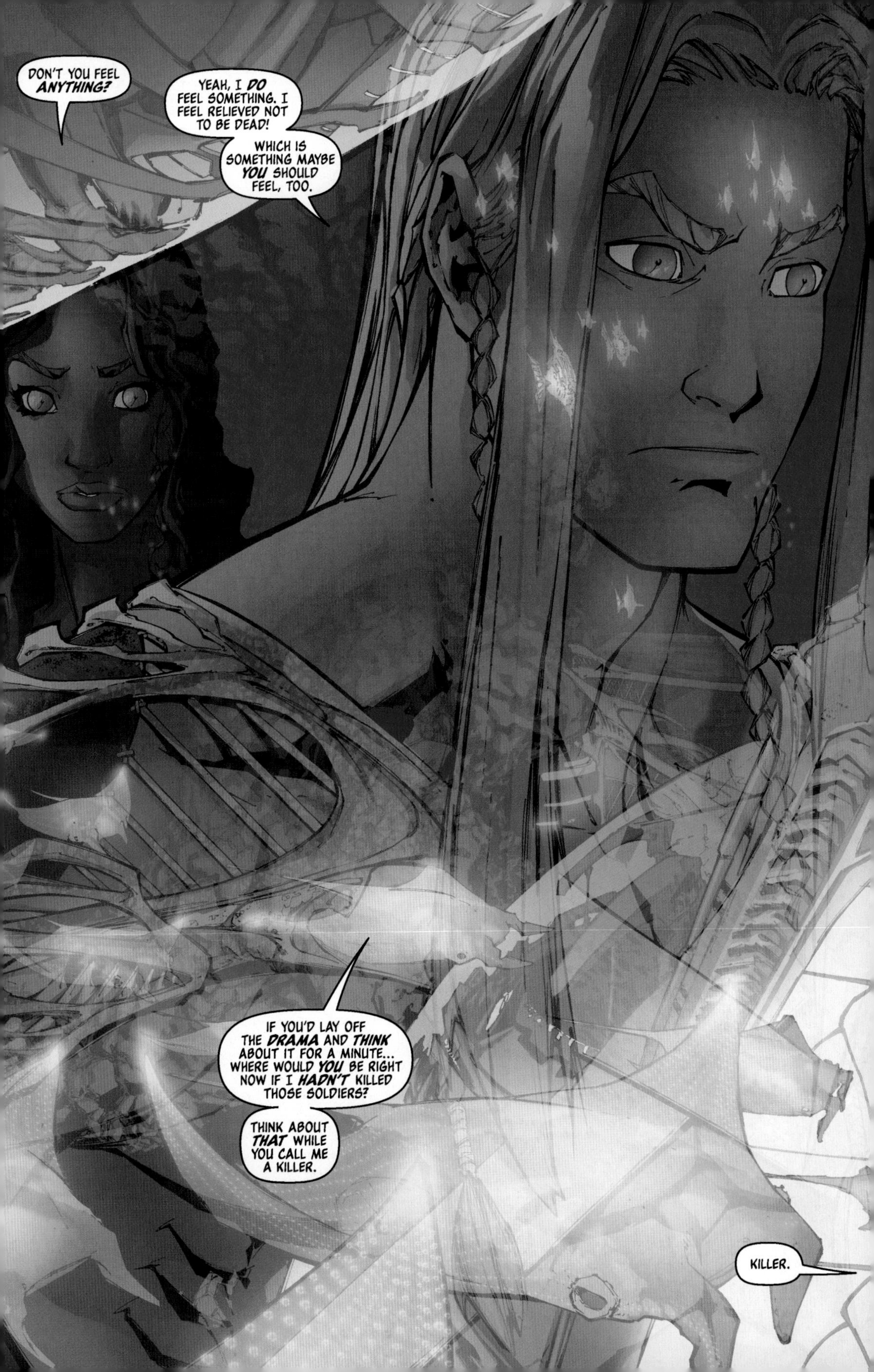
DON'T YOU FEEL ANYTHING?
YEAH, I DO FEEL SOMETHING. I FEEL RELIEVED NOT TO BE DEAD!
WHICH IS SOMETHING MAYBE YOU SHOULD FEEL, TOO.
IF YOU'D LAY OFF THE DRAMA AND THINK ABOUT IT FOR A MINUTE... WHERE WOULD YOU BE RIGHT NOW IF I HADN'T KILLED THOSE SOLDIERS?
THINK ABOUT THAT WHILE YOU CALL ME A KILLER.
KILLER.

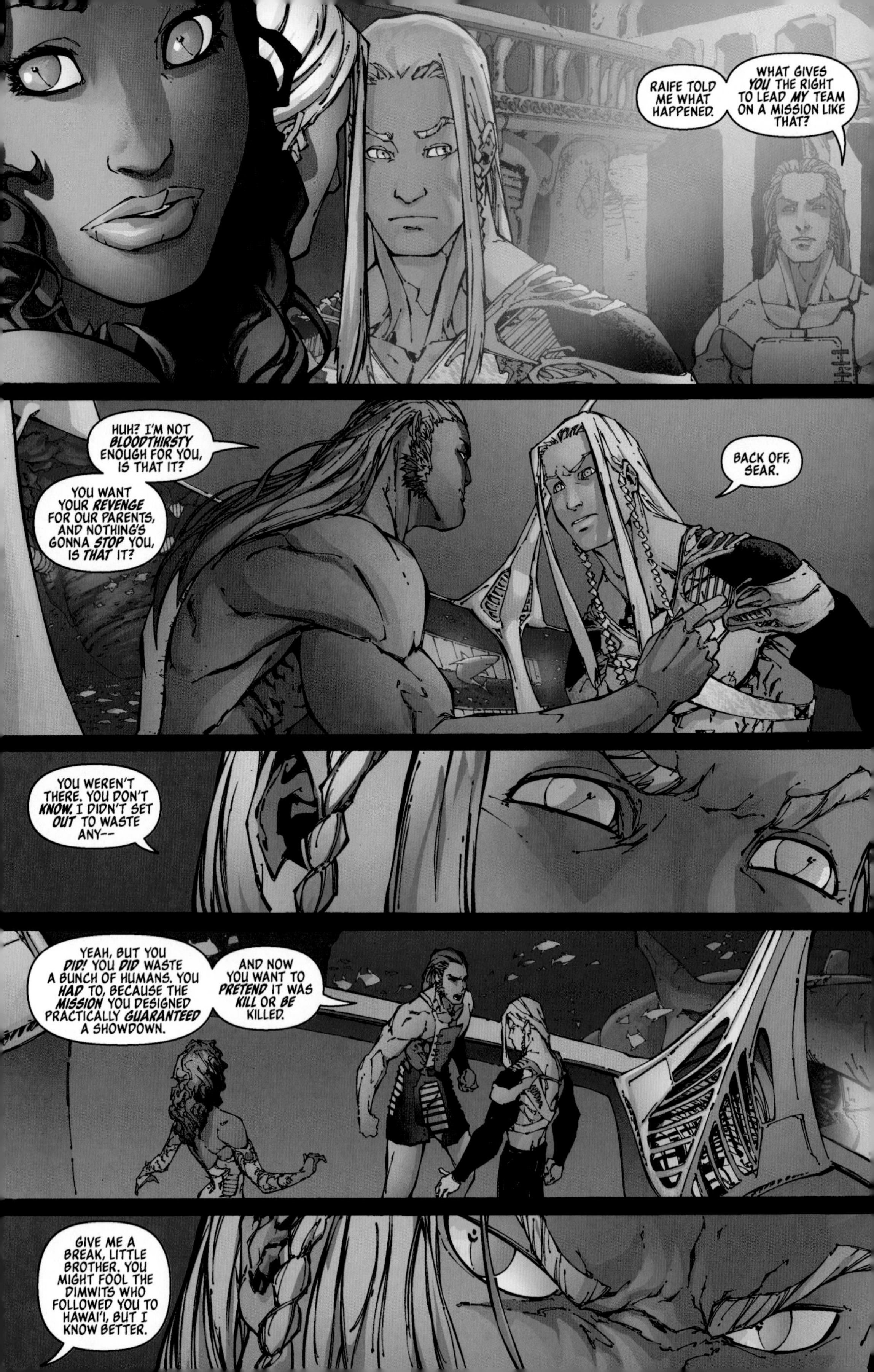
RAIFE TOLD ME WHAT HAPPENED.
WHAT GIVES *YOU* THE RIGHT TO LEAD *MY* TEAM ON A MISSION LIKE THAT?
HUH? I'M NOT *BLOODTHIRSTY* ENOUGH FOR YOU, IS THAT IT?
YOU WANT YOUR *REVENGE* FOR OUR PARENTS, AND NOTHING'S GONNA *STOP* YOU, IS *THAT* IT?
BACK OFF, SEAR.
YOU WEREN'T THERE. YOU DON'T *KNOW.* I DIDN'T SET *OUT* TO WASTE ANY--
YEAH, BUT YOU *DID!* YOU *DID* WASTE A BUNCH OF HUMANS. YOU *HAD* TO, BECAUSE THE *MISSION* YOU DESIGNED PRACTICALLY *GUARANTEED* A SHOWDOWN.
AND NOW YOU WANT TO *PRETEND* IT WAS *KILL* OR *BE* KILLED.
GIVE ME A BREAK, LITTLE BROTHER. YOU MIGHT FOOL THE DIMWITS WHO FOLLOWED YOU TO HAWAI'I, BUT I KNOW BETTER.

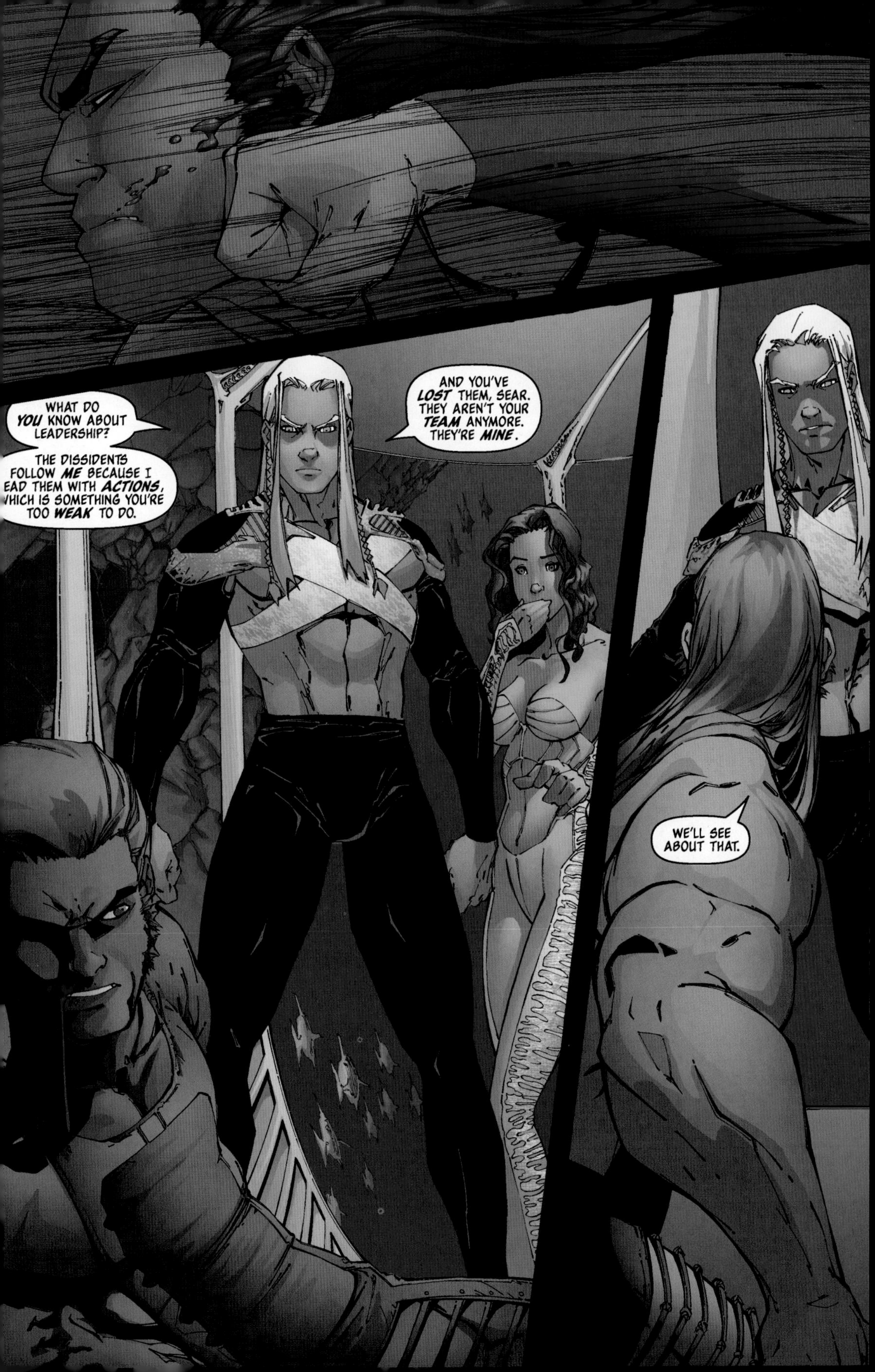
WHAT DO *YOU* KNOW ABOUT LEADERSHIP?
THE DISSIDENTS FOLLOW *ME* BECAUSE I EAD THEM WITH *ACTIONS*, WHICH IS SOMETHING YOU'RE TOO *WEAK* TO DO.
AND YOU'VE *LOST* THEM, SEAR. THEY AREN'T YOUR *TEAM* ANYMORE. THEY'RE *MINE*.
WE'LL SEE ABOUT THAT.

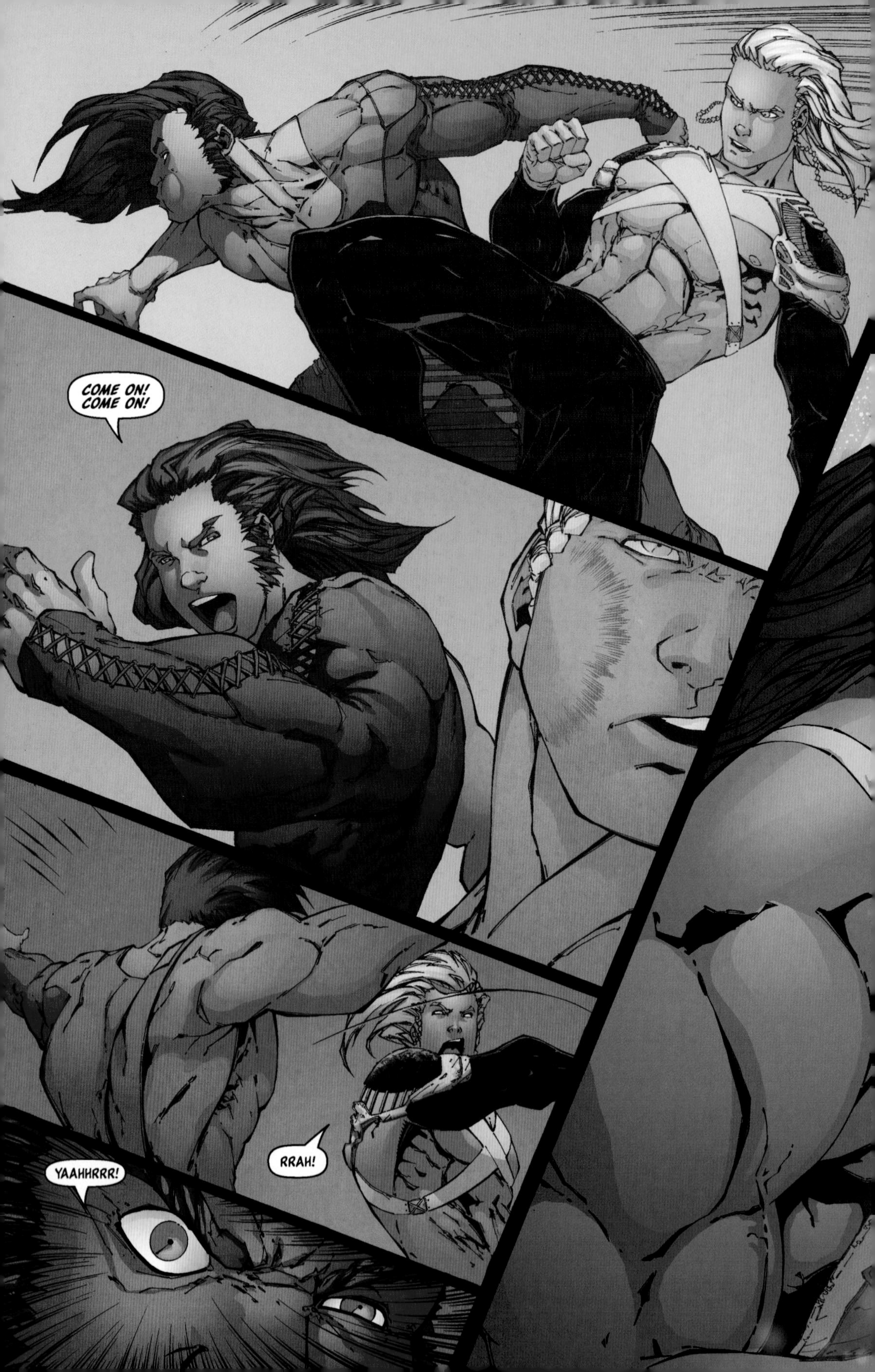
COME ON!
COME ON!
RRAH!
YAAHHRRR!

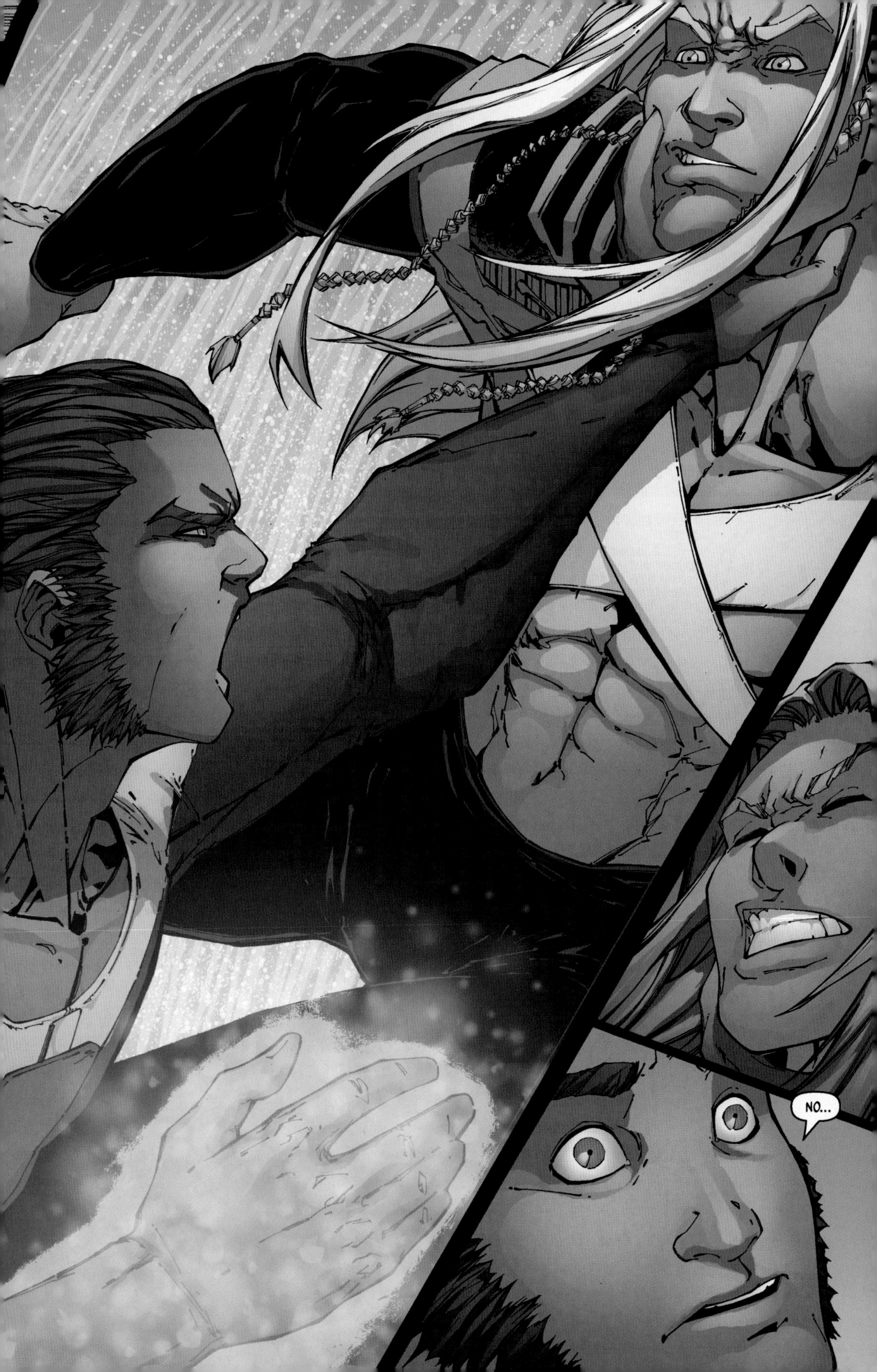
NO...

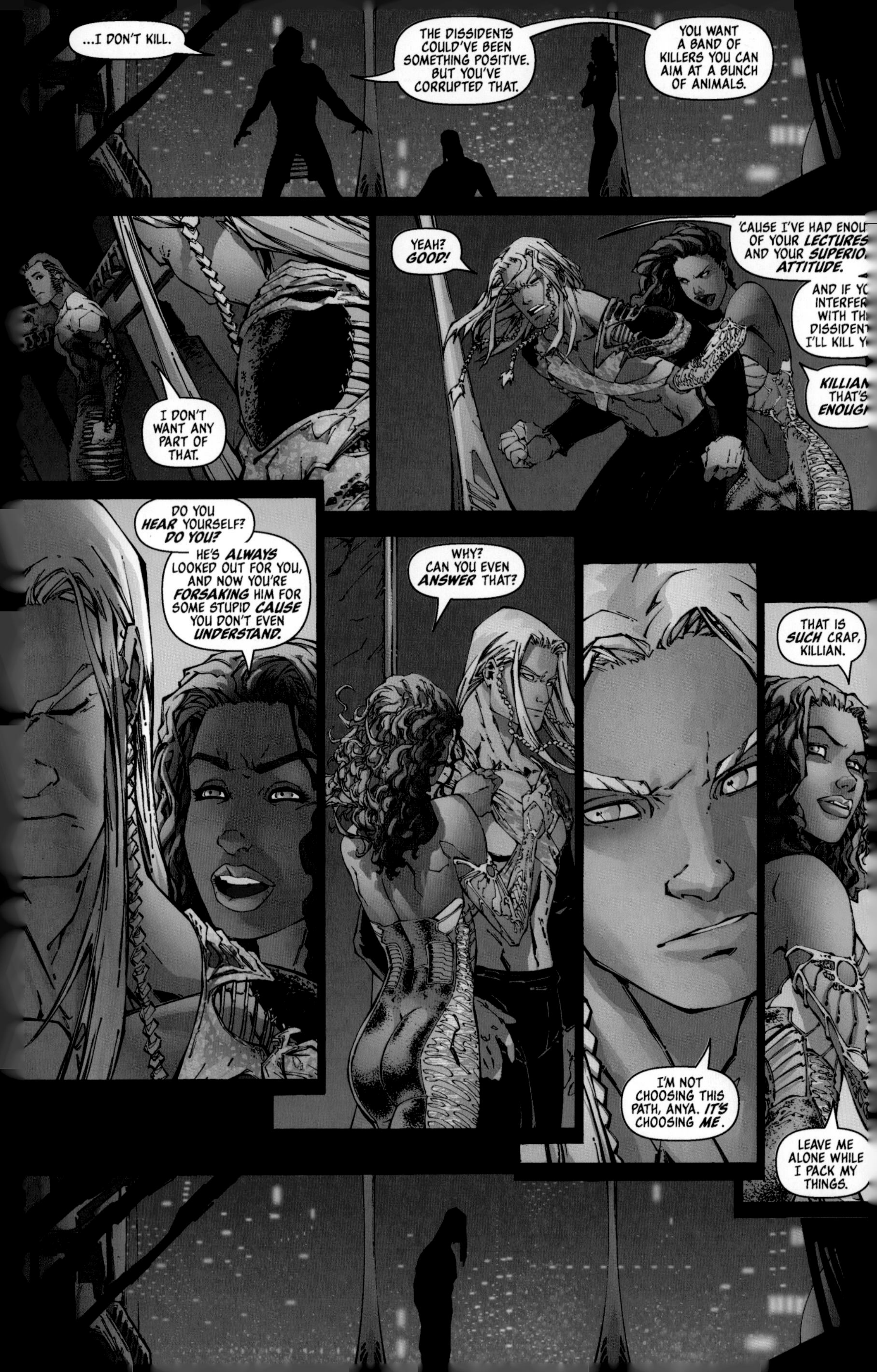

...I DON'T KILL.
THE DISSIDENTS COULD'VE BEEN SOMETHING POSITIVE. BUT YOU'VE CORRUPTED THAT.
YOU WANT A BAND OF KILLERS YOU CAN AIM AT A BUNCH OF ANIMALS.
I DON'T WANT ANY PART OF THAT.
YEAH? GOOD!
'CAUSE I'VE HAD ENOU OF YOUR LECTURES AND YOUR SUPERIO ATTITUDE.
AND IF YO INTERFER WITH THE DISSIDENT I'LL KILL Y
KILLIAN THAT'S ENOUG
DO YOU HEAR YOURSELF? DO YOU?
HE'S ALWAYS LOOKED OUT FOR YOU, AND NOW YOU'RE FORSAKING HIM FOR SOME STUPID CAUSE YOU DON'T EVEN UNDERSTAND.
WHY? CAN YOU EVEN ANSWER THAT?
I'M NOT CHOOSING THIS PATH, ANYA. IT'S CHOOSING ME.
THAT IS SUCH CRAP, KILLIAN.
LEAVE ME ALONE WHILE I PACK MY THINGS.

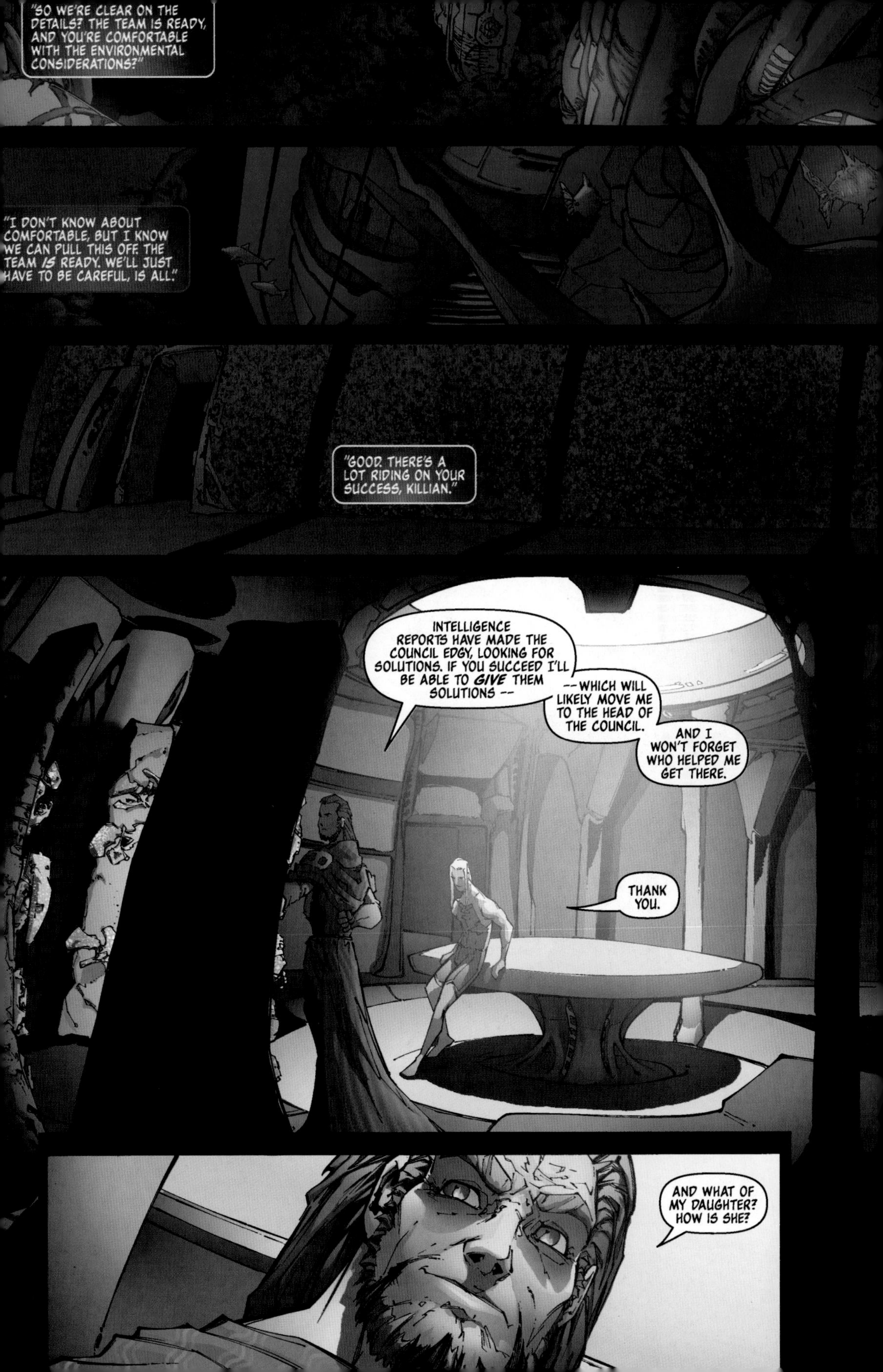
"SO WE'RE CLEAR ON THE DETAILS? THE TEAM IS READY, AND YOU'RE COMFORTABLE WITH THE ENVIRONMENTAL CONSIDERATIONS?"
"I DON'T KNOW ABOUT COMFORTABLE, BUT I KNOW WE CAN PULL THIS OFF. THE TEAM IS READY. WE'LL JUST HAVE TO BE CAREFUL, IS ALL."
"GOOD. THERE'S A LOT RIDING ON YOUR SUCCESS, KILLIAN."
INTELLIGENCE REPORTS HAVE MADE THE COUNCIL EDGY, LOOKING FOR SOLUTIONS. IF YOU SUCCEED I'LL BE ABLE TO GIVE THEM SOLUTIONS --
--WHICH WILL LIKELY MOVE ME TO THE HEAD OF THE COUNCIL.
AND I WON'T FORGET WHO HELPED ME GET THERE.
THANK YOU.
AND WHAT OF MY DAUGHTER? HOW IS SHE?

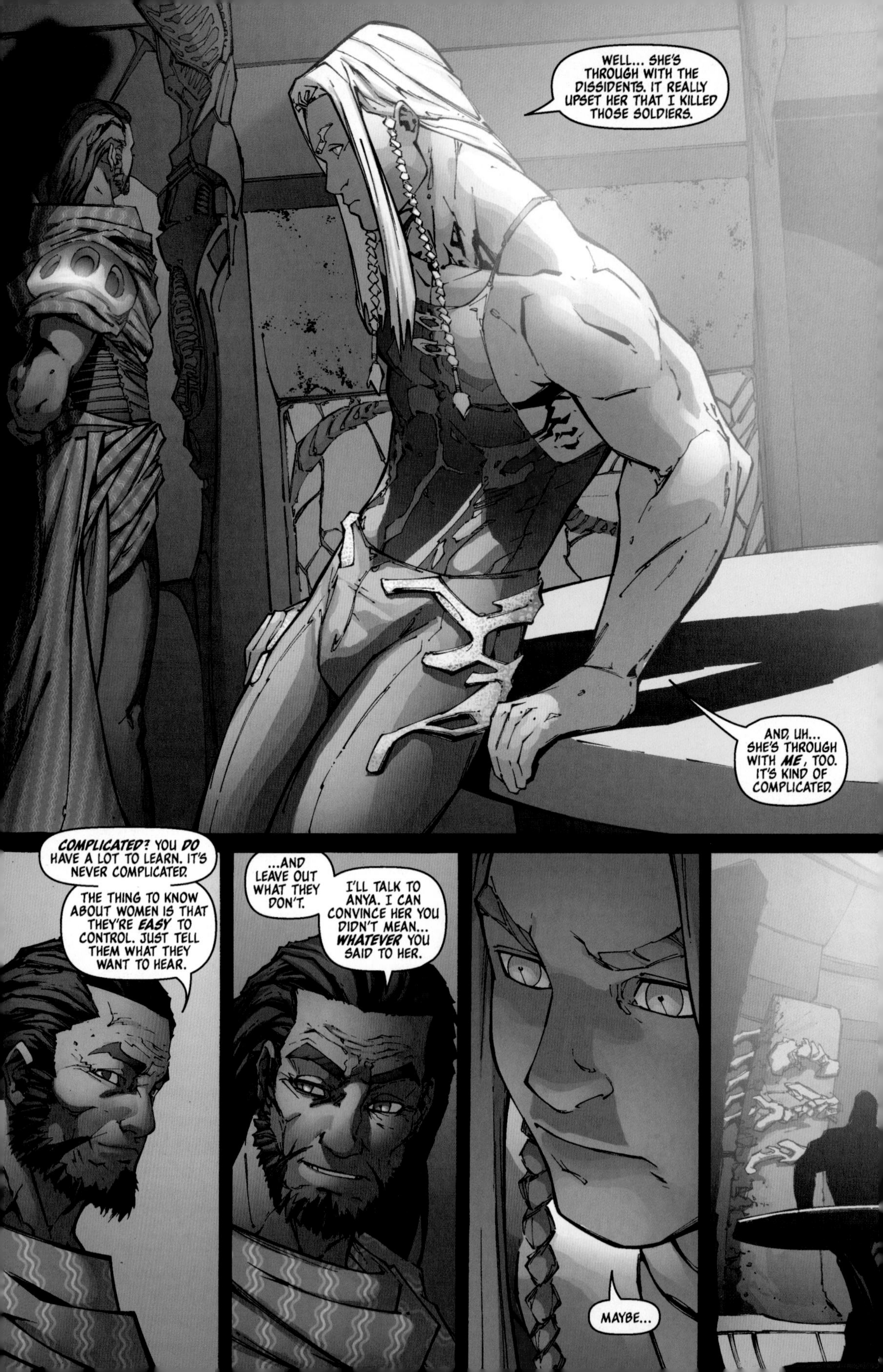
WELL... SHE'S THROUGH WITH THE DISSIDENTS. IT REALLY UPSET HER THAT I KILLED THOSE SOLDIERS.
AND, UH... SHE'S THROUGH WITH *ME*, TOO. IT'S KIND OF COMPLICATED.
COMPLICATED? YOU *DO* HAVE A LOT TO LEARN. IT'S NEVER COMPLICATED.
THE THING TO KNOW ABOUT WOMEN IS THAT THEY'RE *EASY* TO CONTROL. JUST TELL THEM WHAT THEY WANT TO HEAR.
...AND LEAVE OUT WHAT THEY DON'T.
I'LL TALK TO ANYA. I CAN CONVINCE HER YOU DIDN'T MEAN... *WHATEVER* YOU SAID TO HER.
MAYBE...

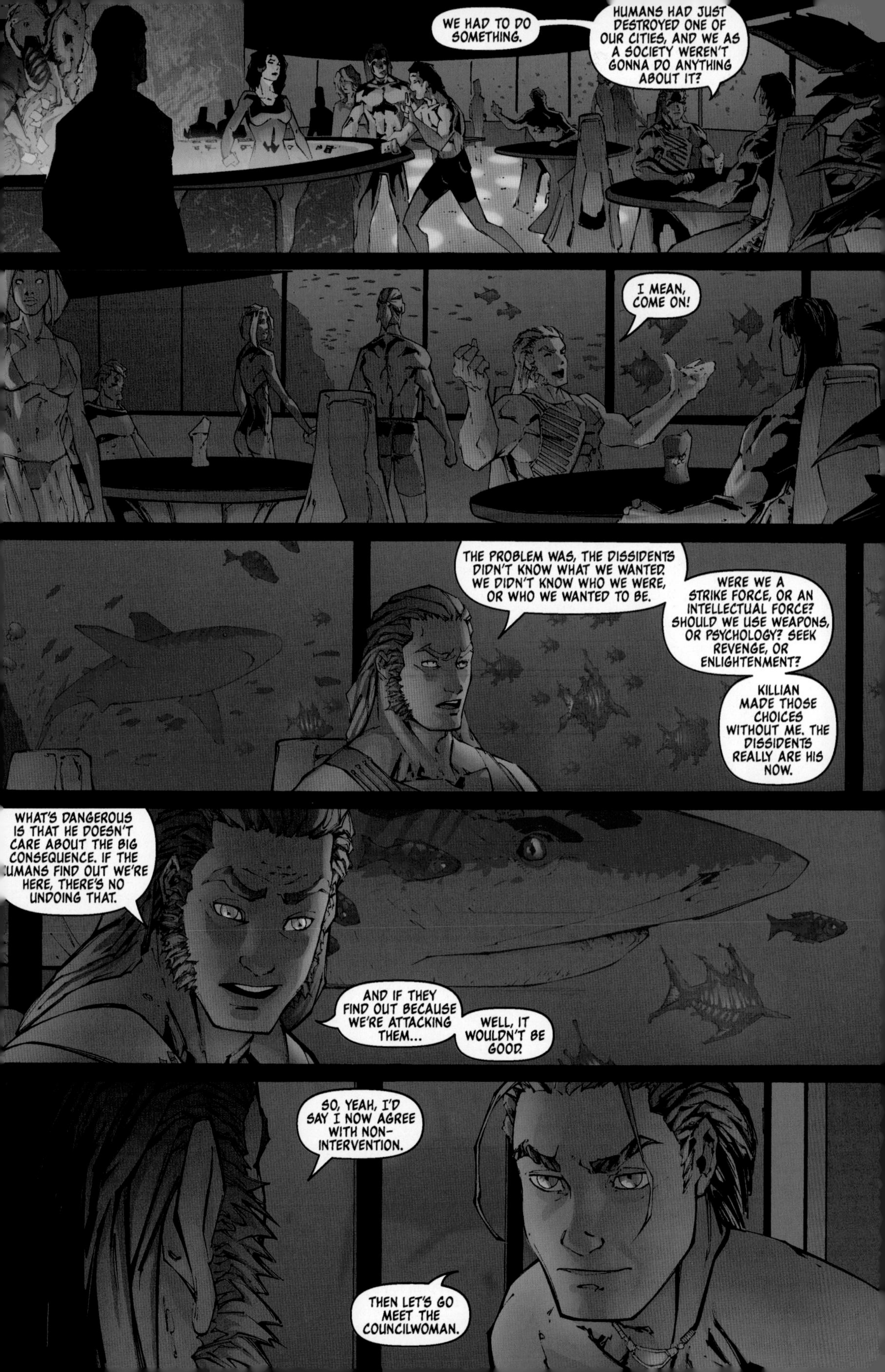
WE HAD TO DO SOMETHING.
HUMANS HAD JUST DESTROYED ONE OF OUR CITIES, AND WE AS A SOCIETY WEREN'T GONNA DO ANYTHING ABOUT IT?
I MEAN, COME ON!
THE PROBLEM WAS, THE DISSIDENTS DIDN'T KNOW WHAT WE WANTED. WE DIDN'T KNOW WHO WE WERE, OR WHO WE WANTED TO BE.
WERE WE A STRIKE FORCE, OR AN INTELLECTUAL FORCE? SHOULD WE USE WEAPONS, OR PSYCHOLOGY? SEEK REVENGE, OR ENLIGHTENMENT?
KILLIAN MADE THOSE CHOICES WITHOUT ME. THE DISSIDENTS REALLY ARE HIS NOW.
WHAT'S DANGEROUS IS THAT HE DOESN'T CARE ABOUT THE BIG CONSEQUENCE. IF THE HUMANS FIND OUT WE'RE HERE, THERE'S NO UNDOING THAT.
AND IF THEY FIND OUT BECAUSE WE'RE ATTACKING THEM...
WELL, IT WOULDN'T BE GOOD.
SO, YEAH, I'D SAY I NOW AGREE WITH NON-INTERVENTION.
THEN LET'S GO MEET THE COUNCILWOMAN.

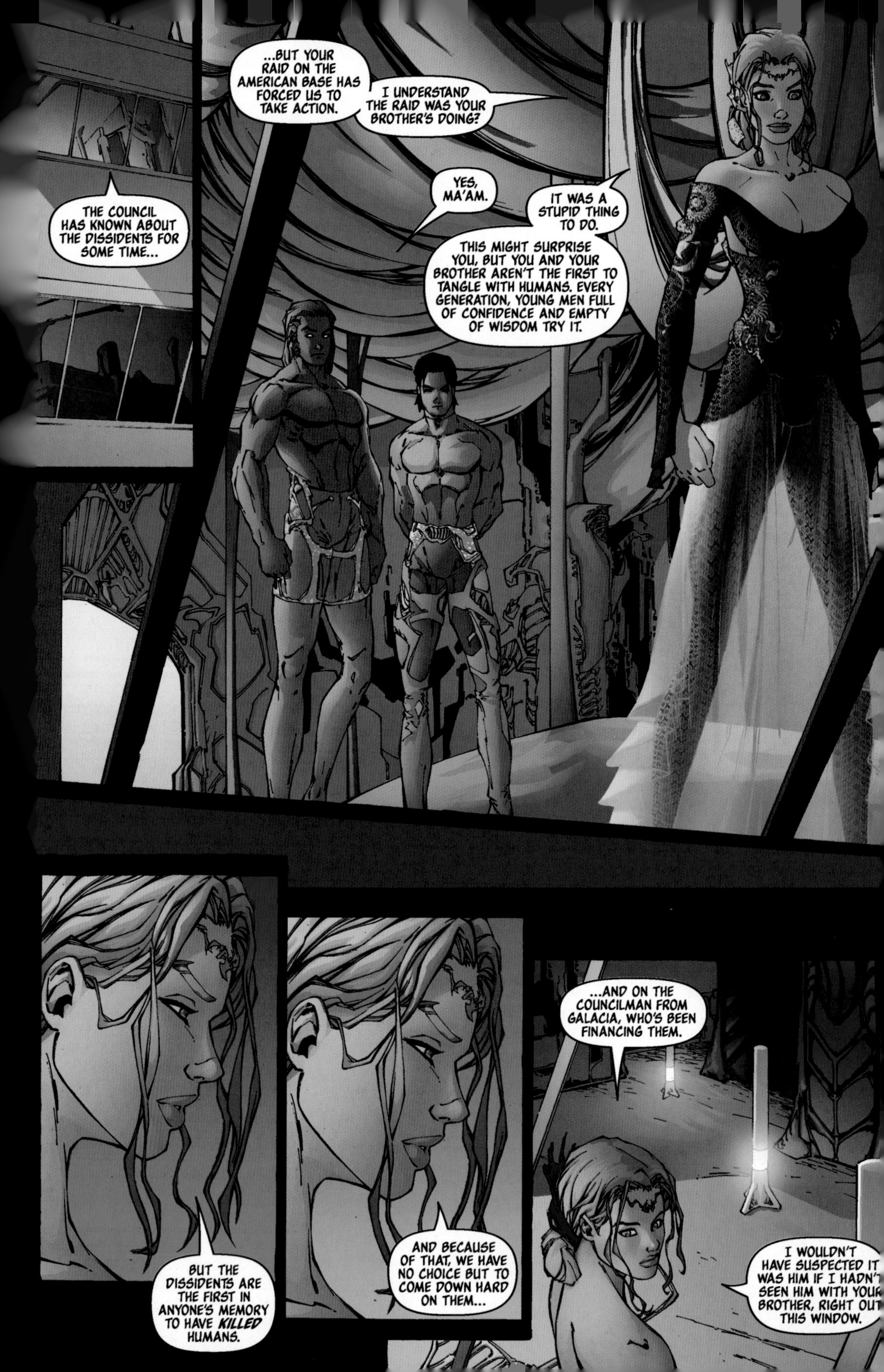
...BUT YOUR RAID ON THE AMERICAN BASE HAS FORCED US TO TAKE ACTION.
I UNDERSTAND THE RAID WAS YOUR BROTHER'S DOING?
THE COUNCIL HAS KNOWN ABOUT THE DISSIDENTS FOR SOME TIME...
YES, MA'AM.
IT WAS A STUPID THING TO DO.
THIS MIGHT SURPRISE YOU, BUT YOU AND YOUR BROTHER AREN'T THE FIRST TO TANGLE WITH HUMANS. EVERY GENERATION, YOUNG MEN FULL OF CONFIDENCE AND EMPTY OF WISDOM TRY IT.
BUT THE DISSIDENTS ARE THE FIRST IN ANYONE'S MEMORY TO HAVE *KILLED* HUMANS.
AND BECAUSE OF THAT, WE HAVE NO CHOICE BUT TO COME DOWN HARD ON THEM...
...AND ON THE COUNCILMAN FROM GALACIA, WHO'S BEEN FINANCING THEM.
I WOULDN'T HAVE SUSPECTED IT WAS HIM IF I HADN'T SEEN HIM WITH YOUR BROTHER, RIGHT OUT THIS WINDOW.

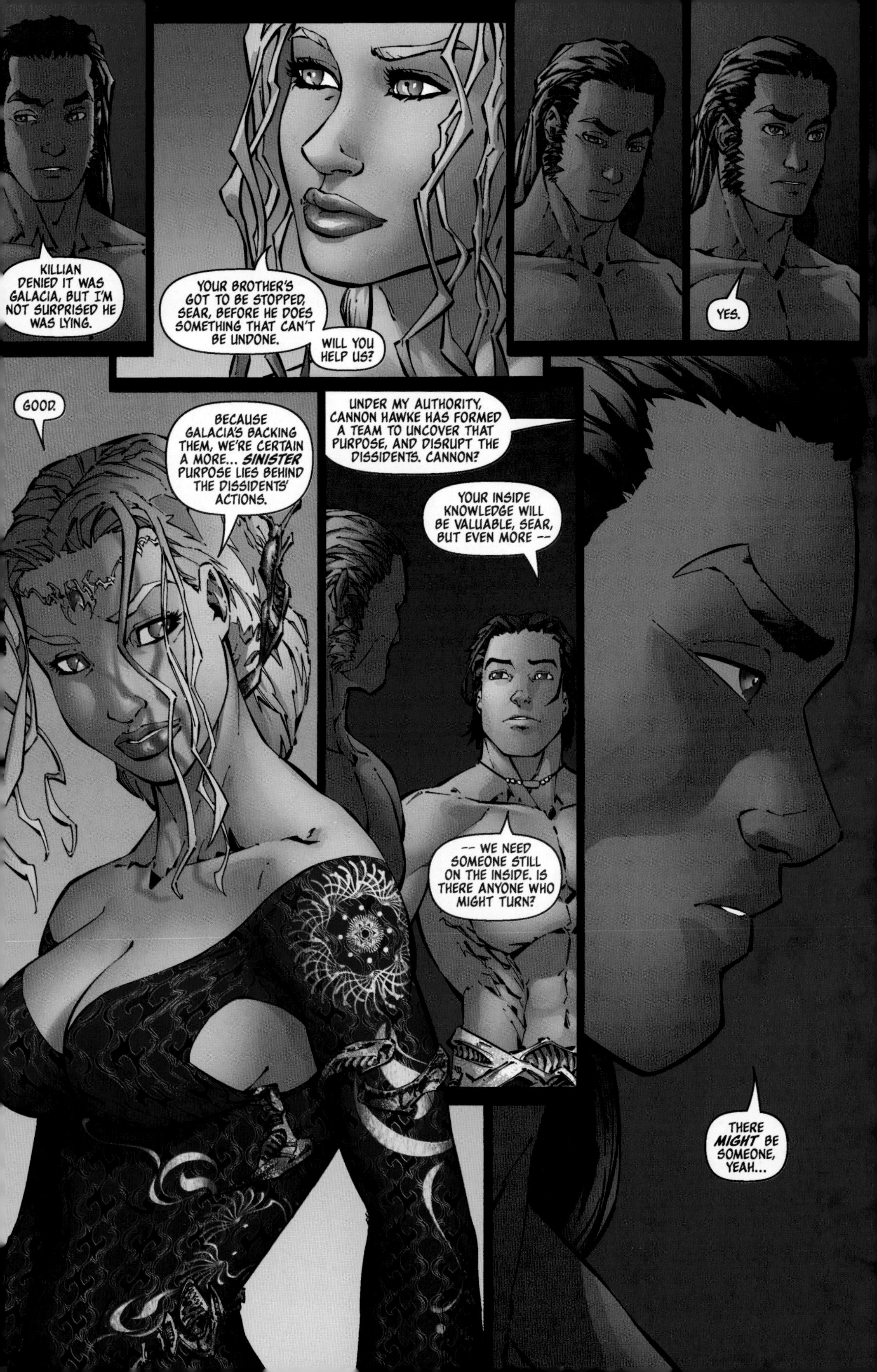
KILLIAN DENIED IT WAS GALACIA, BUT I'M NOT SURPRISED HE WAS LYING.
YOUR BROTHER'S GOT TO BE STOPPED, SEAR, BEFORE HE DOES SOMETHING THAT CAN'T BE UNDONE.
WILL YOU HELP US?
YES.
GOOD.
BECAUSE GALACIA'S BACKING THEM, WE'RE CERTAIN A MORE... *SINISTER* PURPOSE LIES BEHIND THE DISSIDENTS' ACTIONS.
UNDER MY AUTHORITY, CANNON HAWKE HAS FORMED A TEAM TO UNCOVER THAT PURPOSE, AND DISRUPT THE DISSIDENTS. CANNON?
YOUR INSIDE KNOWLEDGE WILL BE VALUABLE, SEAR, BUT EVEN MORE --
-- WE NEED SOMEONE STILL ON THE INSIDE. IS THERE ANYONE WHO MIGHT TURN?
THERE *MIGHT* BE SOMEONE, YEAH...

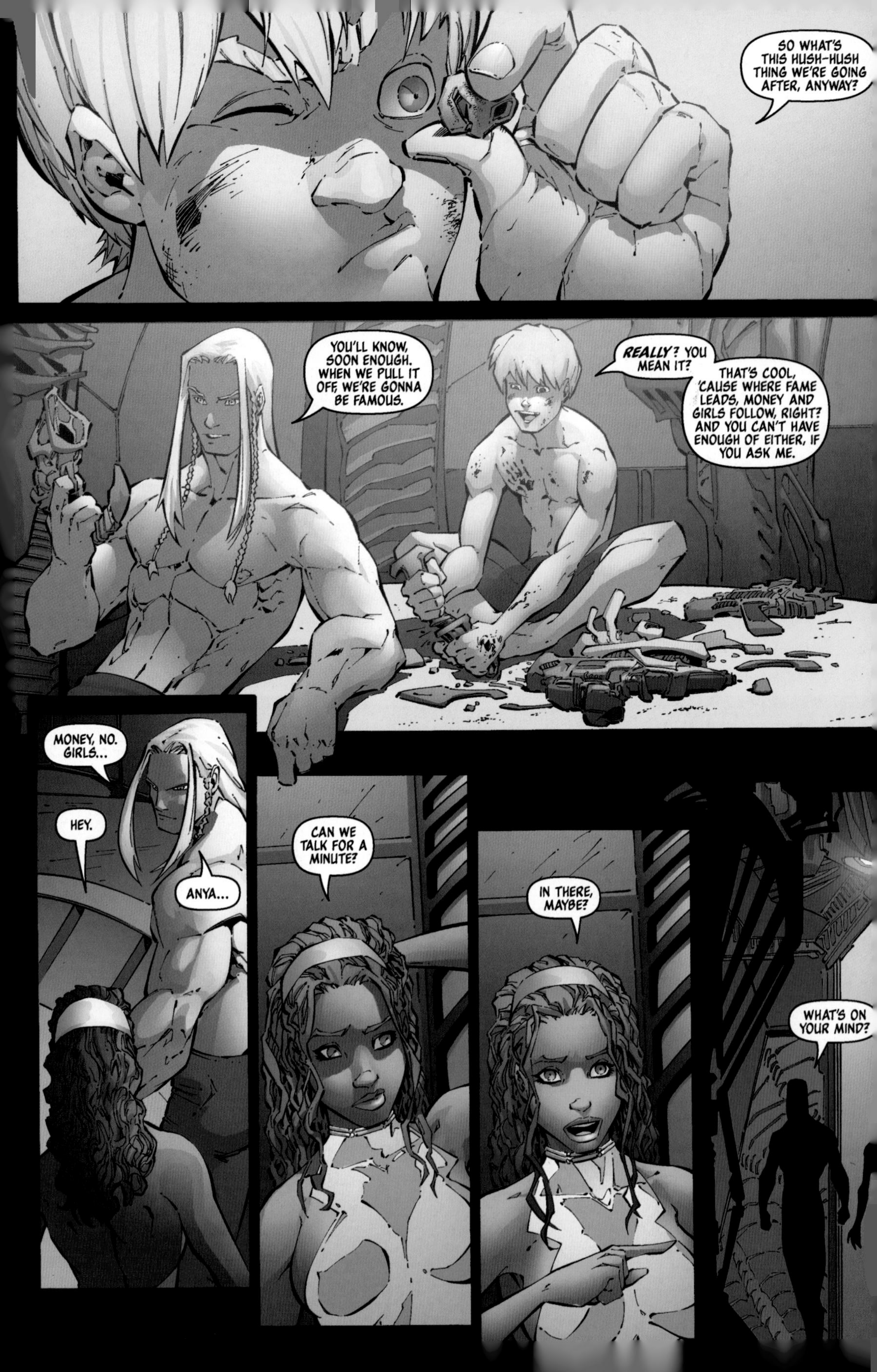
SO WHAT'S THIS HUSH-HUSH THING WE'RE GOING AFTER, ANYWAY?
YOU'LL KNOW, SOON ENOUGH. WHEN WE PULL IT OFF, WE'RE GONNA BE FAMOUS.
REALLY? YOU MEAN IT?
THAT'S COOL, 'CAUSE WHERE FAME LEADS, MONEY AND GIRLS FOLLOW, RIGHT? AND YOU CAN'T HAVE ENOUGH OF EITHER, IF YOU ASK ME.
MONEY, NO. GIRLS...
HEY.
ANYA...
CAN WE TALK FOR A MINUTE?
IN THERE, MAYBE?
WHAT'S ON YOUR MIND?

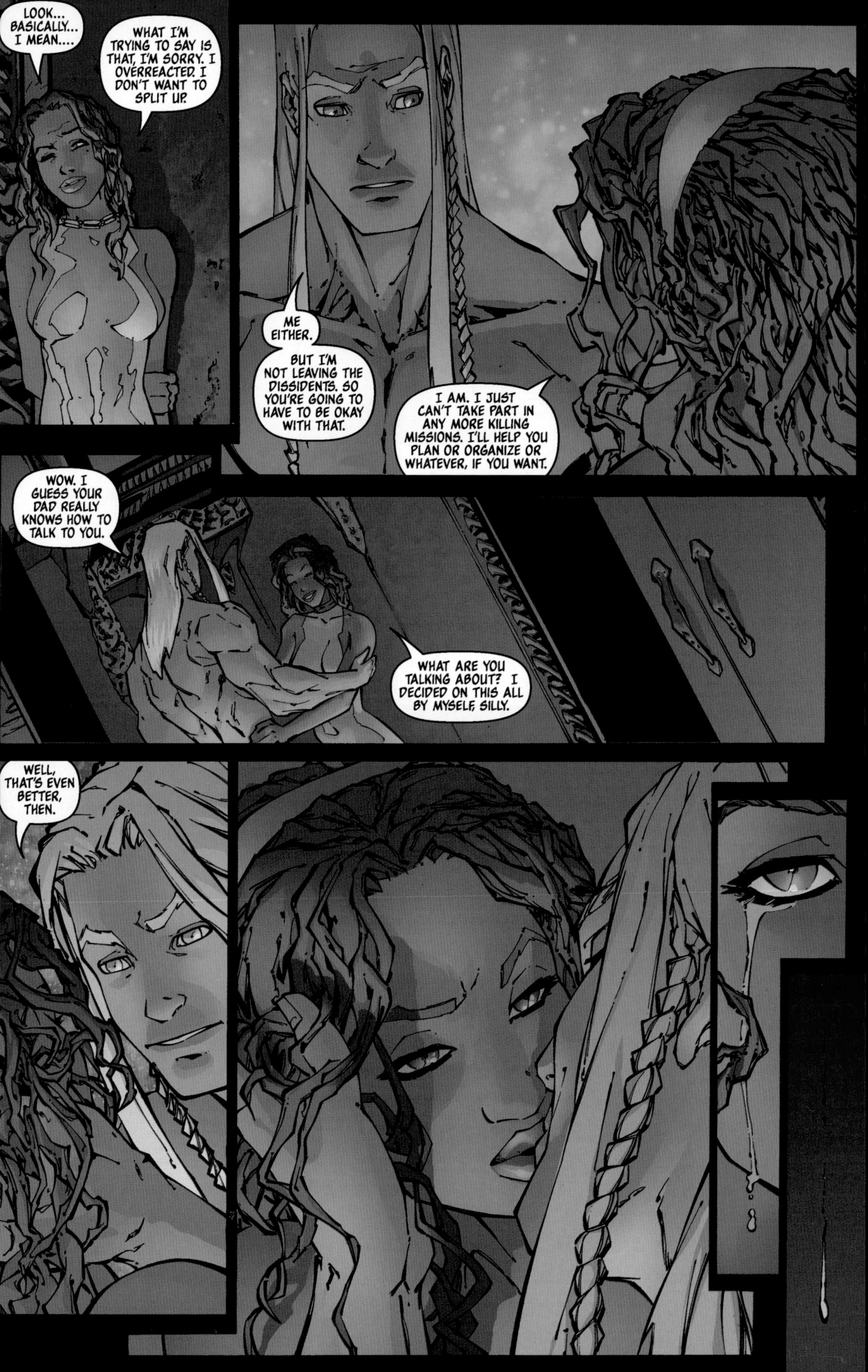
LOOK... BASICALLY... I MEAN....
WHAT I'M TRYING TO SAY IS THAT, I'M SORRY. I OVERREACTED. I DON'T WANT TO SPLIT UP.
ME EITHER.
BUT I'M NOT LEAVING THE DISSIDENTS. SO YOU'RE GOING TO HAVE TO BE OKAY WITH THAT.
I AM. I JUST CAN'T TAKE PART IN ANY MORE KILLING MISSIONS. I'LL HELP YOU PLAN OR ORGANIZE OR WHATEVER, IF YOU WANT.
WOW. I GUESS YOUR DAD REALLY KNOWS HOW TO TALK TO YOU.
WHAT ARE YOU TALKING ABOUT? I DECIDED ON THIS ALL BY MYSELF, SILLY.
WELL, THAT'S EVEN BETTER, THEN.

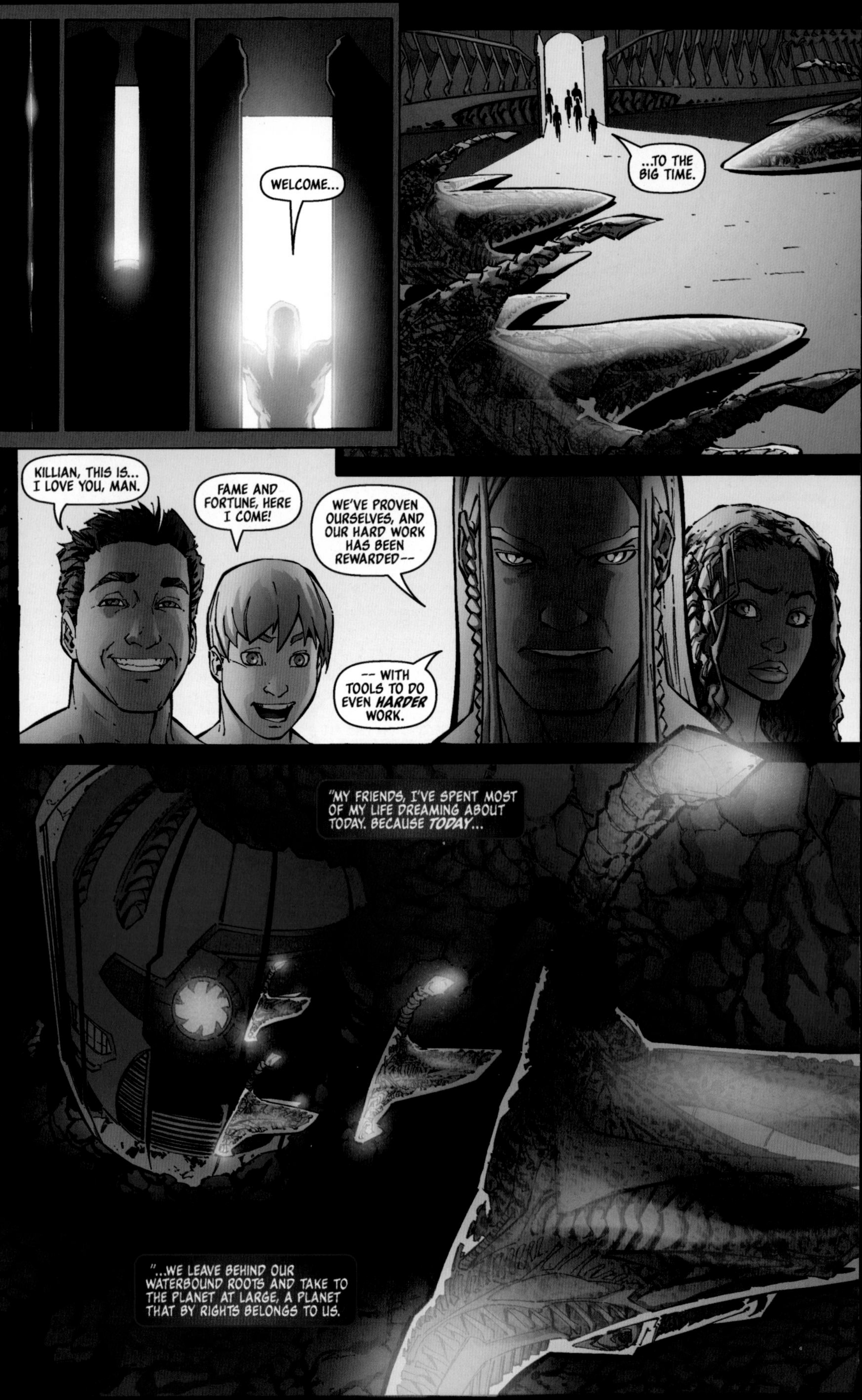
WELCOME...
...TO THE BIG TIME.
KILLIAN, THIS IS... I LOVE YOU, MAN.
FAME AND FORTUNE, HERE I COME!
WE'VE PROVEN OURSELVES, AND OUR HARD WORK HAS BEEN REWARDED--
-- WITH TOOLS TO DO EVEN HARDER WORK.
"MY FRIENDS, I'VE SPENT MOST OF MY LIFE DREAMING ABOUT TODAY. BECAUSE TODAY...
"...WE LEAVE BEHIND OUR WATERBOUND ROOTS AND TAKE TO THE PLANET AT LARGE, A PLANET THAT BY RIGHTS BELONGS TO US.

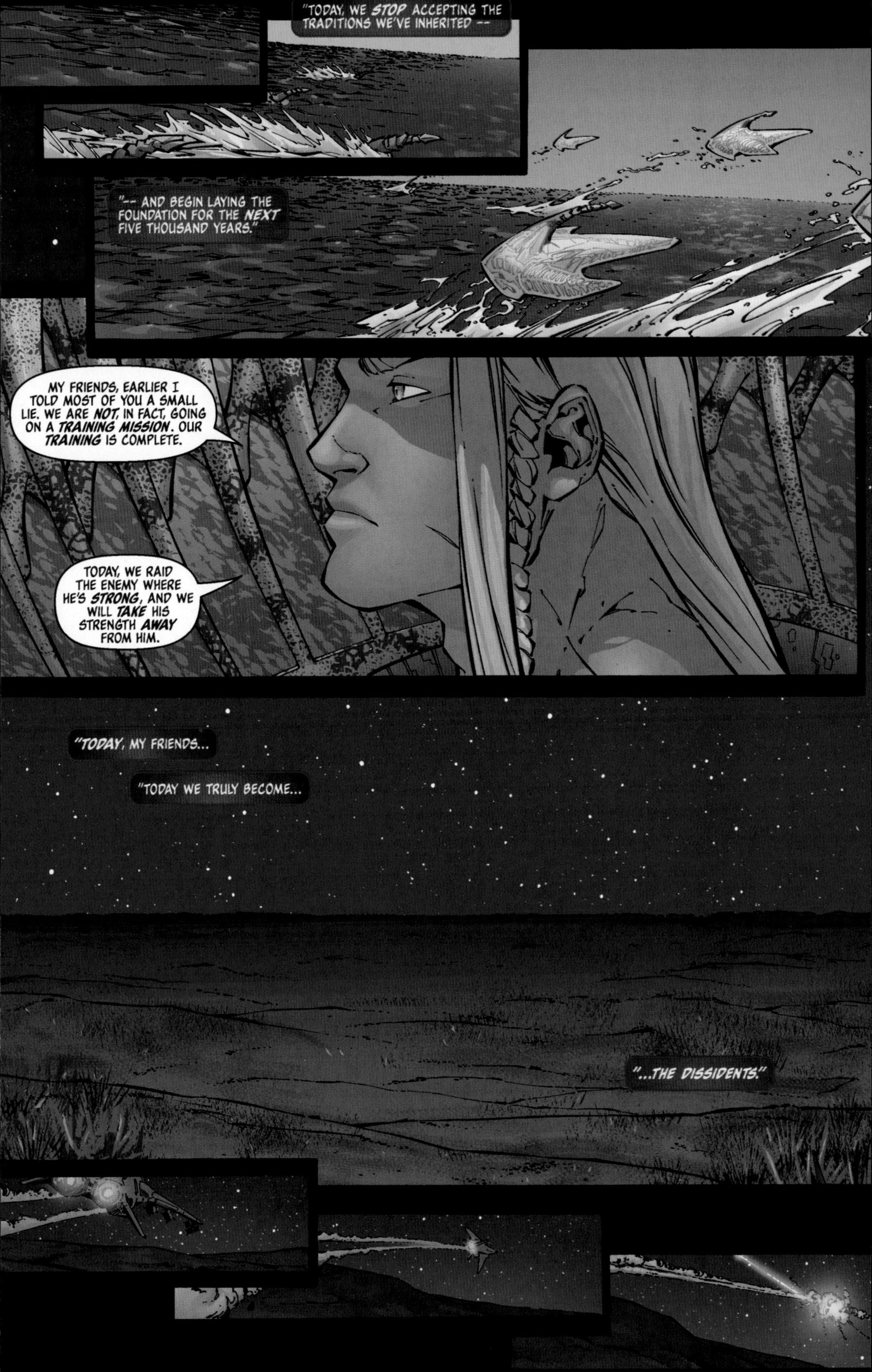
"TODAY, WE STOP ACCEPTING THE TRADITIONS WE'VE INHERITED --
"-- AND BEGIN LAYING THE FOUNDATION FOR THE NEXT FIVE THOUSAND YEARS."
MY FRIENDS, EARLIER I TOLD MOST OF YOU A SMALL LIE. WE ARE NOT, IN FACT, GOING ON A TRAINING MISSION. OUR TRAINING IS COMPLETE.
TODAY, WE RAID THE ENEMY WHERE HE'S STRONG, AND WE WILL TAKE HIS STRENGTH AWAY FROM HIM.
"TODAY, MY FRIENDS...
"TODAY WE TRULY BECOME...
"...THE DISSIDENTS."

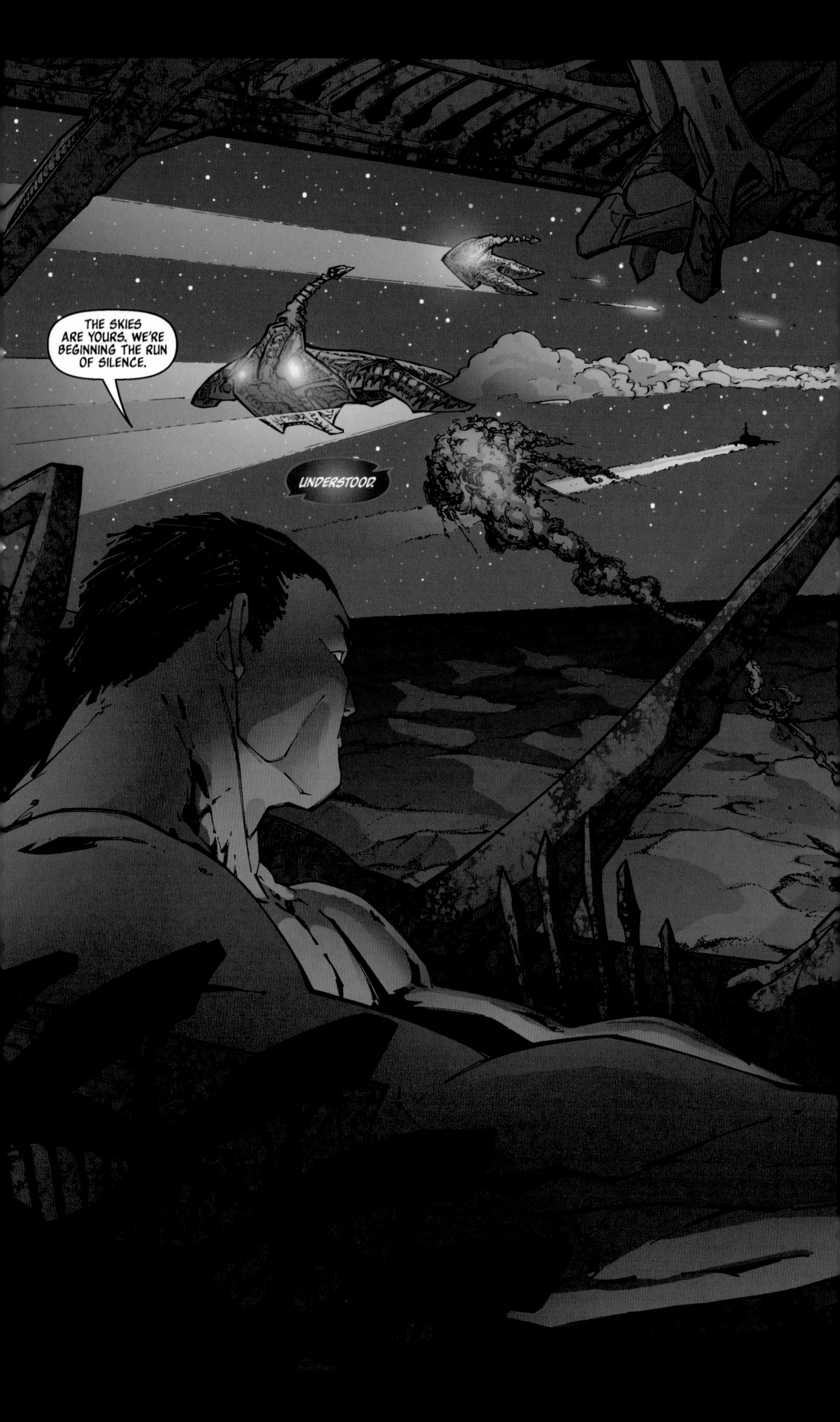
THE SKIES ARE YOURS. WE'RE BEGINNING THE RUN OF SILENCE.
UNDERSTOOD.

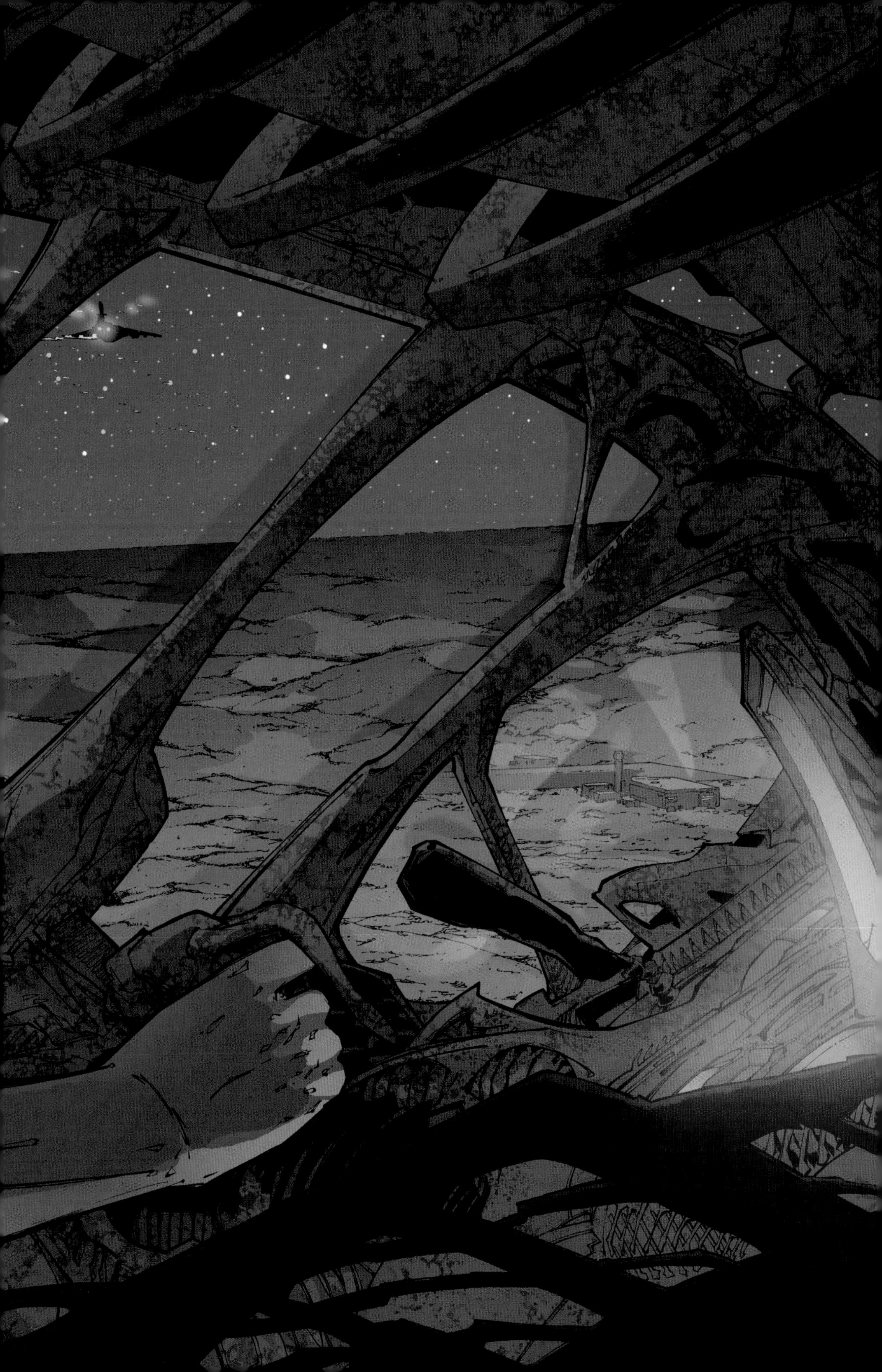

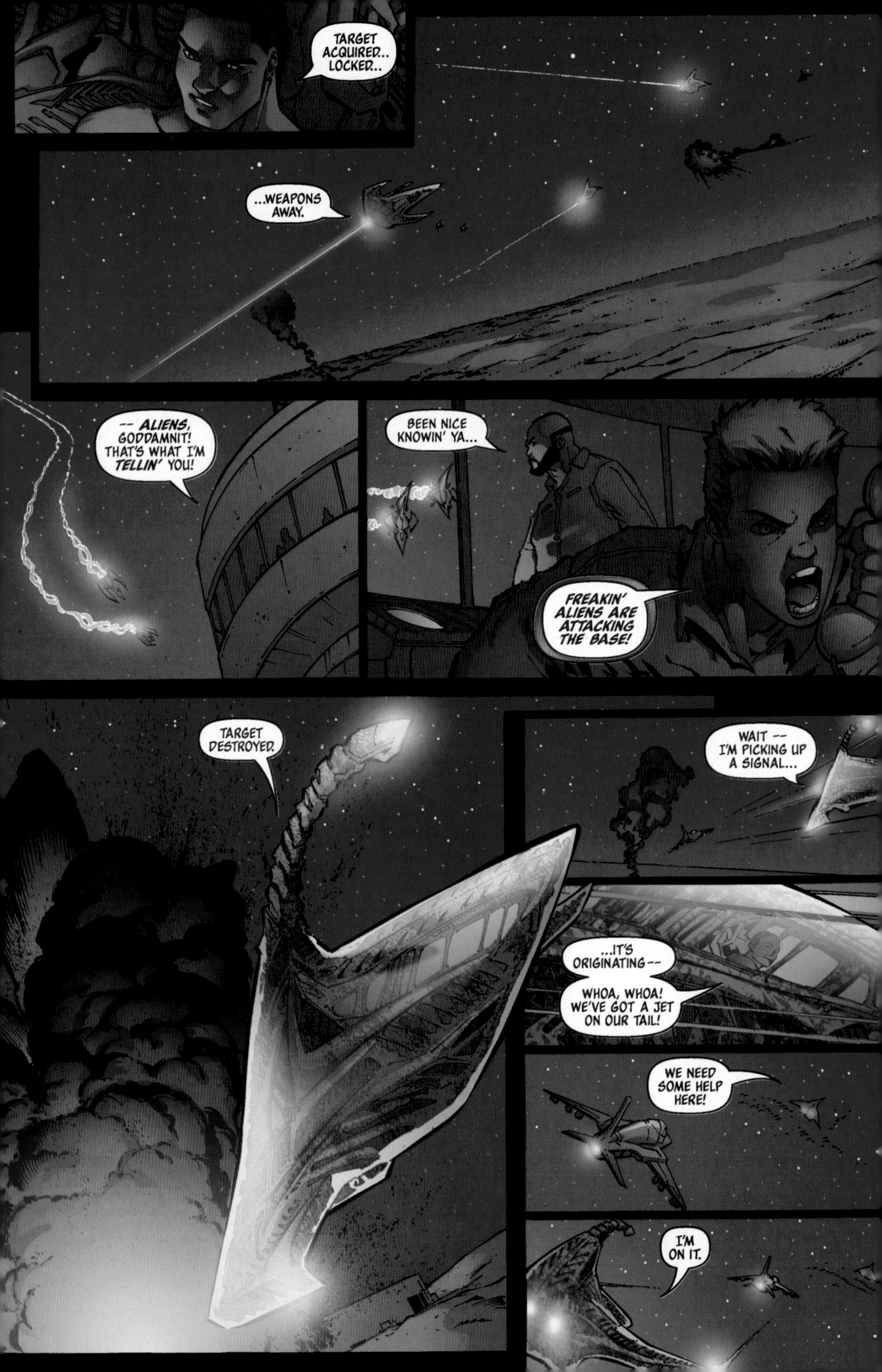
TARGET ACQUIRED... LOCKED...
...WEAPONS AWAY.
-- ALIENS, GODDAMNIT! THAT'S WHAT I'M TELLIN' YOU!
BEEN NICE KNOWIN' YA...
FREAKIN' ALIENS ARE ATTACKING THE BASE!
TARGET DESTROYED.
WAIT -- I'M PICKING UP A SIGNAL...
...IT'S ORIGINATING--
WHOA, WHOA! WE'VE GOT A JET ON OUR TAIL!
WE NEED SOME HELP HERE!
I'M ON IT.

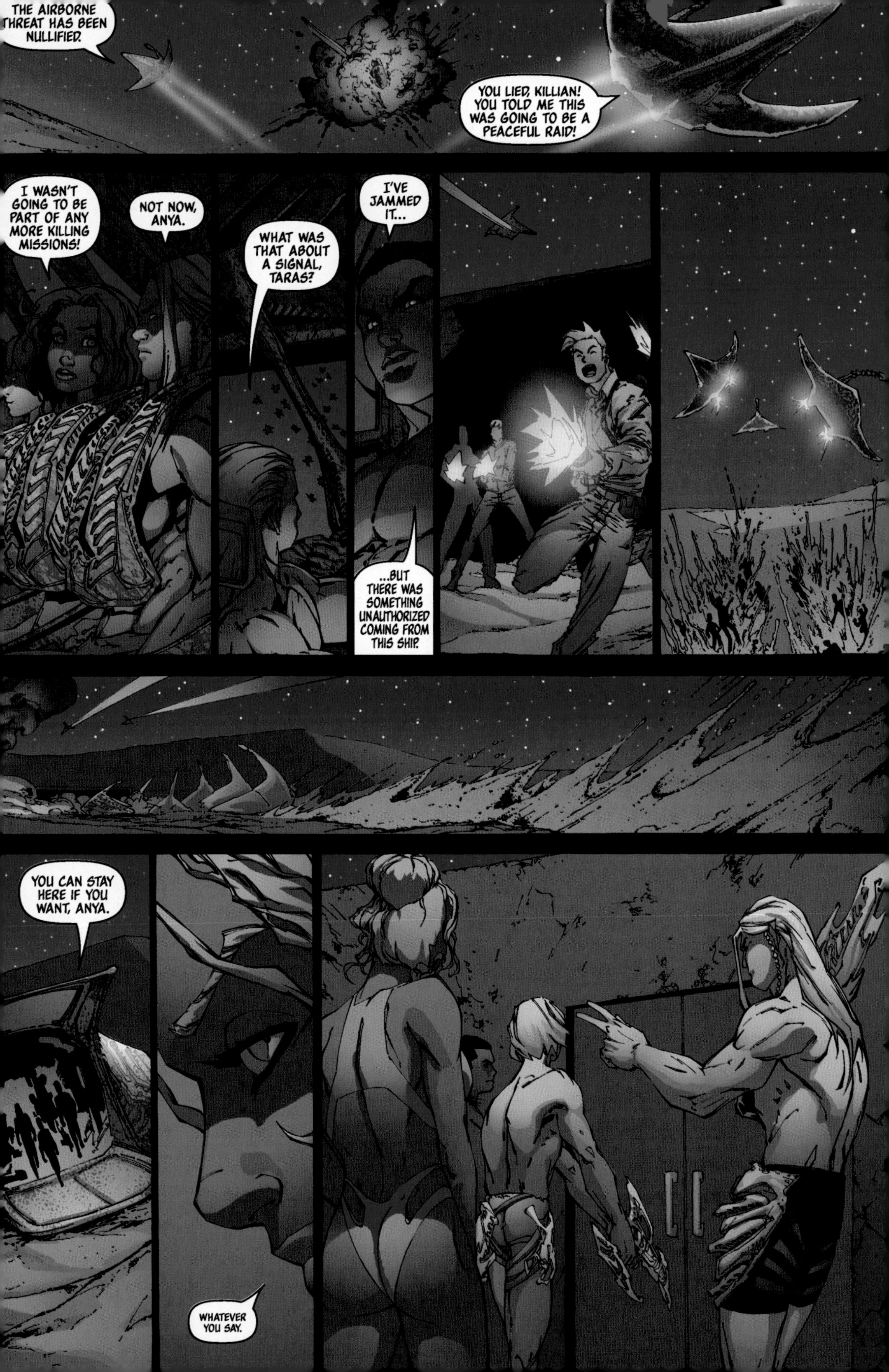

THE AIRBORNE THREAT HAS BEEN NULLIFIED.
YOU LIED, KILLIAN! YOU TOLD ME THIS WAS GOING TO BE A PEACEFUL RAID!
I WASN'T GOING TO BE PART OF ANY MORE KILLING MISSIONS!
NOT NOW, ANYA.
WHAT WAS THAT ABOUT A SIGNAL, TARAS?
I'VE JAMMED IT...
...BUT THERE WAS SOMETHING UNAUTHORIZED COMING FROM THIS SHIP.
YOU CAN STAY HERE IF YOU WANT, ANYA.
WHATEVER YOU SAY.

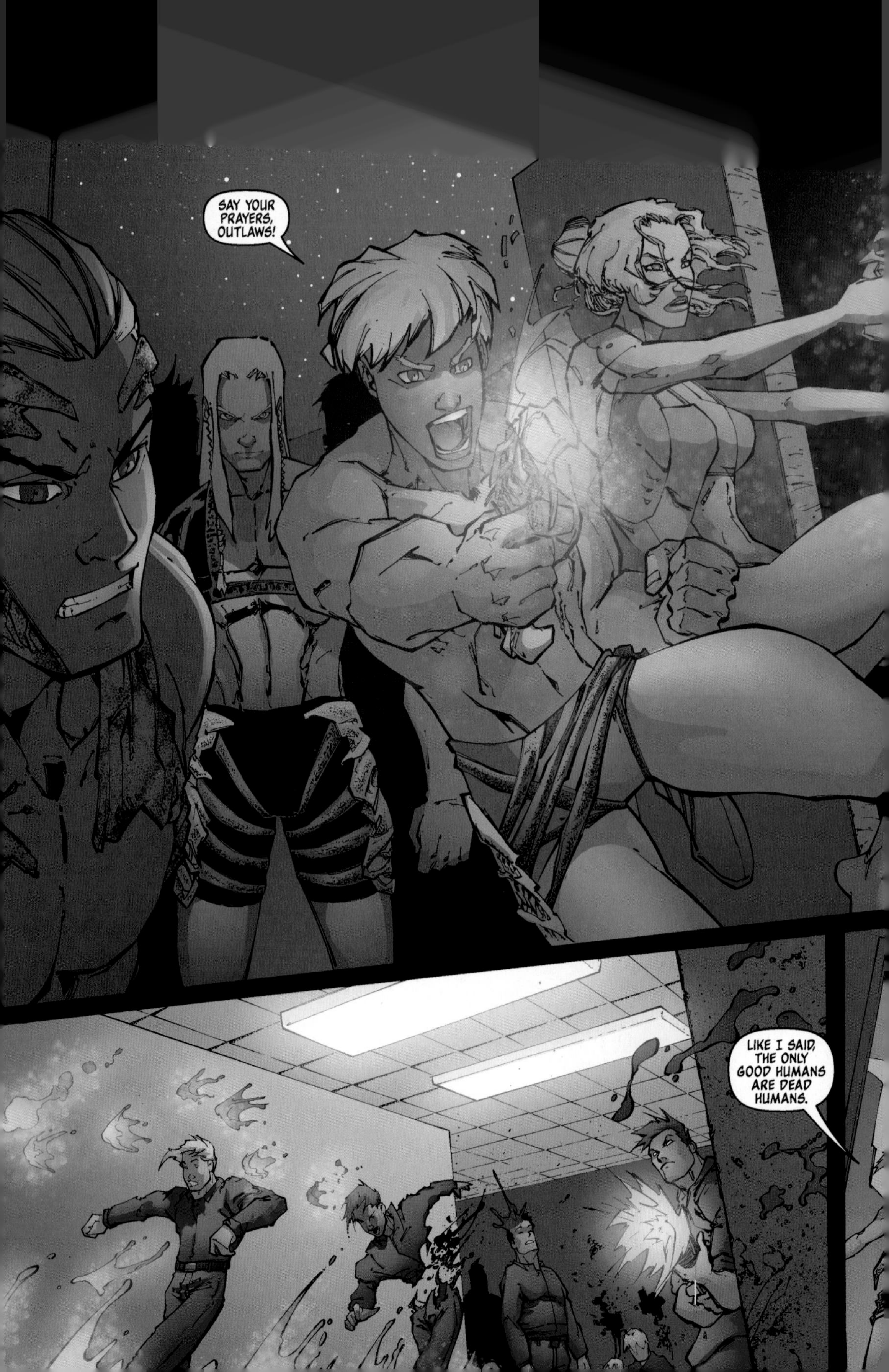
SAY YOUR PRAYERS, OUTLAWS!
LIKE I SAID, THE ONLY GOOD HUMANS ARE DEAD HUMANS.

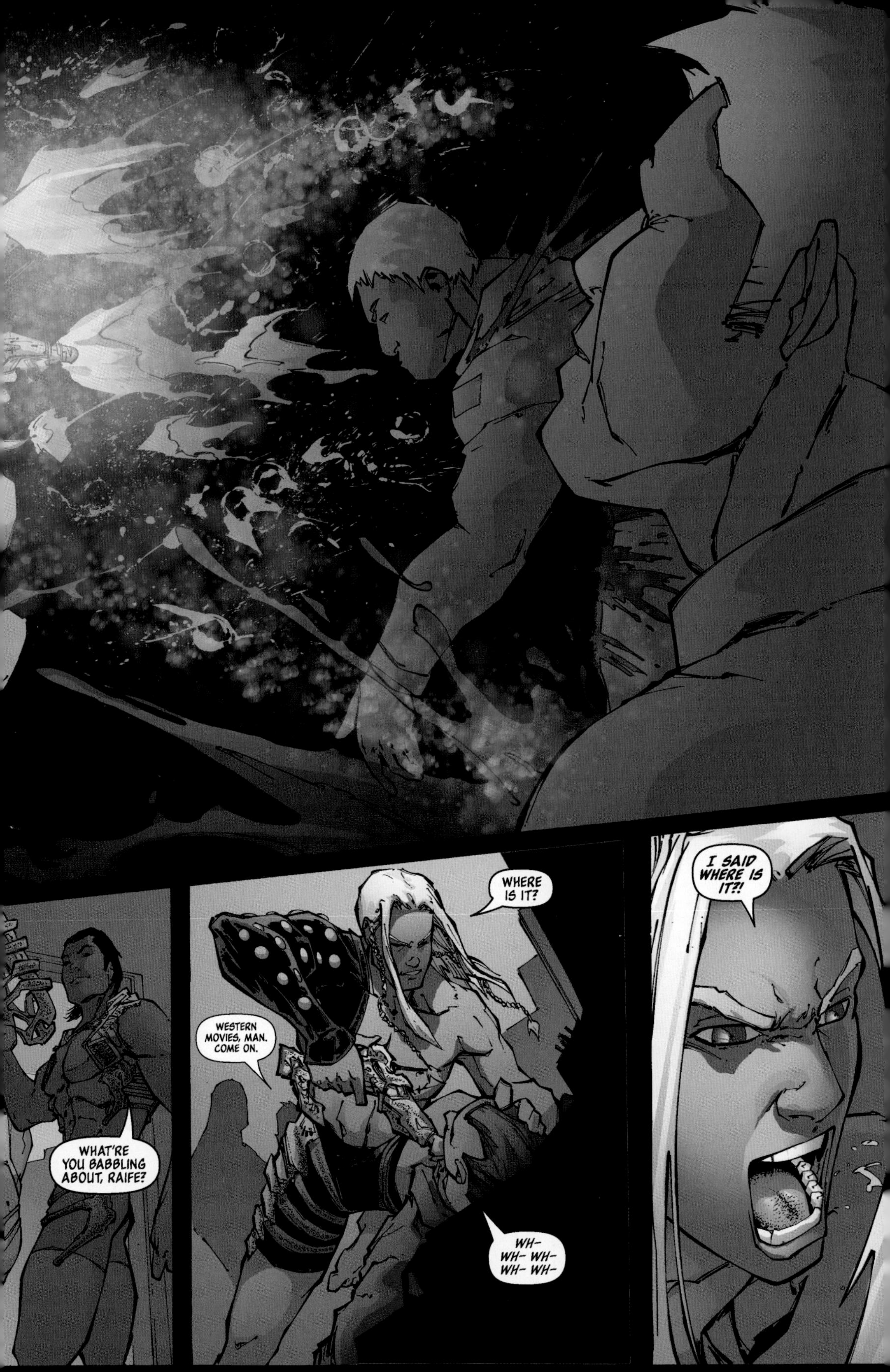
WHAT'RE YOU BABBLING ABOUT, RAIFE?
WHERE IS IT?
WESTERN MOVIES, MAN. COME ON.
WH- WH- WH- WH- WH-
I SAID WHERE IS IT?!

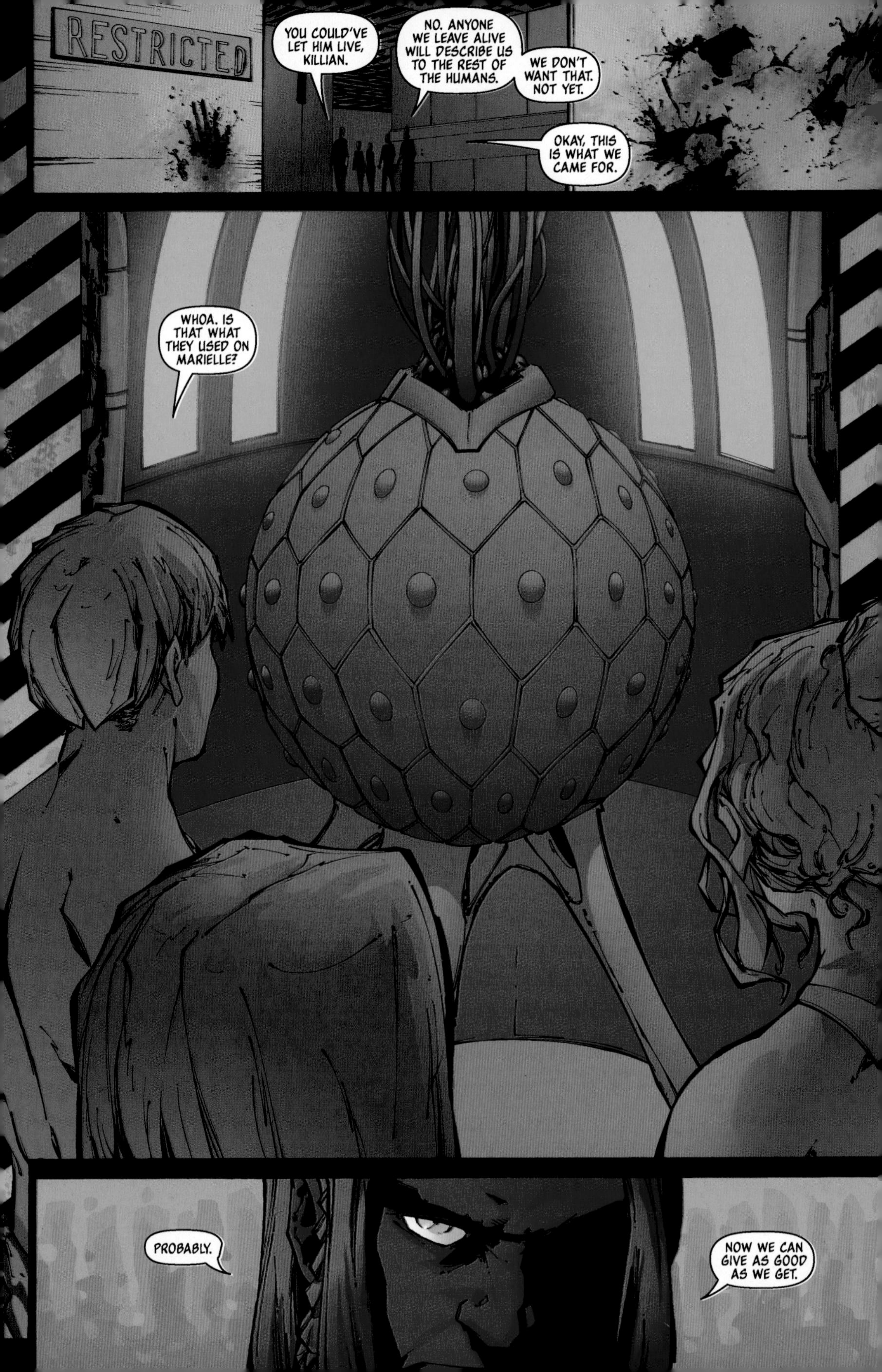
RESTRICTED
YOU COULD'VE LET HIM LIVE, KILLIAN.
NO. ANYONE WE LEAVE ALIVE WILL DESCRIBE US TO THE REST OF THE HUMANS.
WE DON'T WANT THAT. NOT YET.
OKAY, THIS IS WHAT WE CAME FOR.
WHOA. IS THAT WHAT THEY USED ON MARIELLE?
PROBABLY.
NOW WE CAN GIVE AS GOOD AS WE GET.

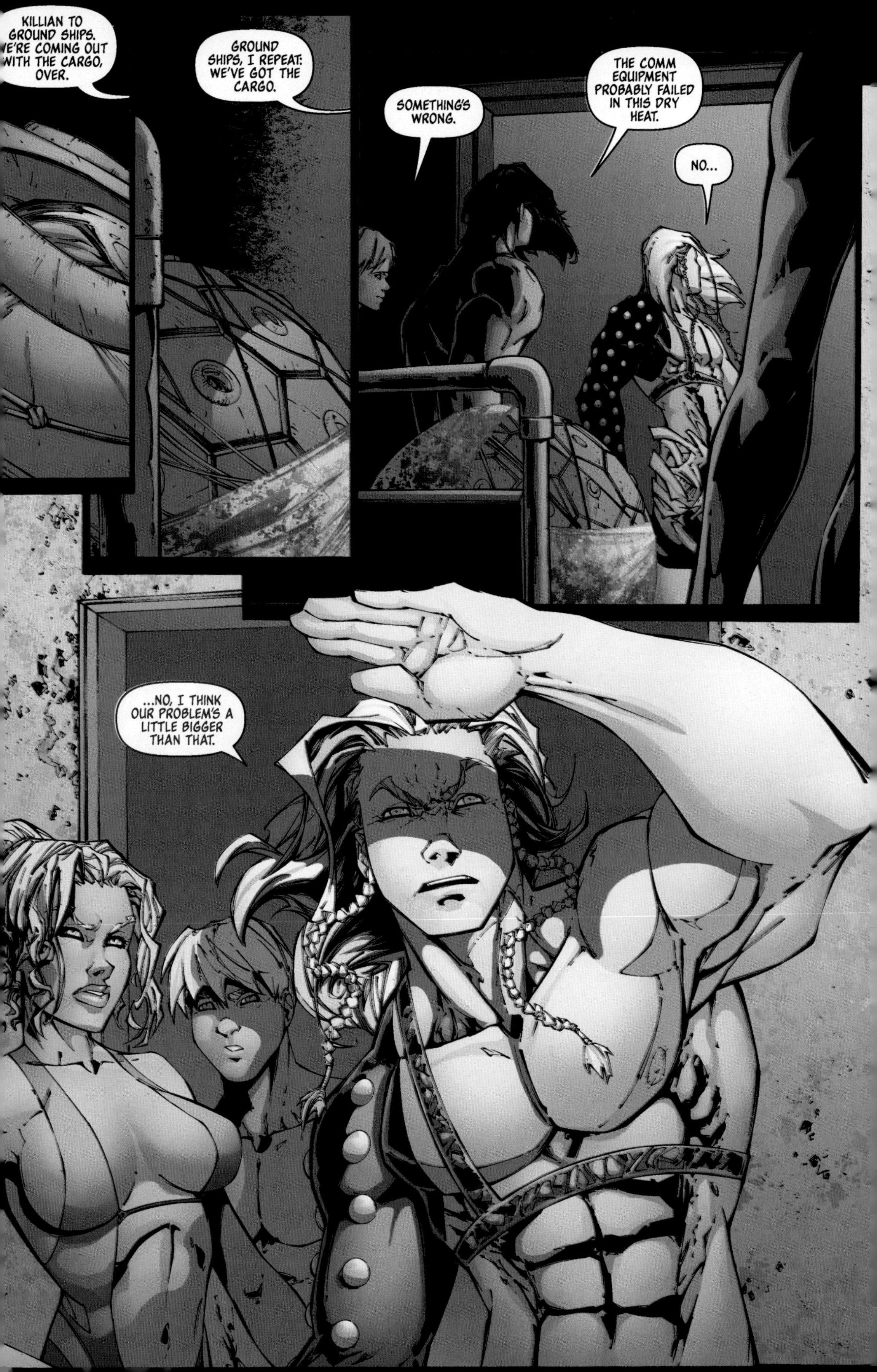
KILLIAN TO GROUND SHIPS. WE'RE COMING OUT WITH THE CARGO, OVER.
GROUND SHIPS, I REPEAT: WE'VE GOT THE CARGO.
SOMETHING'S WRONG.
THE COMM EQUIPMENT PROBABLY FAILED IN THIS DRY HEAT.
NO...
...NO, I THINK OUR PROBLEM'S A LITTLE BIGGER THAN THAT.

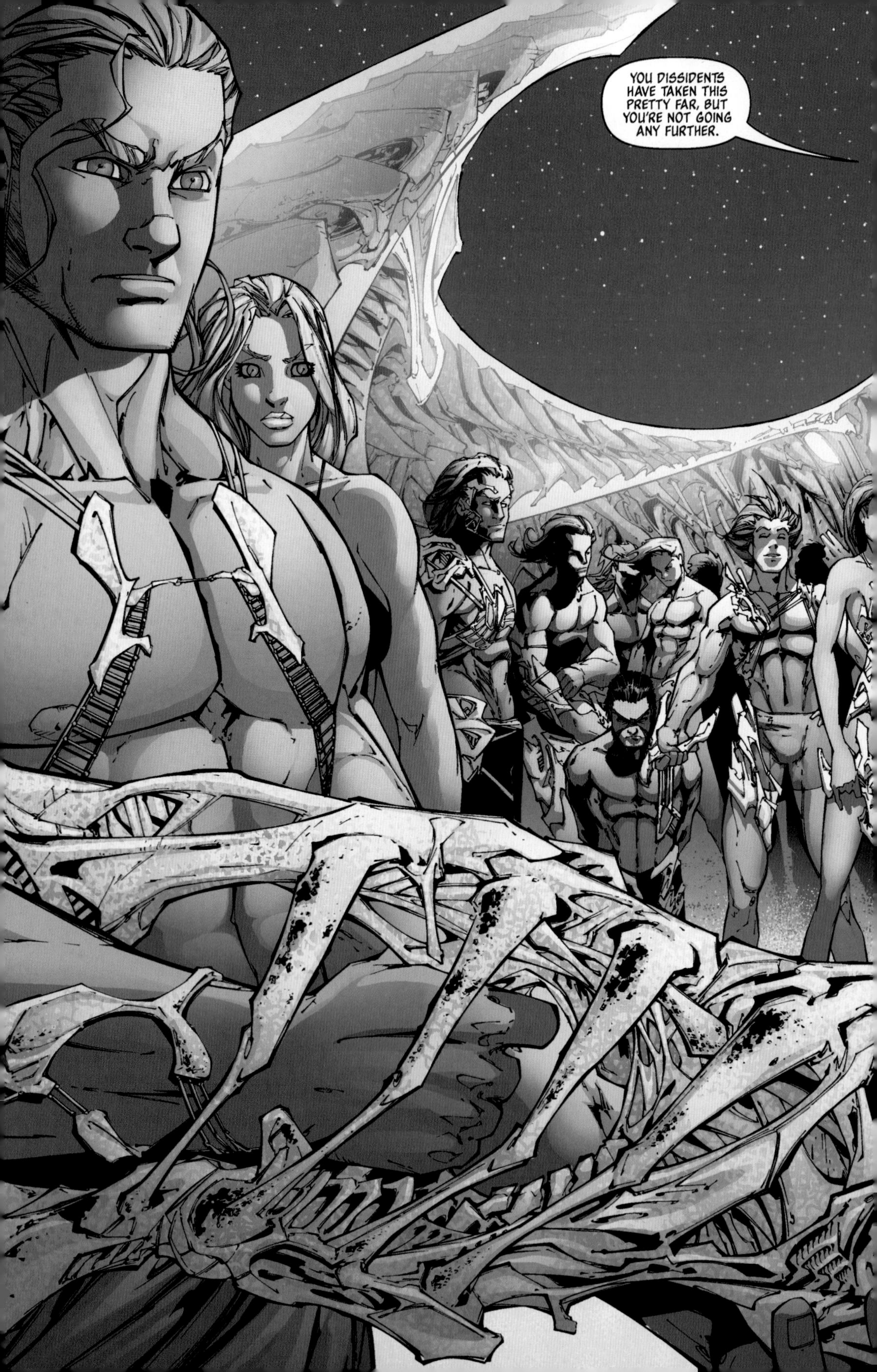
YOU DISSIDENTS HAVE TAKEN THIS PRETTY FAR, BUT YOU'RE NOT GOING ANY FURTHER.

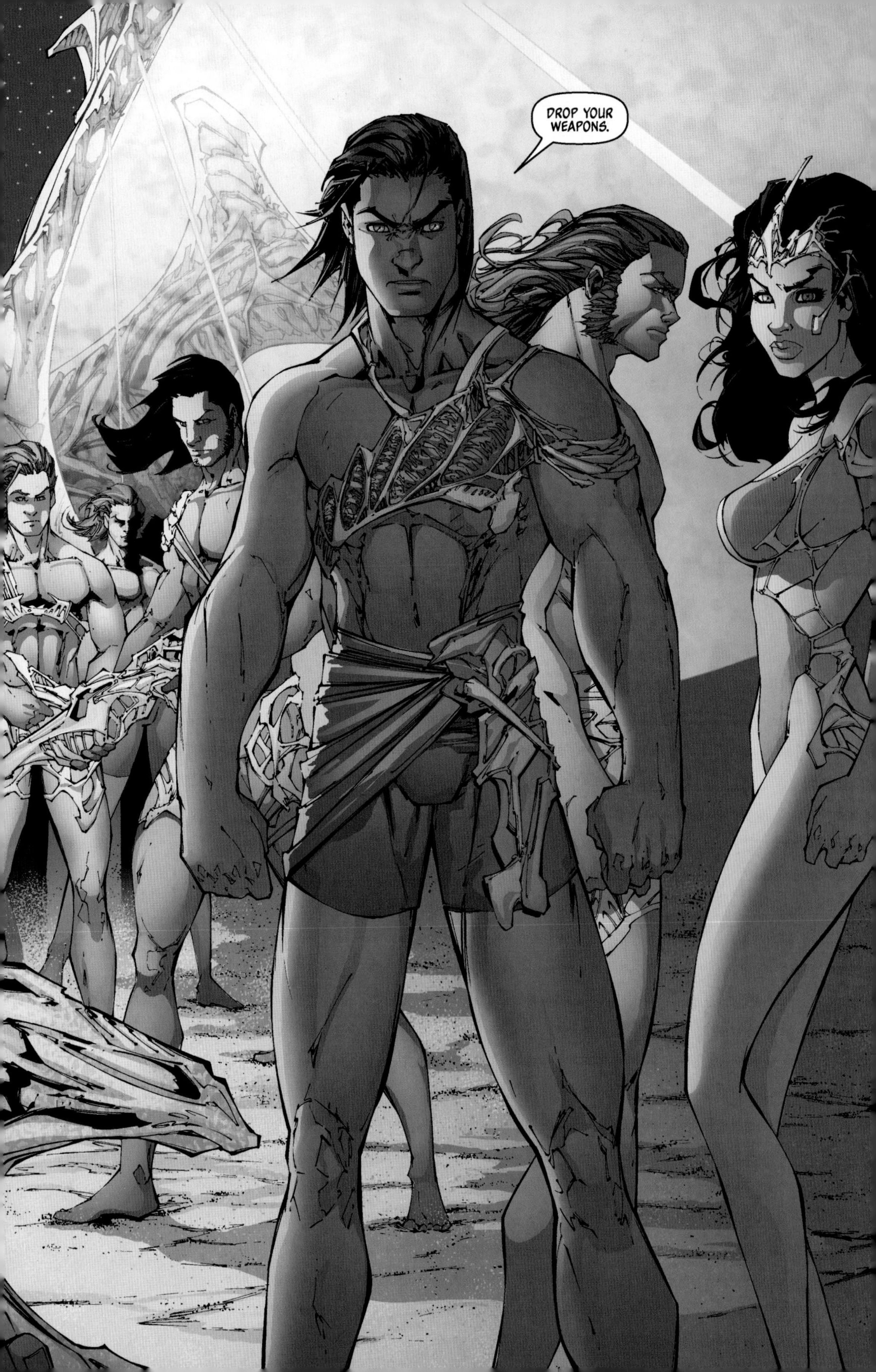
DROP YOUR WEAPONS.

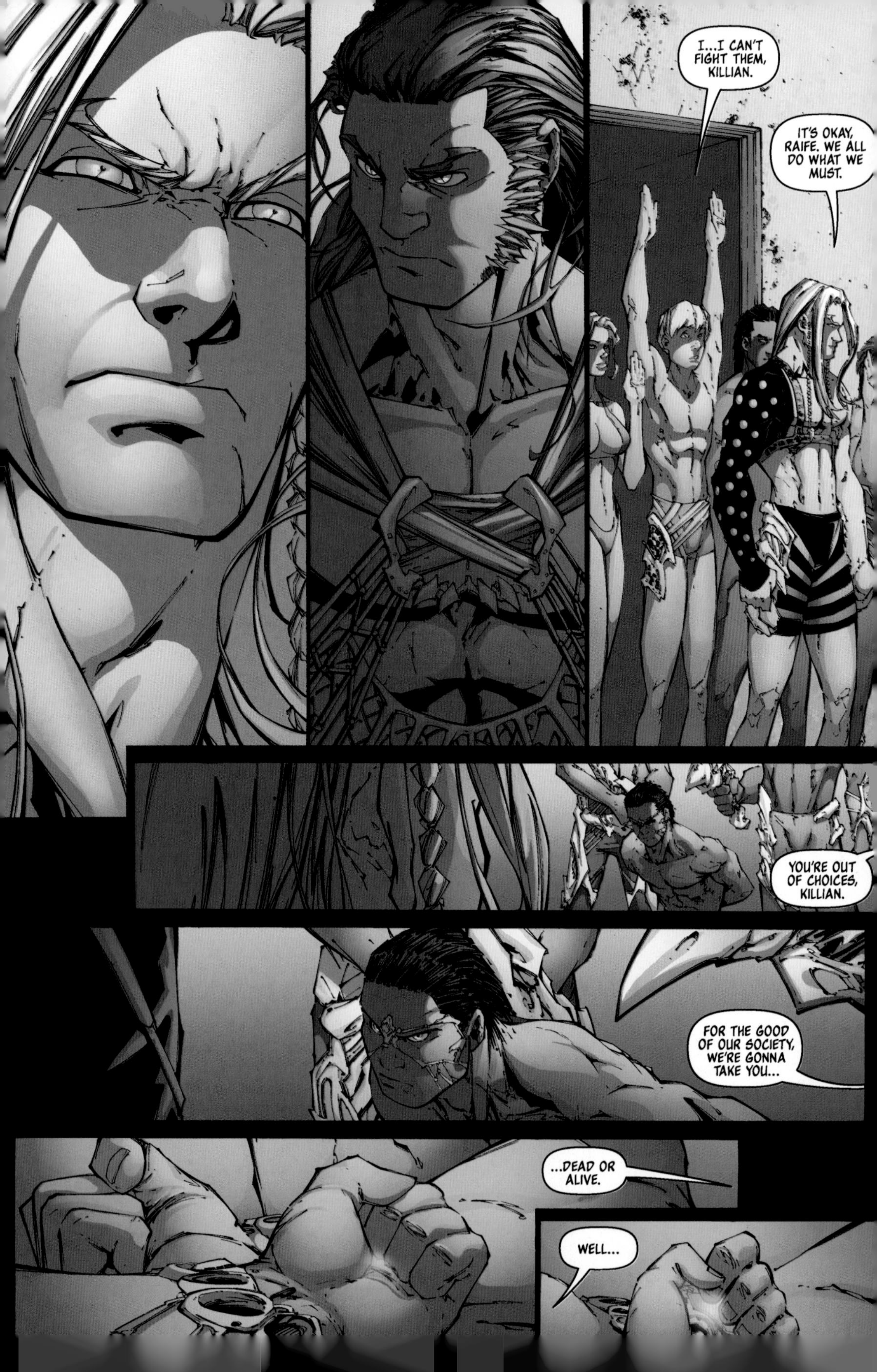
I...I CAN'T FIGHT THEM, KILLIAN.
IT'S OKAY, RAIFE. WE ALL DO WHAT WE MUST.
YOU'RE OUT OF CHOICES, KILLIAN.
FOR THE GOOD OF OUR SOCIETY, WE'RE GONNA TAKE YOU...
...DEAD OR ALIVE.
WELL...

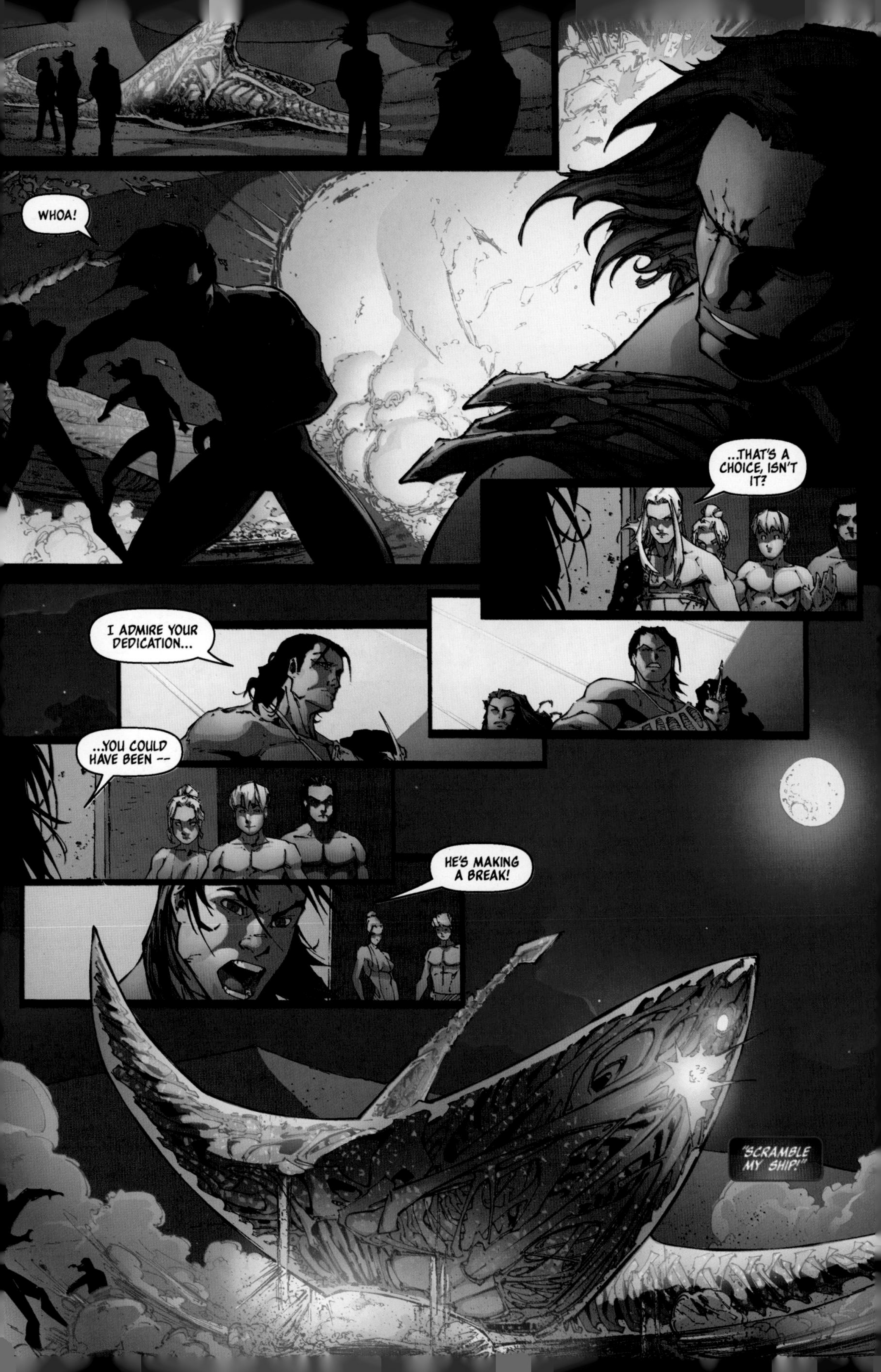
WHOA!
...THAT'S A CHOICE, ISN'T IT?
I ADMIRE YOUR DEDICATION...
...YOU COULD HAVE BEEN --
HE'S MAKING A BREAK!
"SCRAMBLE MY SHIP!"

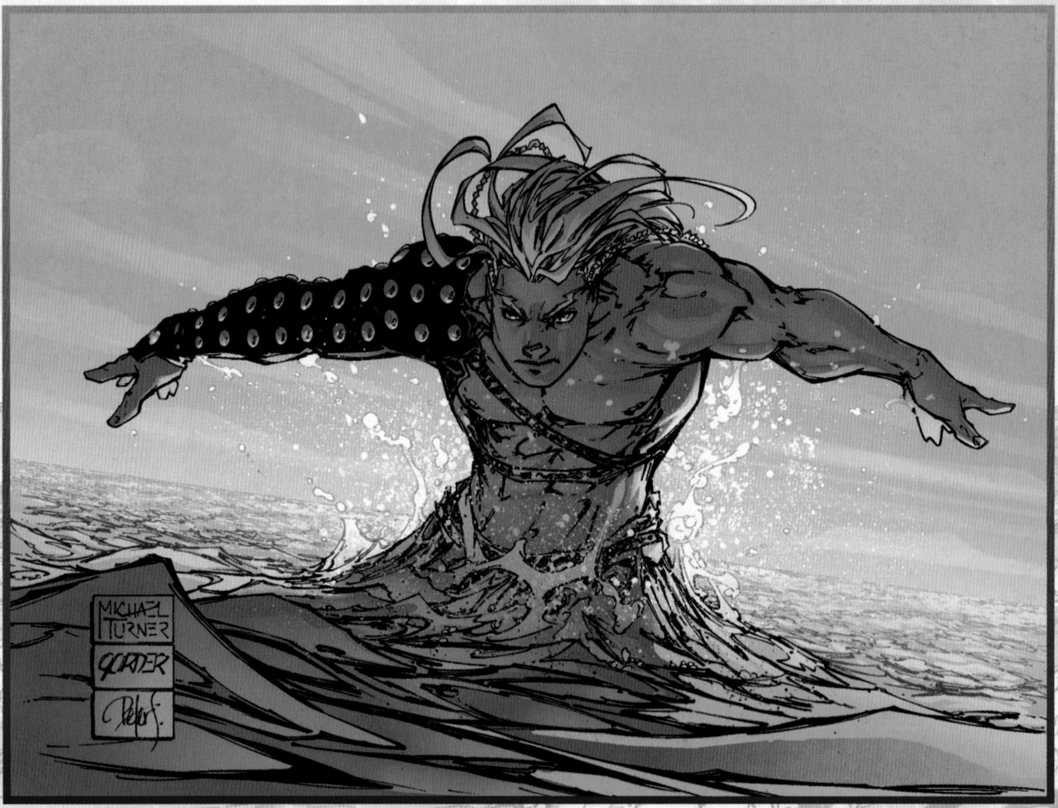
MICHAEL TURNER
GORDER

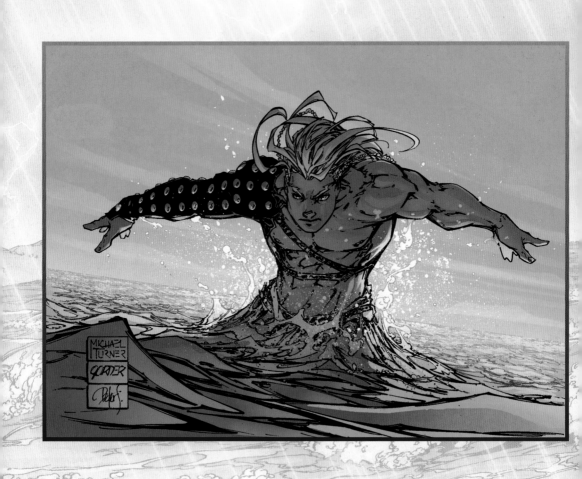

MICHAEL TURNER'S FATHOM TRADING CARD SET:
KILLIAN *BY*
• MICHAEL TURNER • JASON GORDER • PETER STEIGERWALD •

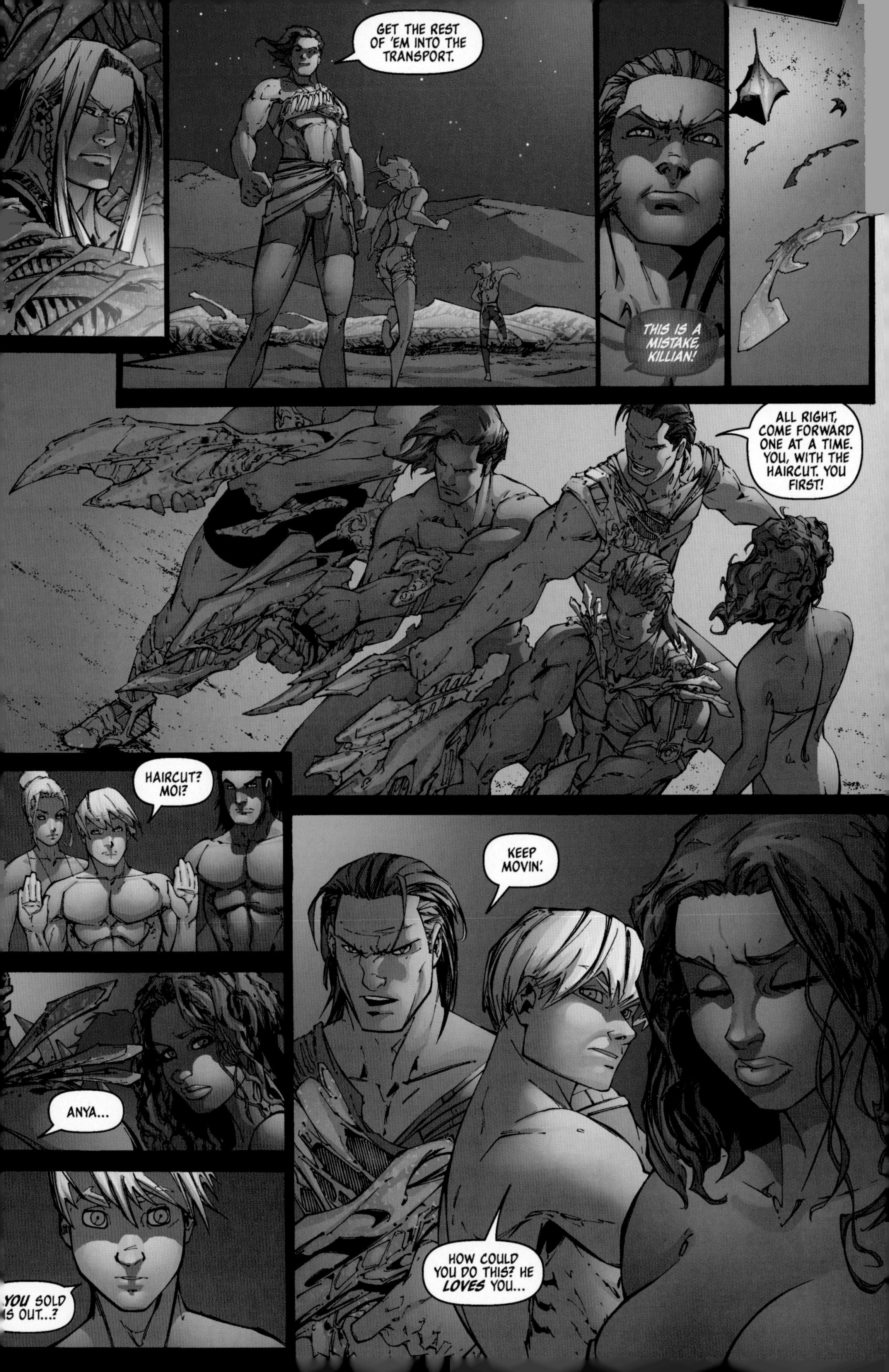
GET THE REST OF 'EM INTO THE TRANSPORT.
THIS IS A MISTAKE, KILLIAN!
ALL RIGHT, COME FORWARD ONE AT A TIME. YOU, WITH THE HAIRCUT. YOU FIRST!
HAIRCUT? MOI?
KEEP MOVIN'.
ANYA...
YOU SOLD
S OUT...?
HOW COULD YOU DO THIS? HE LOVES YOU...

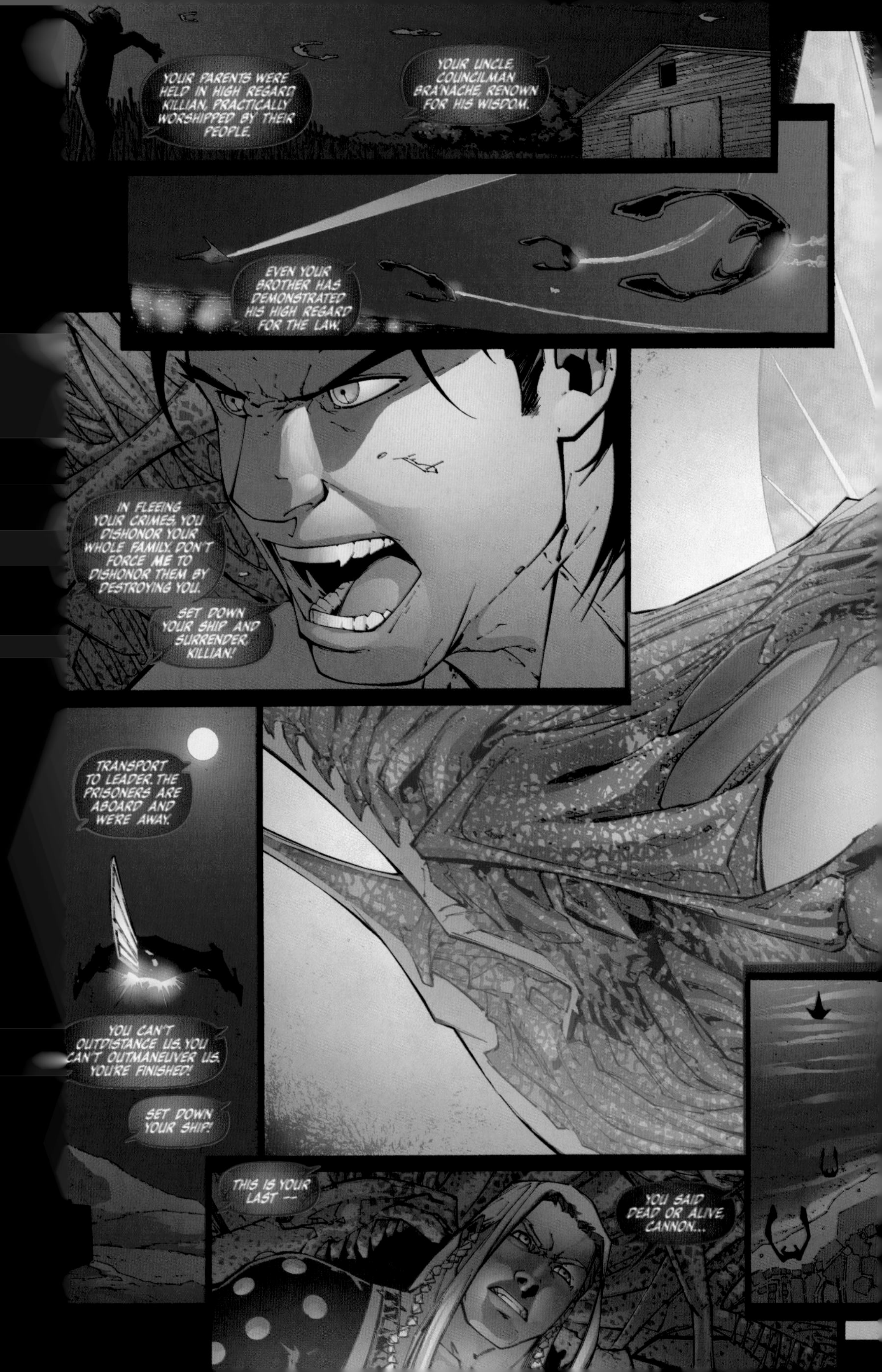
YOUR PARENTS WERE HELD IN HIGH REGARD KILLIAN, PRACTICALLY WORSHIPPED BY THEIR PEOPLE.
YOUR UNCLE, COUNCILMAN BRA'NACHE, RENOWN FOR HIS WISDOM.
EVEN YOUR BROTHER HAS DEMONSTRATED HIS HIGH REGARD FOR THE LAW.
IN FLEEING YOUR CRIMES, YOU DISHONOR YOUR WHOLE FAMILY. DON'T FORCE ME TO DISHONOR THEM BY DESTROYING YOU.
SET DOWN YOUR SHIP AND SURRENDER, KILLIAN!
TRANSPORT TO LEADER. THE PRISONERS ARE ABOARD AND WE'RE AWAY.
YOU CAN'T OUTDISTANCE US. YOU CAN'T OUTMANEUVER US. YOU'RE FINISHED!
SET DOWN YOUR SHIP!
THIS IS YOUR LAST --
YOU SAID DEAD OR ALIVE, CANNON...

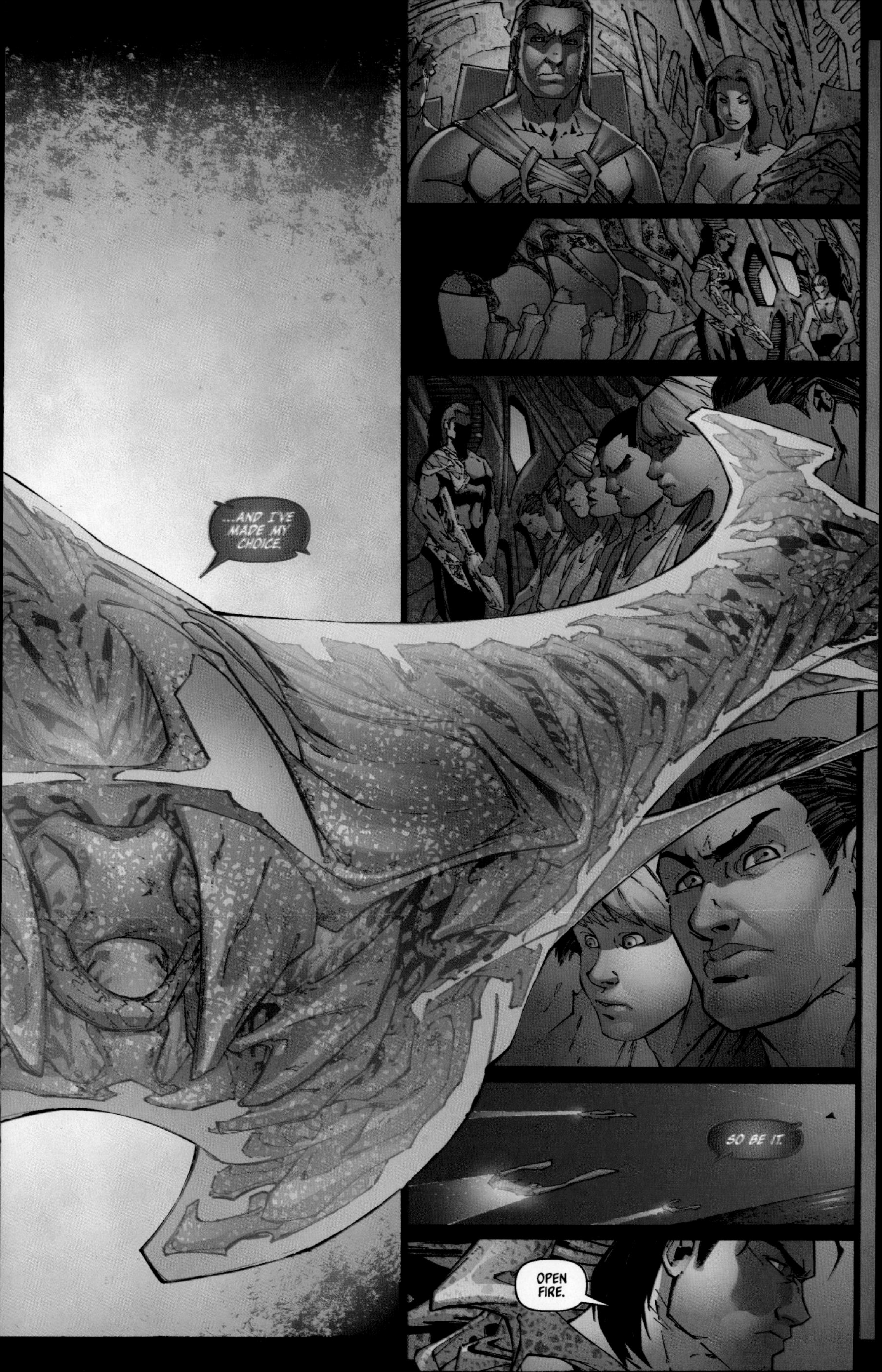
...AND I'VE MADE MY CHOICE.
SO BE IT.
OPEN FIRE.

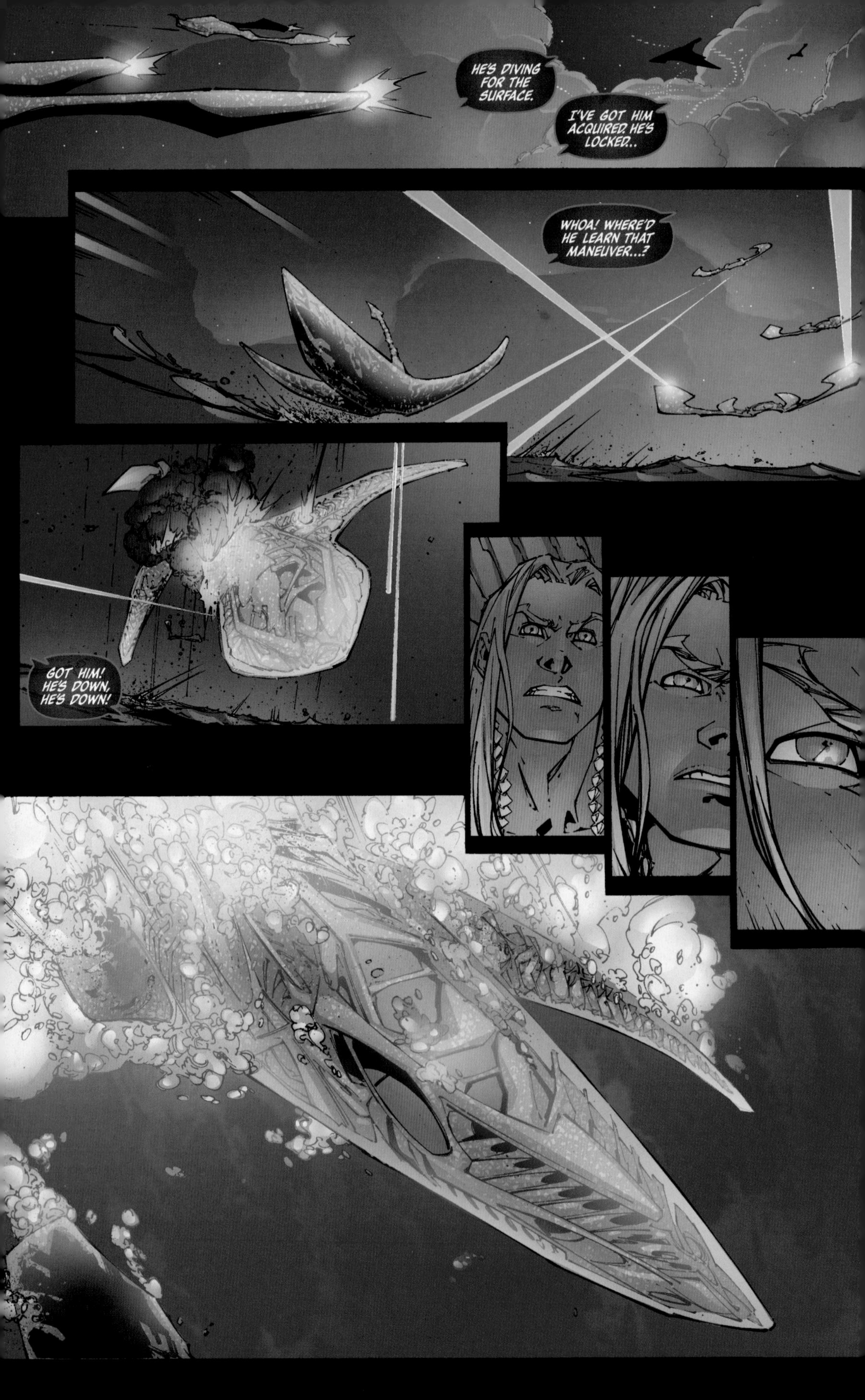
HE'S DIVING FOR THE SURFACE.
I'VE GOT HIM ACQUIRED. HE'S LOCKED...
WHOA! WHERE'D HE LEARN THAT MANEUVER...?
GOT HIM! HE'S DOWN, HE'S DOWN!

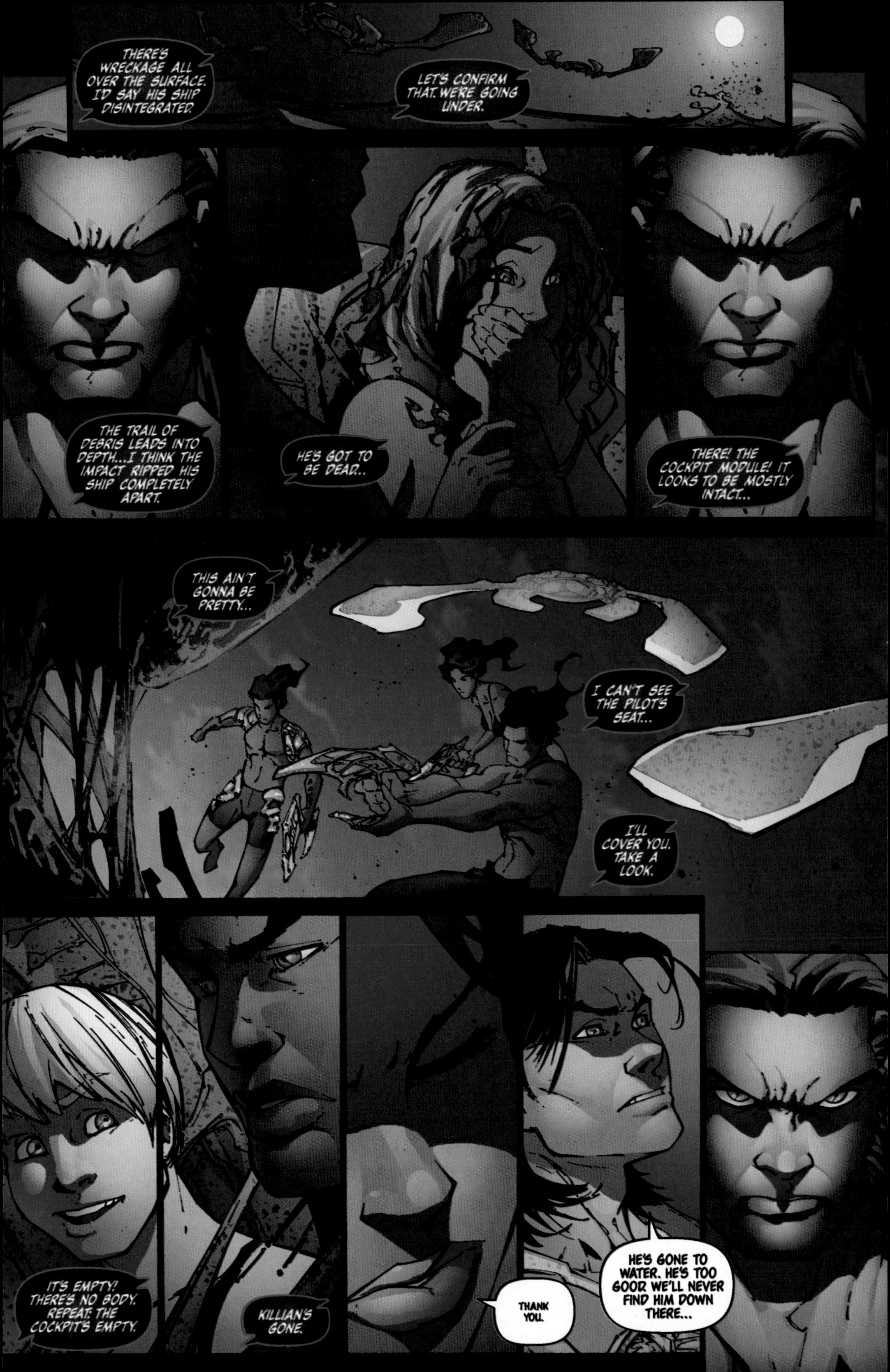
THERE'S WRECKAGE ALL OVER THE SURFACE. I'D SAY HIS SHIP DISINTEGRATED.
LET'S CONFIRM THAT. WE'RE GOING UNDER.
THE TRAIL OF DEBRIS LEADS INTO DEPTH...I THINK THE IMPACT RIPPED HIS SHIP COMPLETELY APART.
HE'S GOT TO BE DEAD..
THERE! THE COCKPIT MODULE! IT LOOKS TO BE MOSTLY INTACT...
THIS AIN'T GONNA BE PRETTY...
I CAN'T SEE THE PILOT'S SEAT...
I'LL COVER YOU. TAKE A LOOK.
IT'S EMPTY! THERE'S NO BODY. REPEAT: THE COCKPIT'S EMPTY.
KILLIAN'S GONE.
THANK YOU.
HE'S GONE TO WATER. HE'S TOO GOOD. WE'LL NEVER FIND HIM DOWN THERE...

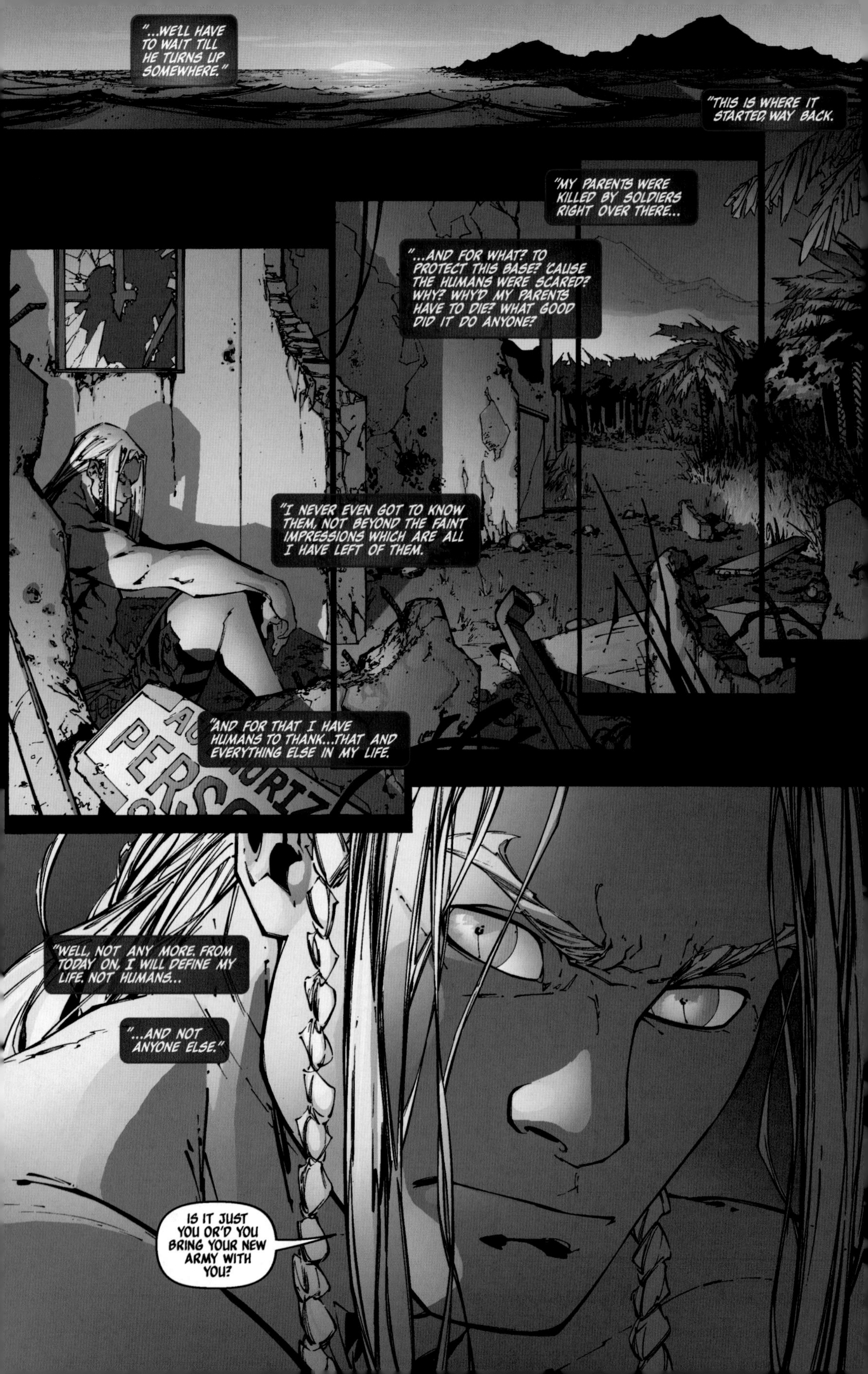
"...WE'LL HAVE TO WAIT TILL HE TURNS UP SOMEWHERE."
"THIS IS WHERE IT STARTED, WAY BACK.
"MY PARENTS WERE KILLED BY SOLDIERS RIGHT OVER THERE...
"...AND FOR WHAT? TO PROTECT THIS BASE? 'CAUSE THE HUMANS WERE SCARED? WHY? WHY'D MY PARENTS HAVE TO DIE? WHAT GOOD DID IT DO ANYONE?
"I NEVER EVEN GOT TO KNOW THEM, NOT BEYOND THE FAINT IMPRESSIONS WHICH ARE ALL I HAVE LEFT OF THEM.
"AND FOR THAT I HAVE HUMANS TO THANK...THAT AND EVERYTHING ELSE IN MY LIFE.
"WELL, NOT ANY MORE. FROM TODAY ON, I WILL DEFINE MY LIFE. NOT HUMANS...
"...AND NOT ANYONE ELSE."
IS IT JUST YOU OR'D YOU BRING YOUR NEW ARMY WITH YOU?

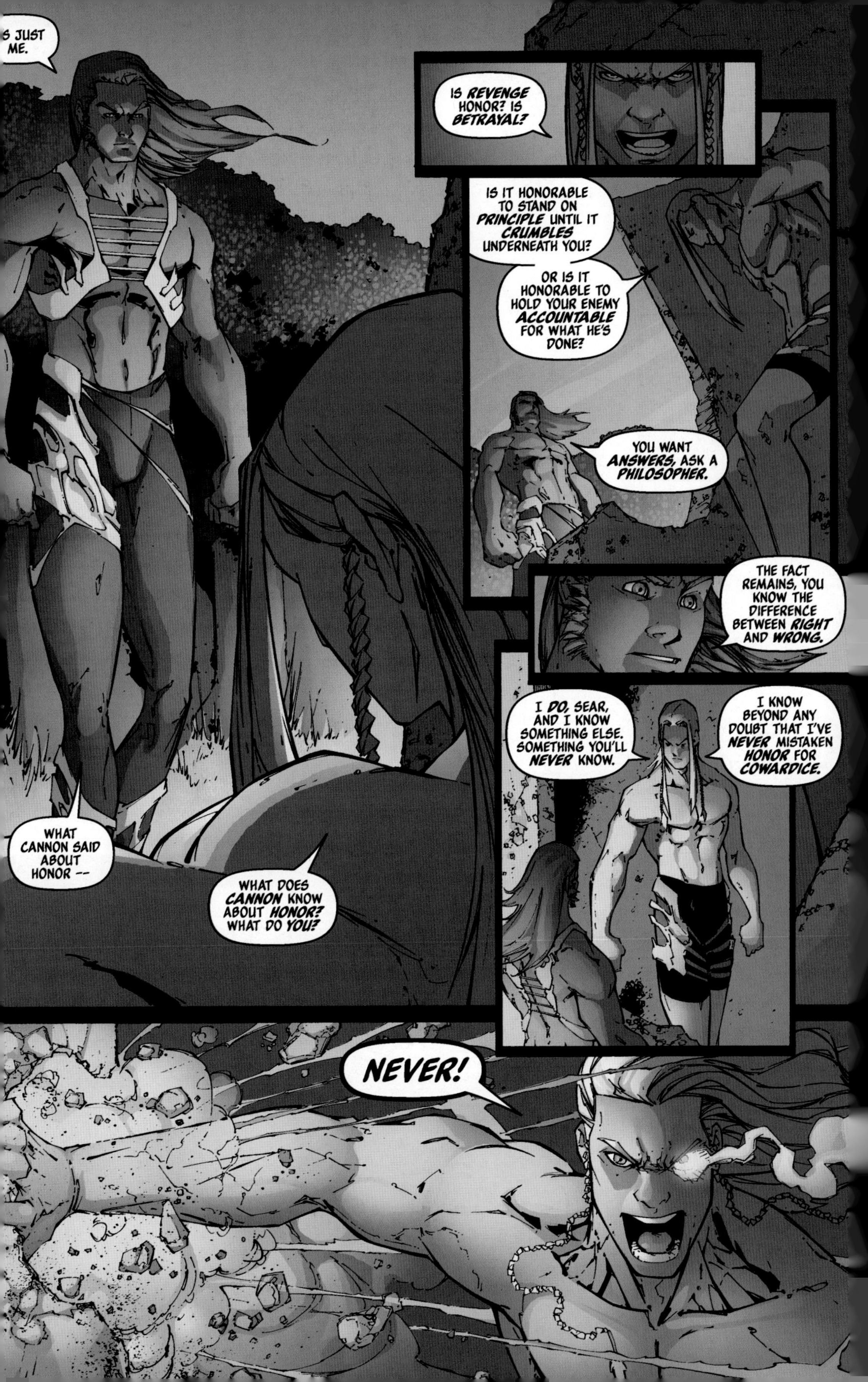

S JUST ME.
IS REVENGE HONOR? IS BETRAYAL?
IS IT HONORABLE TO STAND ON PRINCIPLE UNTIL IT CRUMBLES UNDERNEATH YOU?
OR IS IT HONORABLE TO HOLD YOUR ENEMY ACCOUNTABLE FOR WHAT HE'S DONE?
YOU WANT ANSWERS, ASK A PHILOSOPHER.
WHAT CANNON SAID ABOUT HONOR --
WHAT DOES CANNON KNOW ABOUT HONOR? WHAT DO YOU?
THE FACT REMAINS, YOU KNOW THE DIFFERENCE BETWEEN RIGHT AND WRONG.
I DO, SEAR, AND I KNOW SOMETHING ELSE. SOMETHING YOU'LL NEVER KNOW.
I KNOW BEYOND ANY DOUBT THAT I'VE NEVER MISTAKEN HONOR FOR COWARDICE.
NEVER!

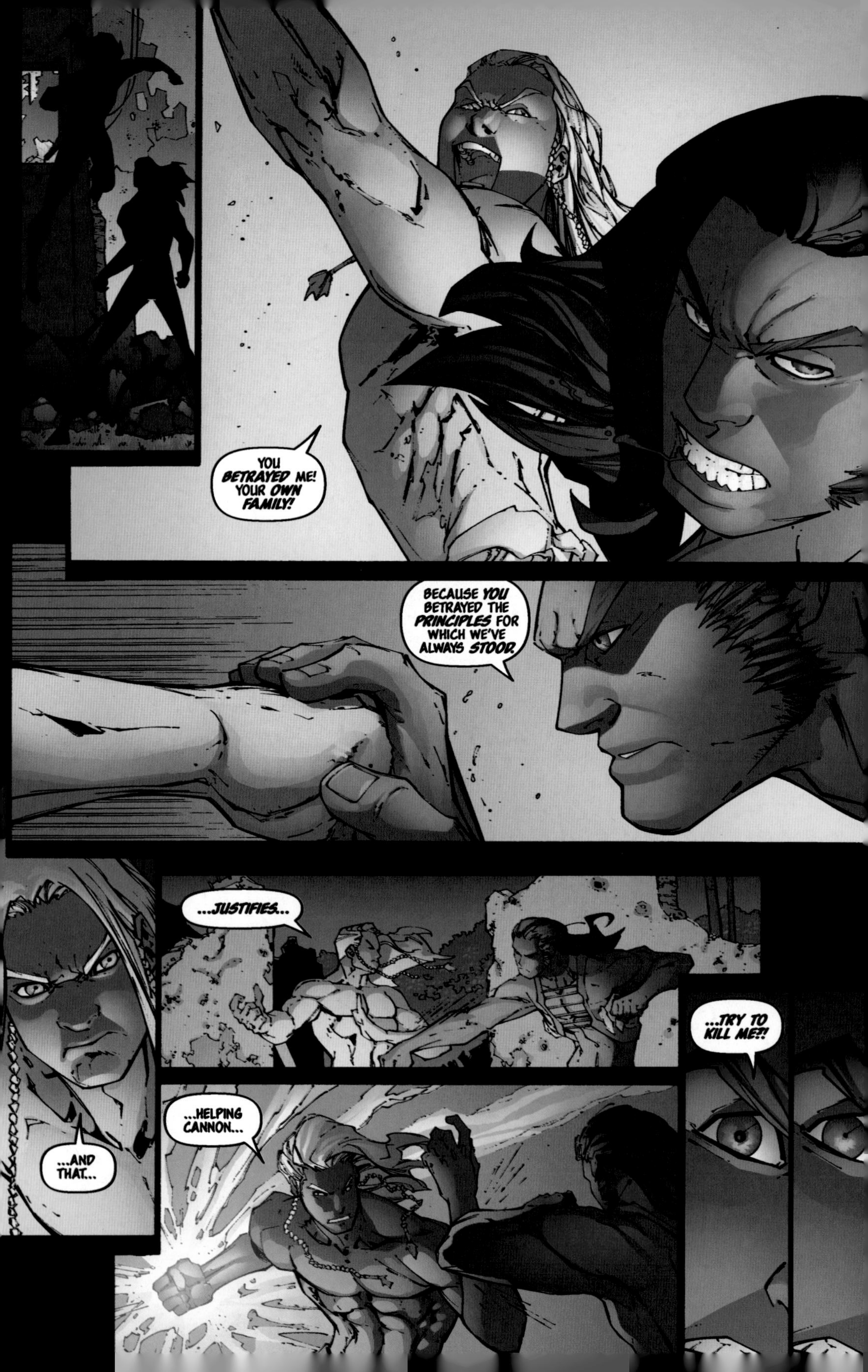
YOU BETRAYED ME! YOUR OWN FAMILY!
BECAUSE YOU BETRAYED THE PRINCIPLES FOR WHICH WE'VE ALWAYS STOOD.
...AND THAT...
...JUSTIFIES...
...HELPING CANNON...
...TRY TO KILL ME?!

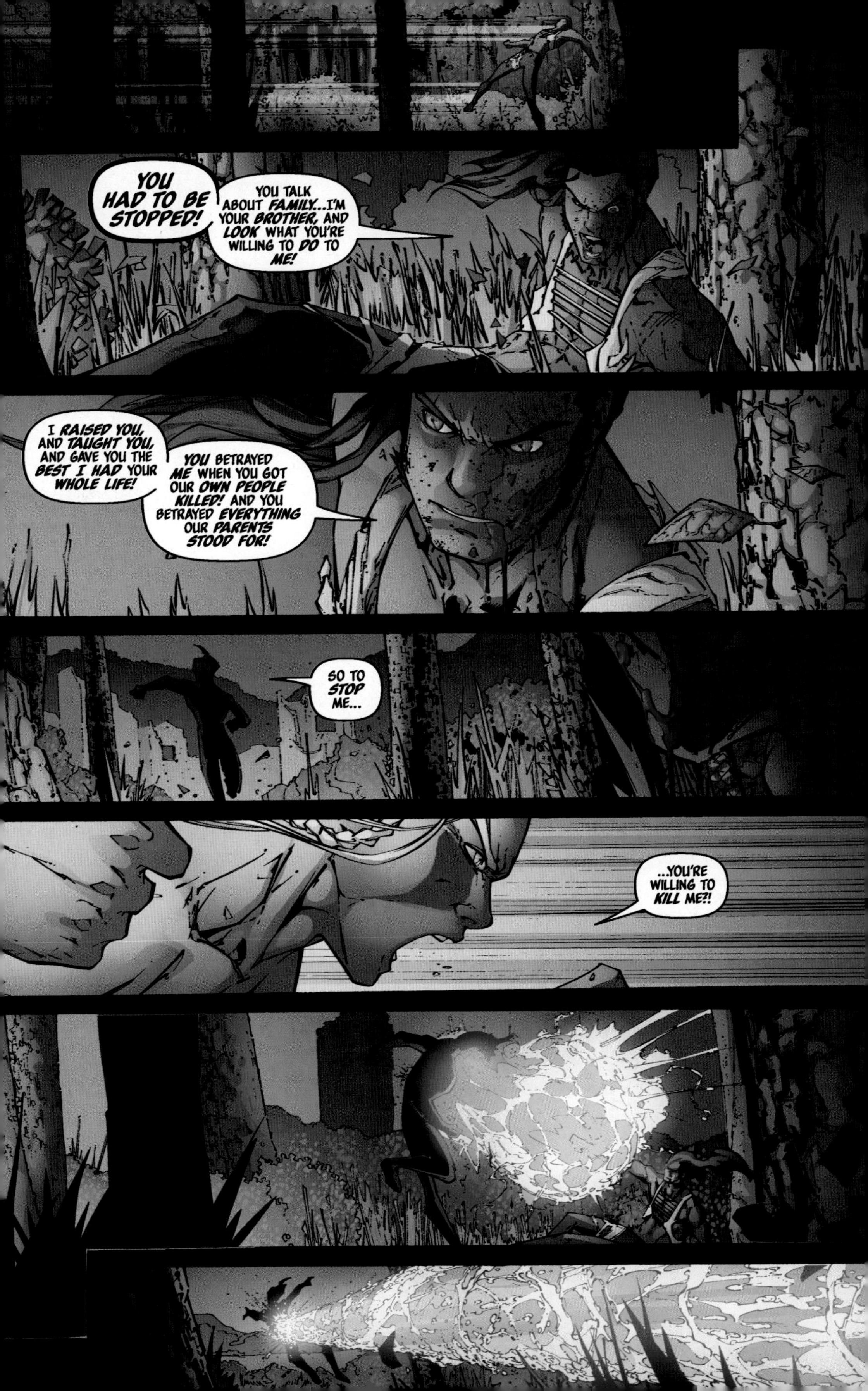
YOU HAD TO BE STOPPED!
YOU TALK ABOUT FAMILY...I'M YOUR BROTHER, AND LOOK WHAT YOU'RE WILLING TO DO TO ME!
I RAISED YOU, AND TAUGHT YOU, AND GAVE YOU THE BEST I HAD YOUR WHOLE LIFE!
YOU BETRAYED ME WHEN YOU GOT OUR OWN PEOPLE KILLED! AND YOU BETRAYED EVERYTHING OUR PARENTS STOOD FOR!
SO TO STOP ME...
...YOU'RE WILLING TO KILL ME?!

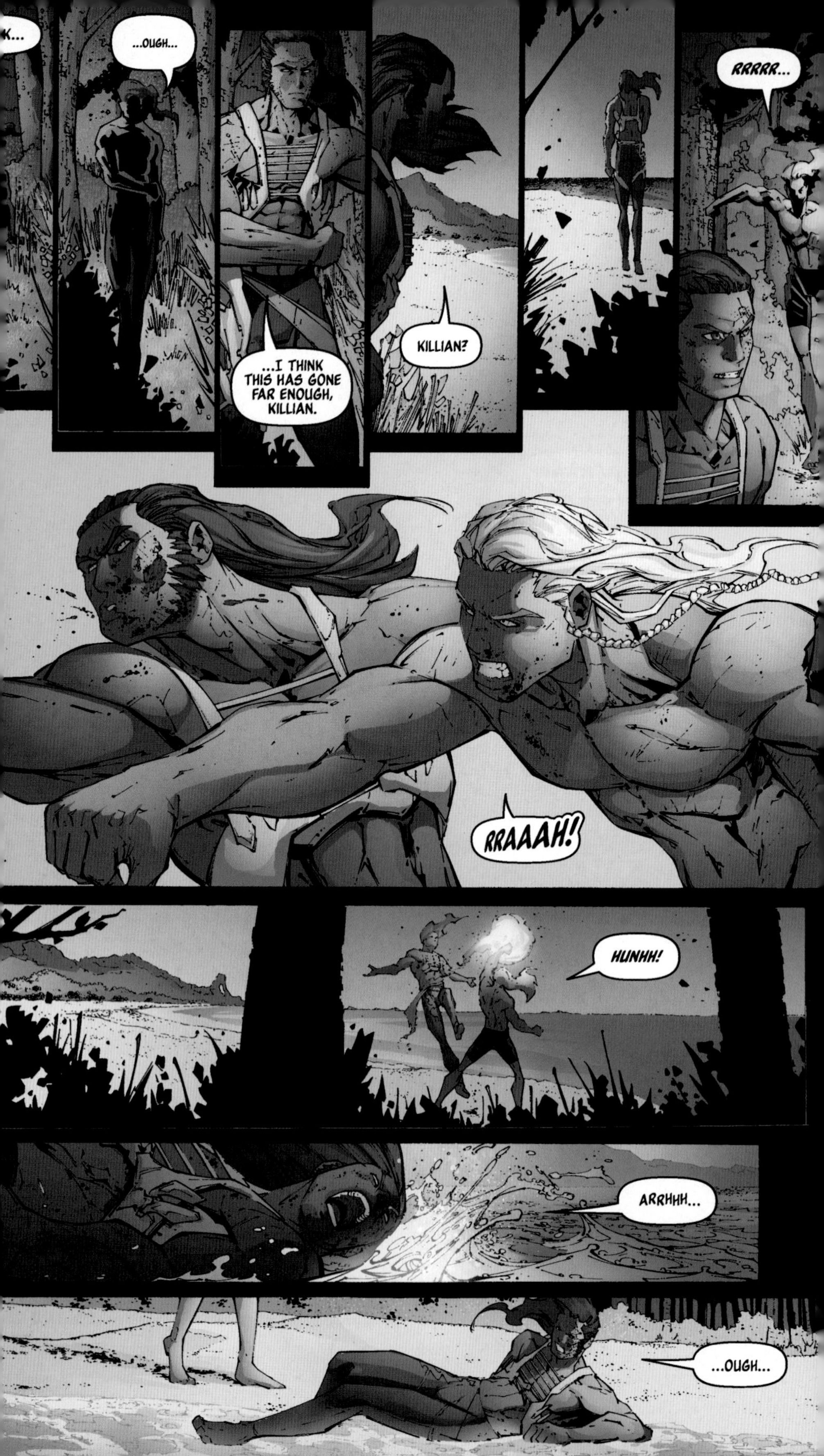
K...
...OUGH...
...I THINK THIS HAS GONE FAR ENOUGH, KILLIAN.
KILLIAN?
RRRRR...
RRAAAH!
HUNHH!
ARRHHH...
...OUGH...

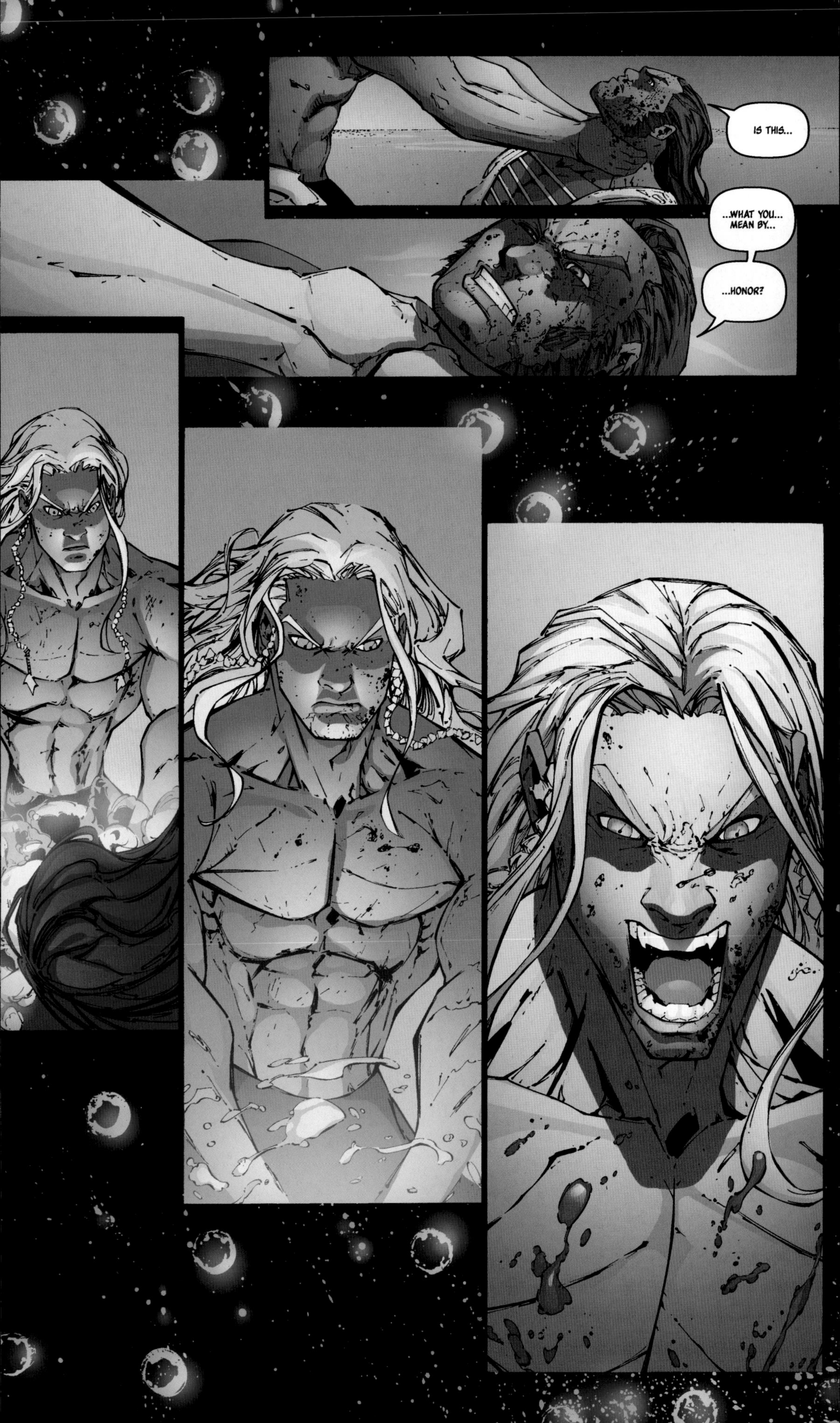
IS THIS...
...WHAT YOU... MEAN BY...
...HONOR?

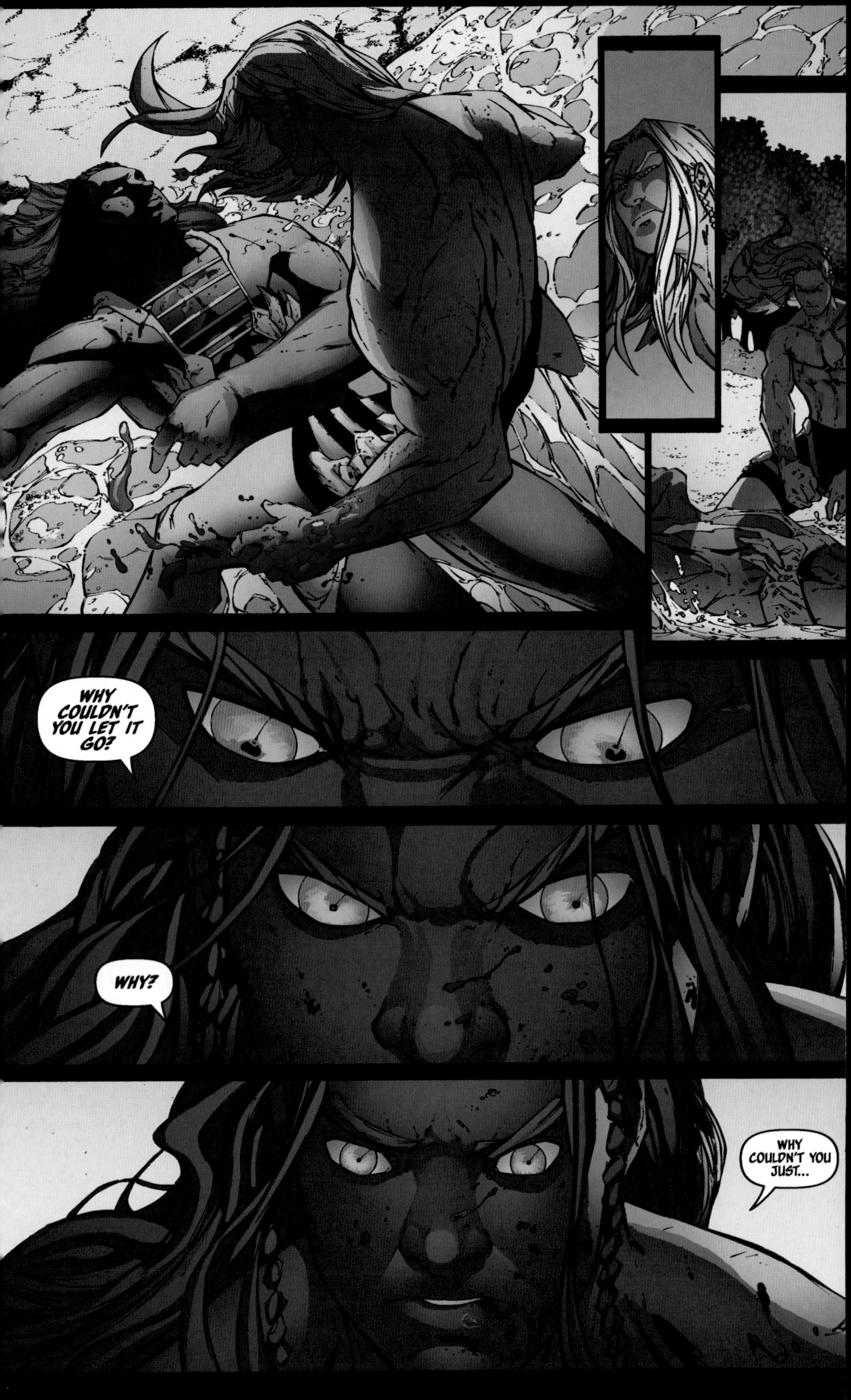
WHY COULDN'T YOU LET IT GO?
WHY?
WHY COULDN'T YOU JUST...

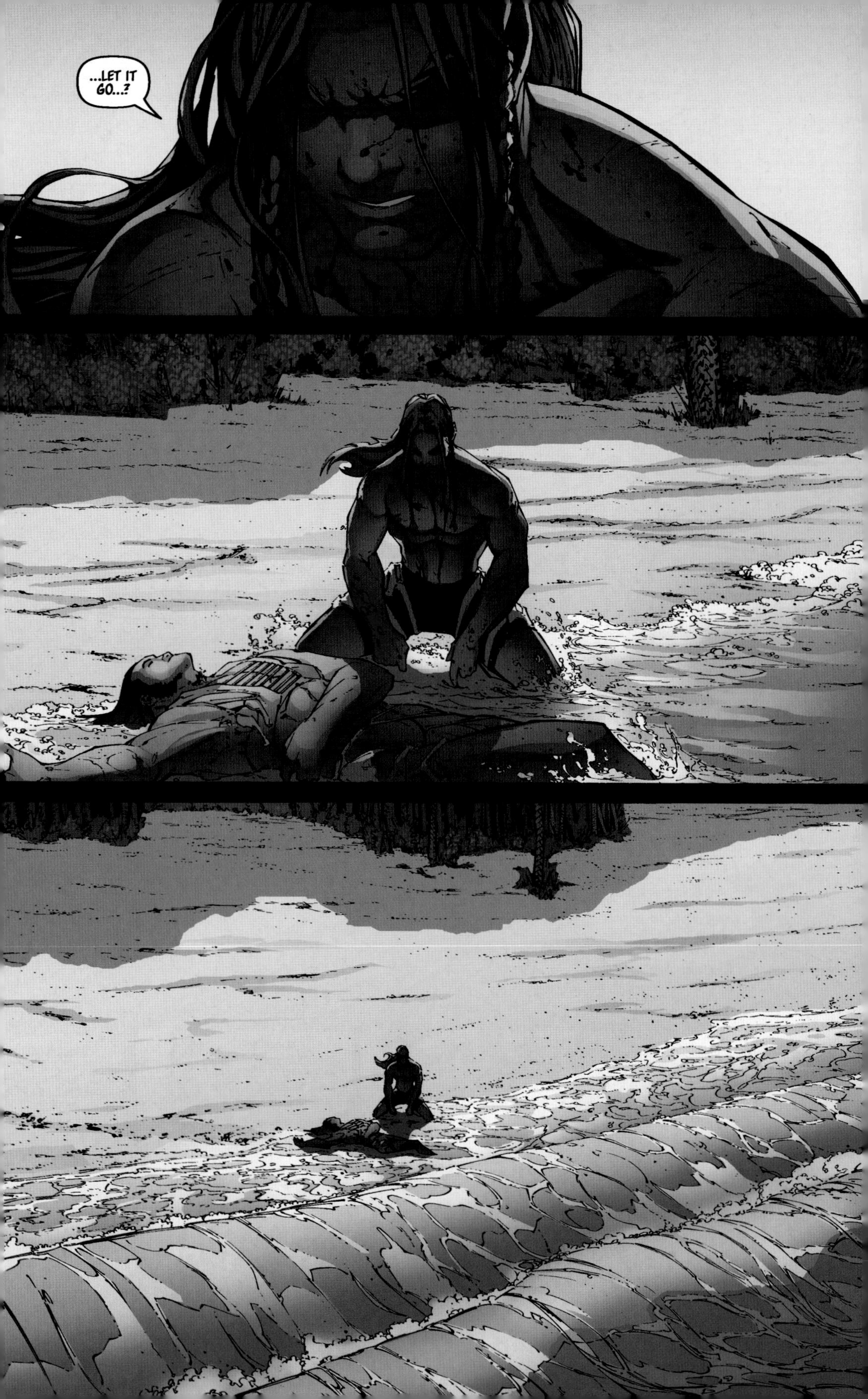
...LET IT GO...?

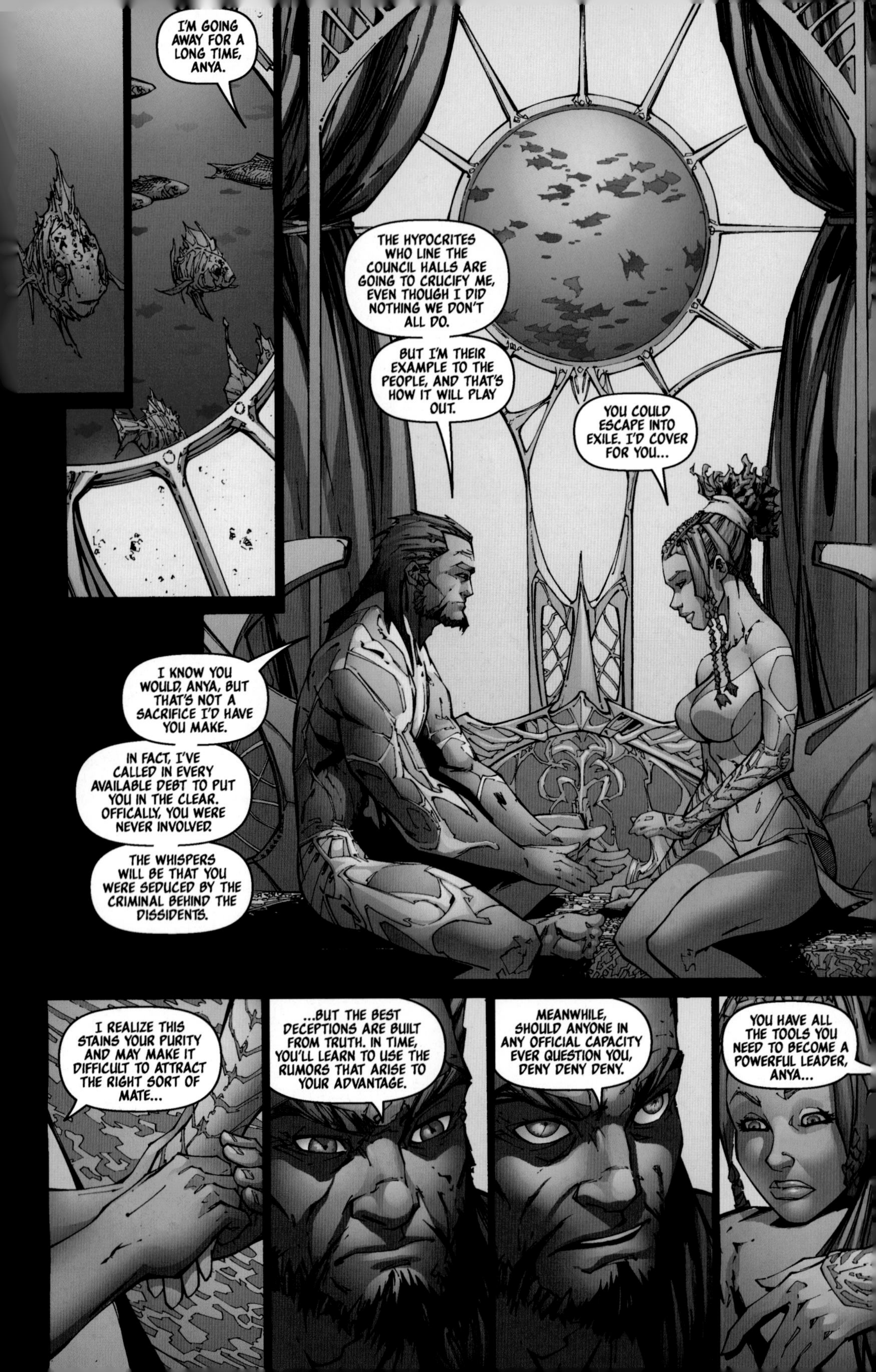
I'M GOING AWAY FOR A LONG TIME, ANYA.
THE HYPOCRITES WHO LINE THE COUNCIL HALLS ARE GOING TO CRUCIFY ME, EVEN THOUGH I DID NOTHING WE DON'T ALL DO.
BUT I'M THEIR EXAMPLE TO THE PEOPLE, AND THAT'S HOW IT WILL PLAY OUT.
YOU COULD ESCAPE INTO EXILE. I'D COVER FOR YOU...
I KNOW YOU WOULD, ANYA, BUT THAT'S NOT A SACRIFICE I'D HAVE YOU MAKE.
IN FACT, I'VE CALLED IN EVERY AVAILABLE DEBT TO PUT YOU IN THE CLEAR. OFFICALLY, YOU WERE NEVER INVOLVED.
THE WHISPERS WILL BE THAT YOU WERE SEDUCED BY THE CRIMINAL BEHIND THE DISSIDENTS.
I REALIZE THIS STAINS YOUR PURITY AND MAY MAKE IT DIFFICULT TO ATTRACT THE RIGHT SORT OF MATE...
...BUT THE BEST DECEPTIONS ARE BUILT FROM TRUTH. IN TIME, YOU'LL LEARN TO USE THE RUMORS THAT ARISE TO YOUR ADVANTAGE.
MEANWHILE, SHOULD ANYONE IN ANY OFFICIAL CAPACITY EVER QUESTION YOU, DENY DENY DENY.
YOU HAVE ALL THE TOOLS YOU NEED TO BECOME A POWERFUL LEADER, ANYA...

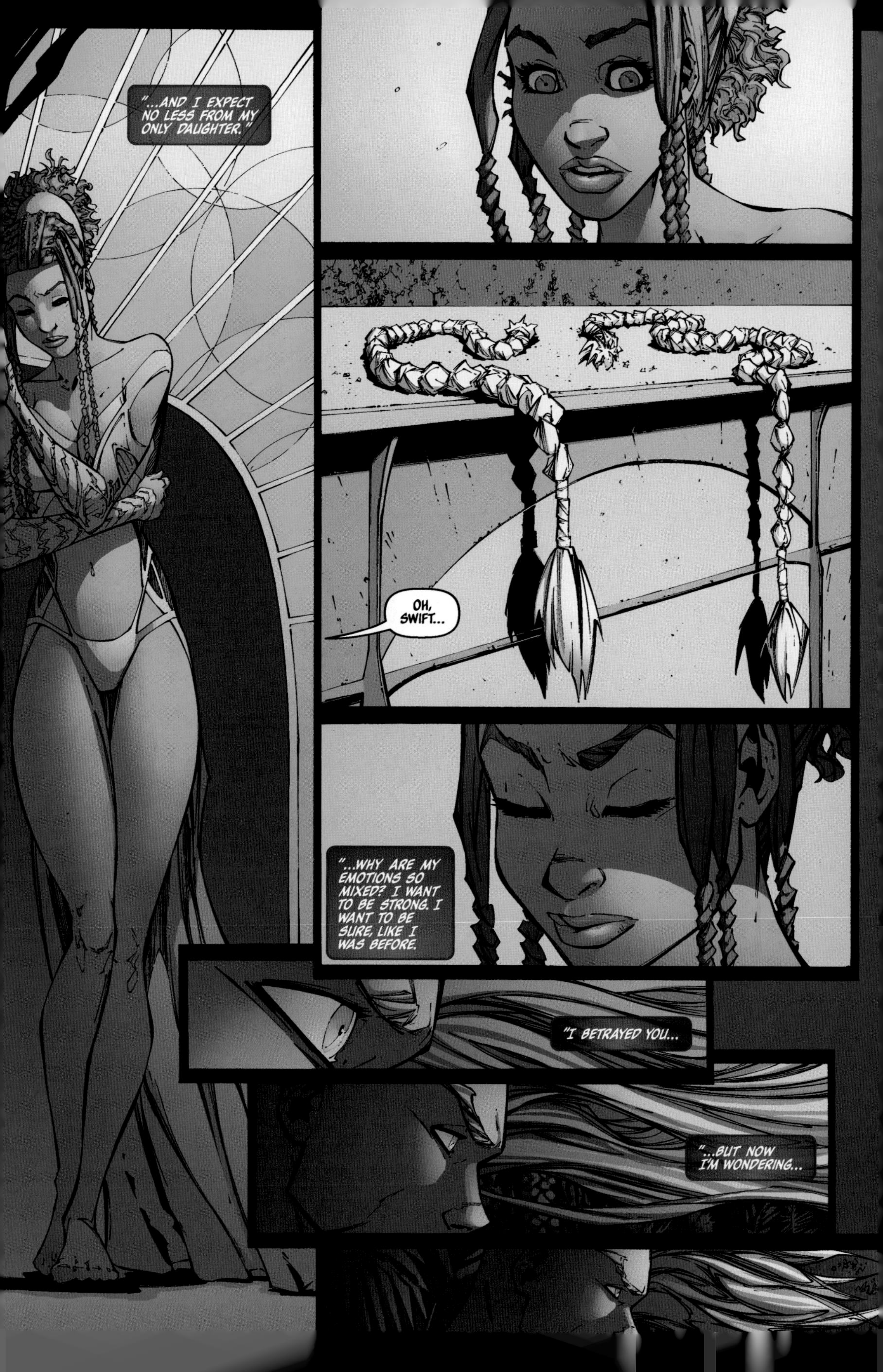
"...AND I EXPECT NO LESS FROM MY ONLY DAUGHTER."
OH, SWIFT...
"...WHY ARE MY EMOTIONS SO MIXED? I WANT TO BE STRONG. I WANT TO BE SURE, LIKE I WAS BEFORE.
"I BETRAYED YOU...
"...BUT NOW I'M WONDERING...

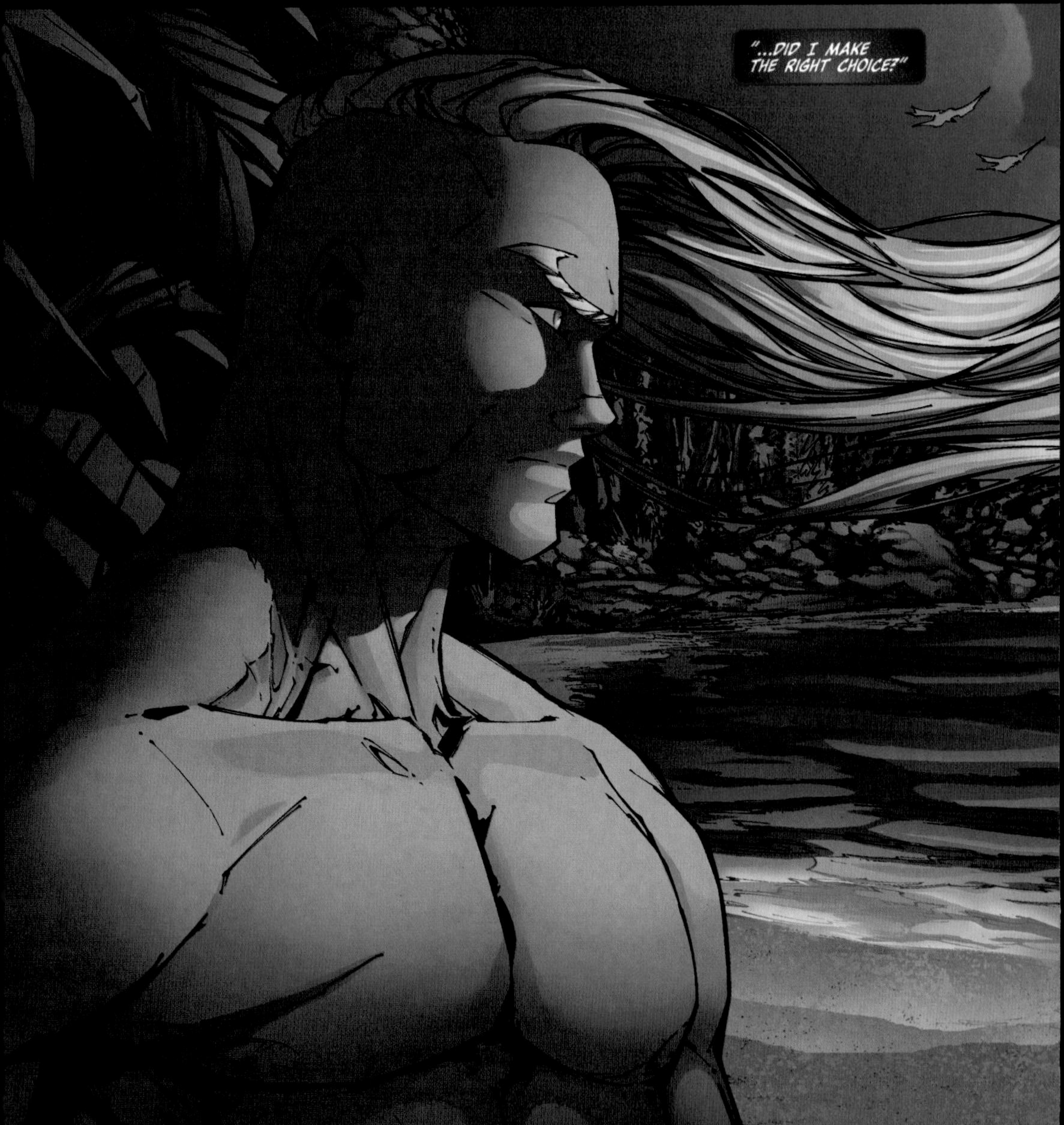
"...DID I MAKE THE RIGHT CHOICE?"

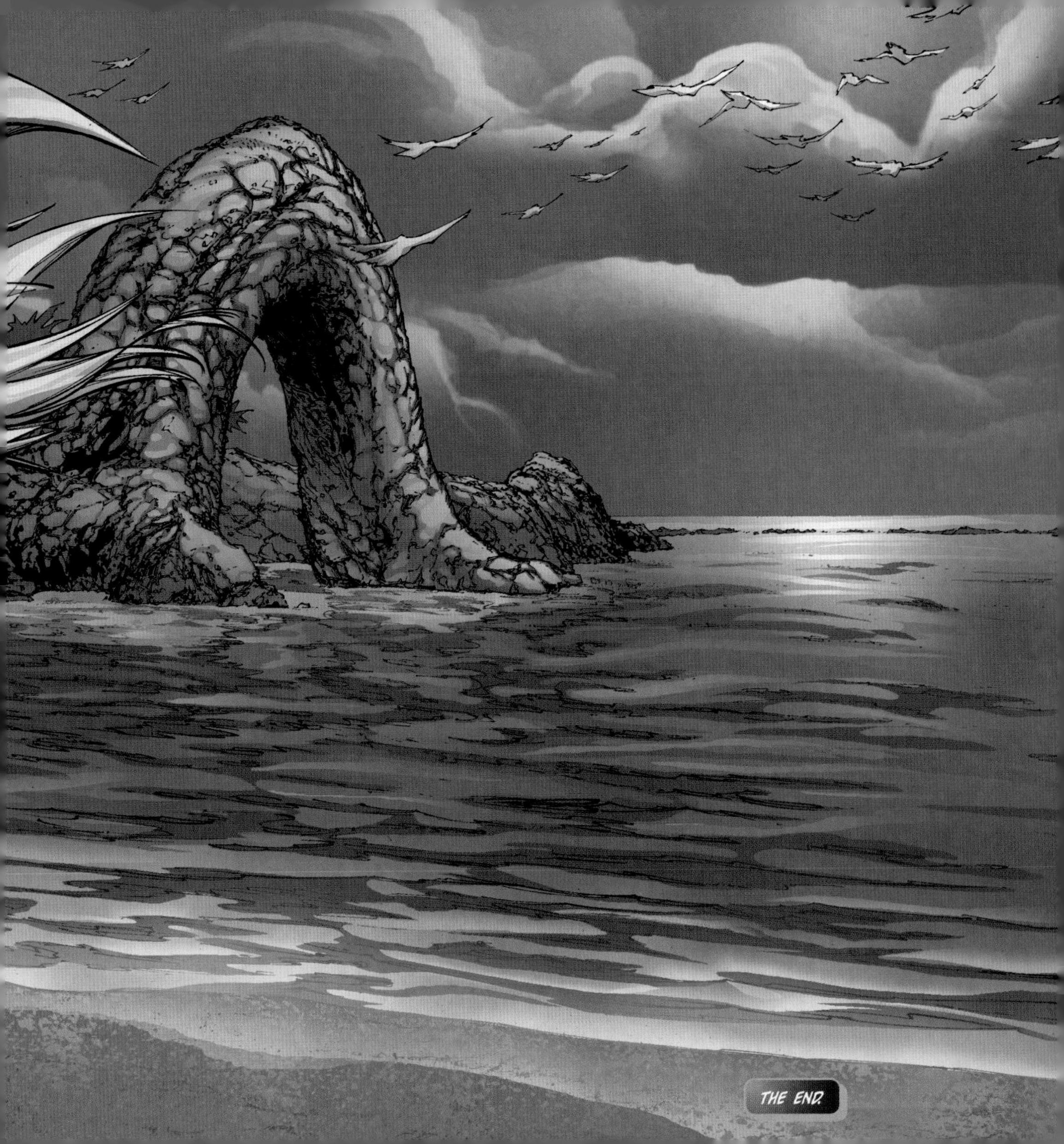
THE END.

MICHAEL TURNER'S
FATHOM™
Killian's Vessel

WRITTEN BY:
Vince Hernandez

PENCILS BY:
Ryan Odagawa

COLORS BY:
John Starr

LETTERING BY:
Josh Reed

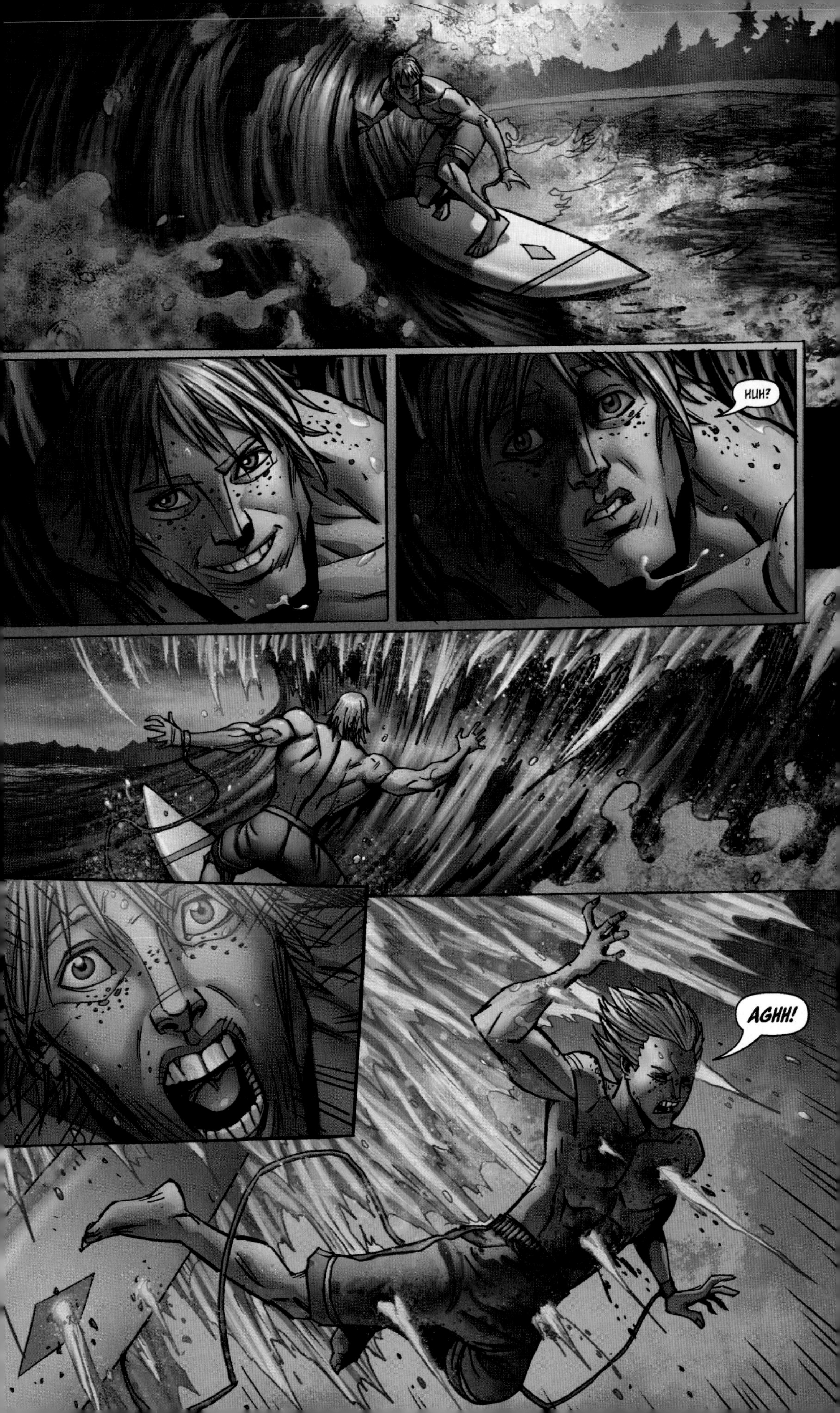
HUH?
AGHH!

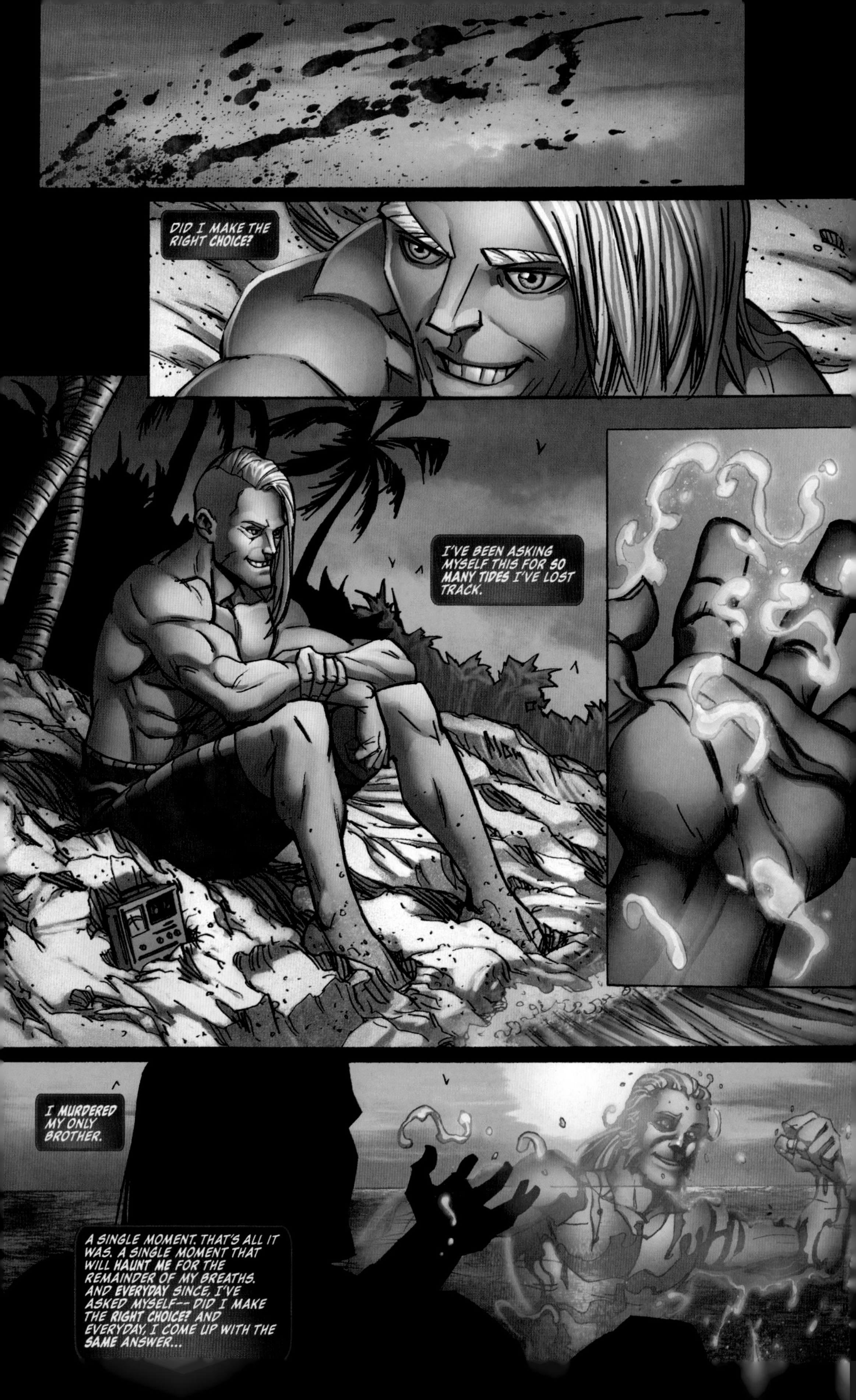
DID I MAKE THE RIGHT CHOICE?
I'VE BEEN ASKING MYSELF THIS FOR SO MANY TIDES I'VE LOST TRACK.
I MURDERED MY ONLY BROTHER.
A SINGLE MOMENT. THAT'S ALL IT WAS. A SINGLE MOMENT THAT WILL HAUNT ME FOR THE REMAINDER OF MY BREATHS. AND EVERYDAY SINCE, I'VE ASKED MYSELF-- DID I MAKE THE RIGHT CHOICE? AND EVERYDAY, I COME UP WITH THE SAME ANSWER...

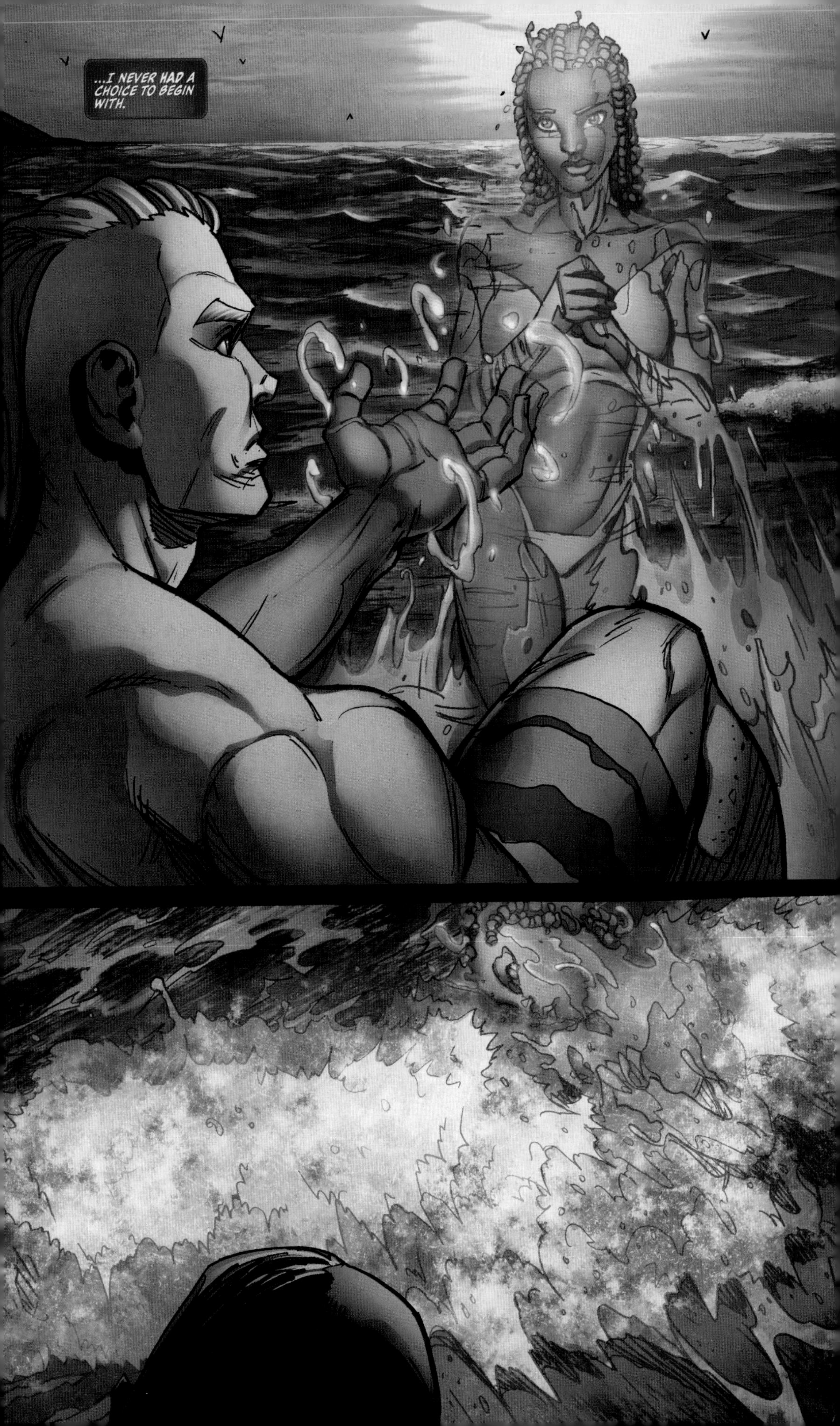
...I NEVER HAD A CHOICE TO BEGIN WITH.

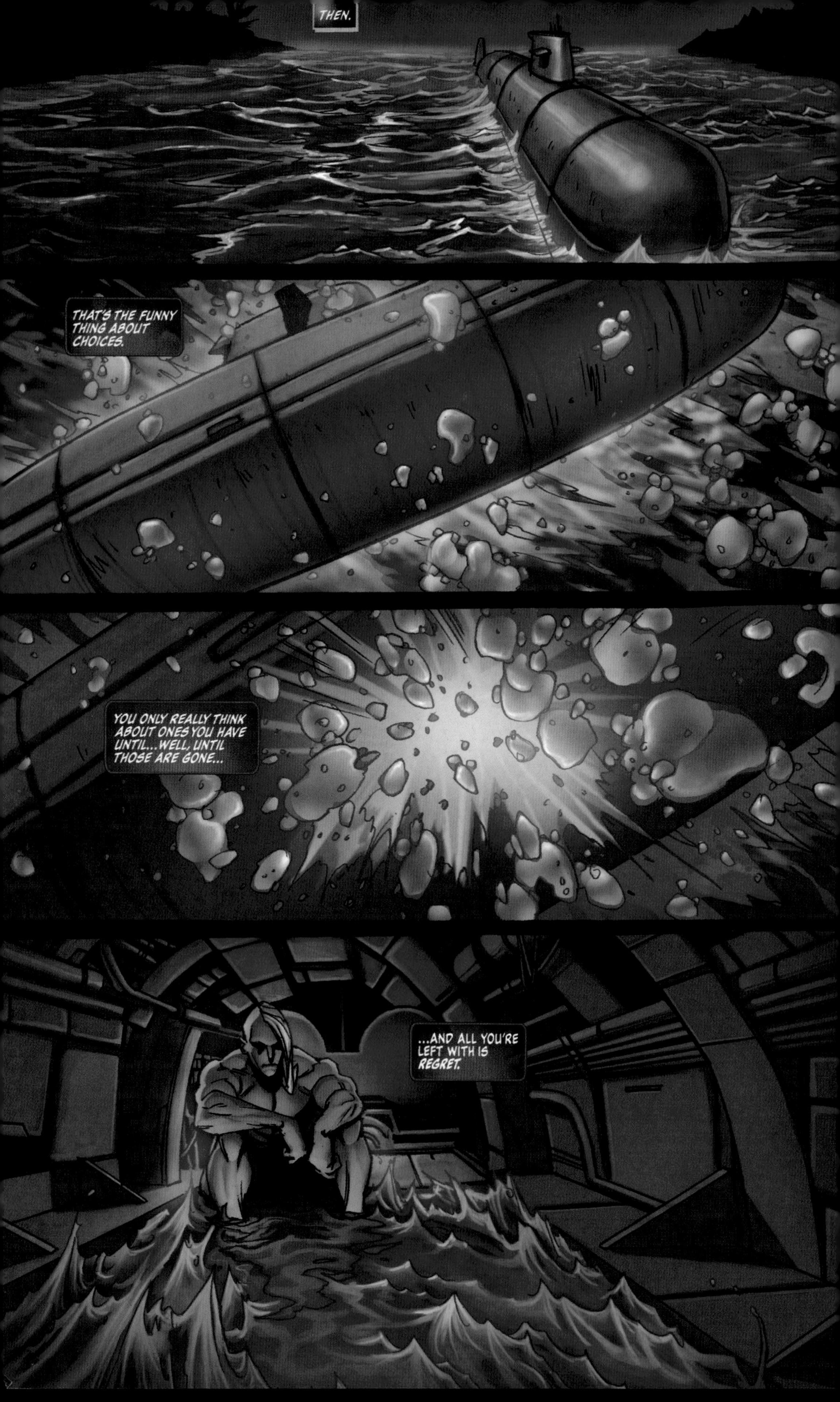
THEN.
THAT'S THE FUNNY THING ABOUT CHOICES.
YOU ONLY REALLY THINK ABOUT ONES YOU HAVE UNTIL...WELL, UNTIL THOSE ARE GONE...
...AND ALL YOU'RE LEFT WITH IS REGRET.

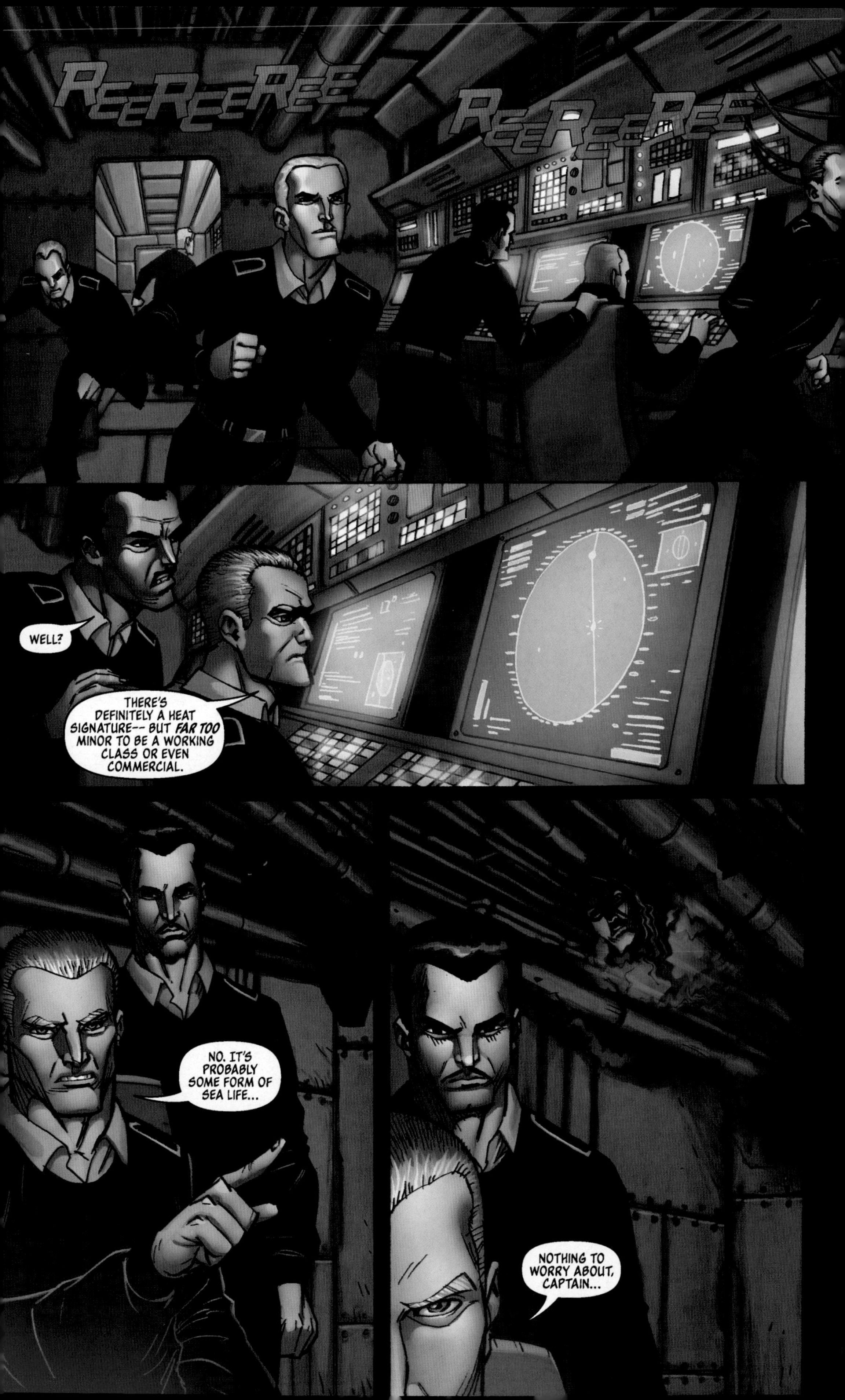
REEREEREE
REEREEREE
WELL?
THERE'S DEFINITELY A HEAT SIGNATURE-- BUT FAR TOO MINOR TO BE A WORKING CLASS OR EVEN COMMERCIAL.
NO. IT'S PROBABLY SOME FORM OF SEA LIFE...
NOTHING TO WORRY ABOUT, CAPTAIN...

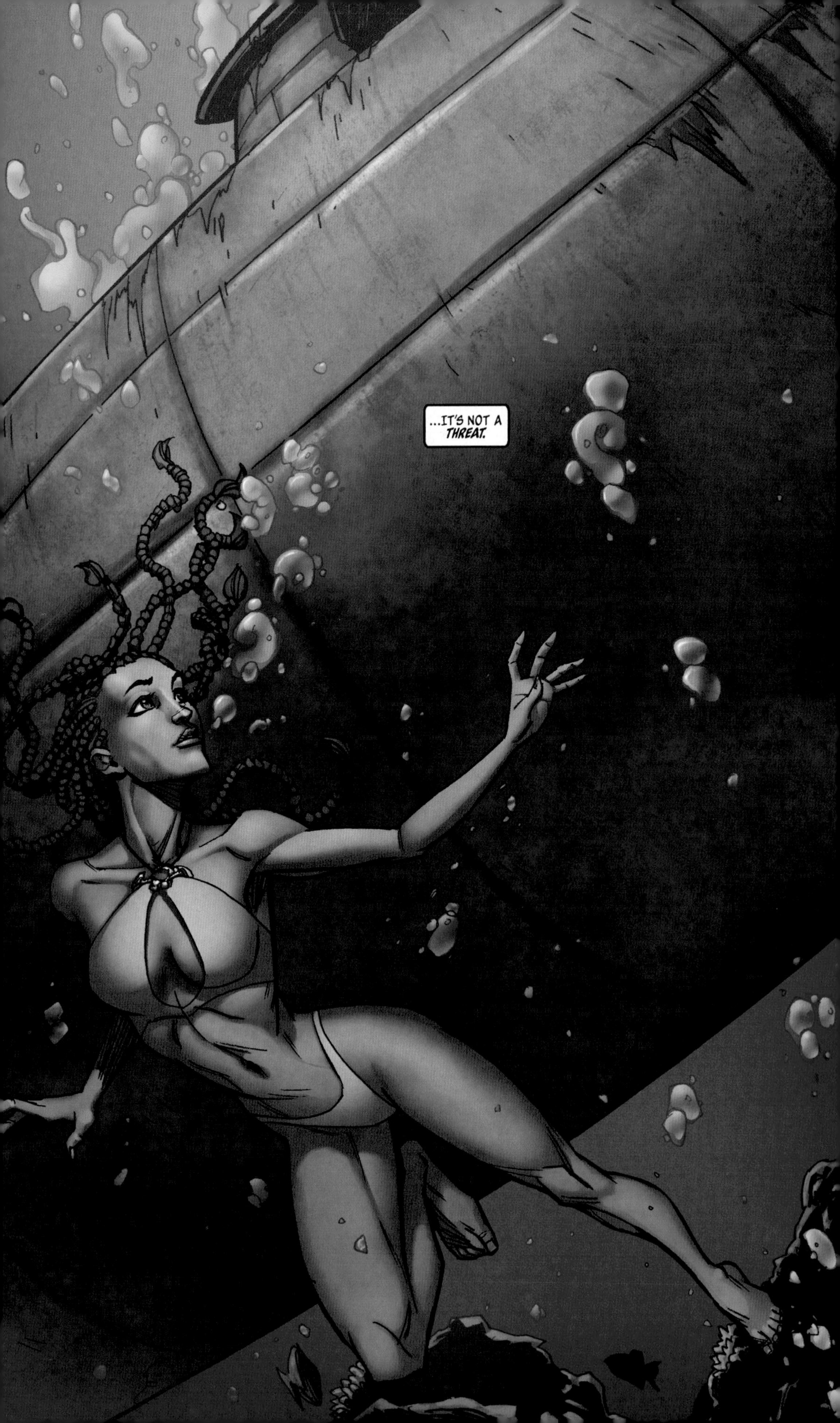
...IT'S NOT A THREAT.

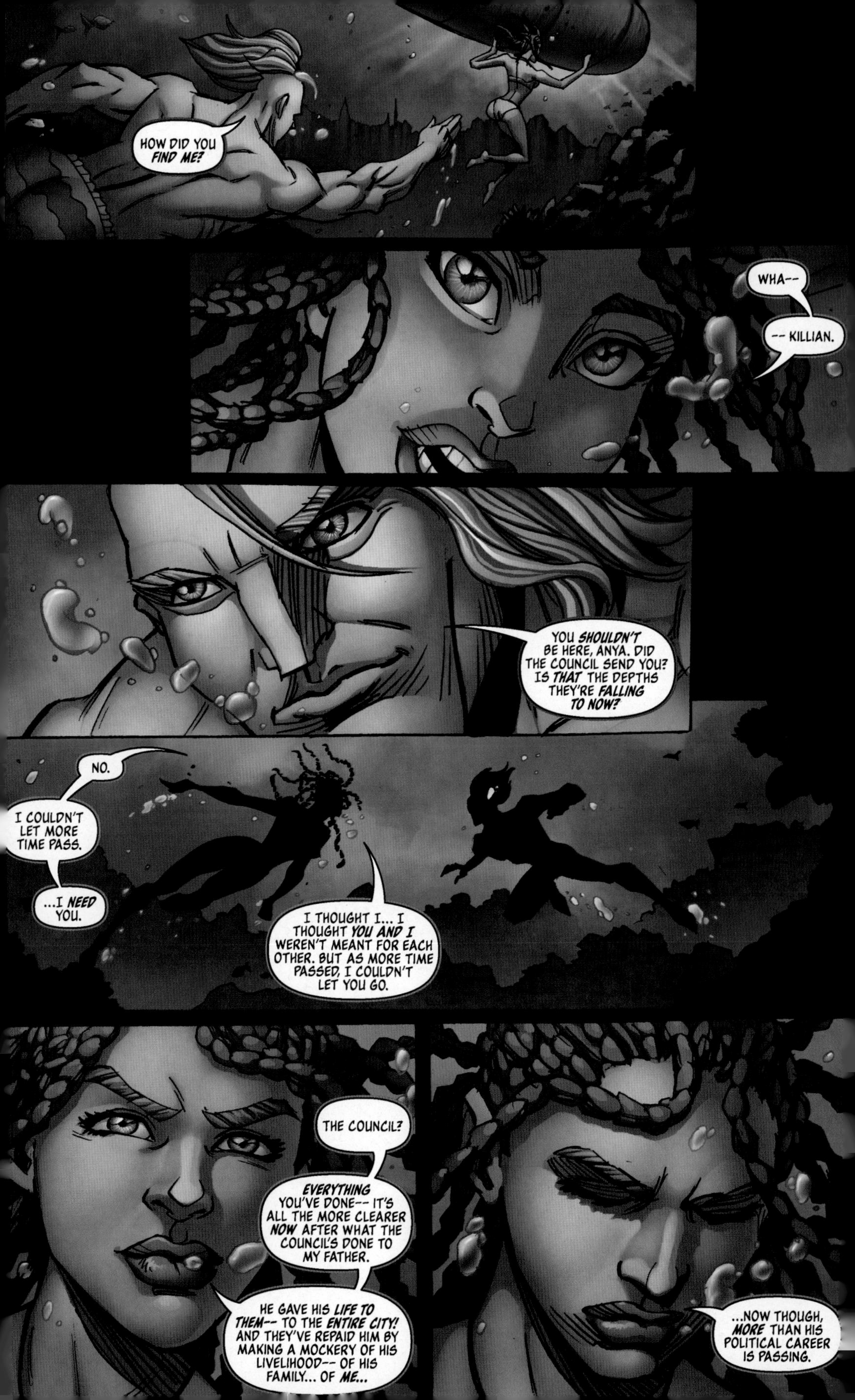
HOW DID YOU FIND ME?
WHA--
-- KILLIAN.
YOU SHOULDN'T BE HERE, ANYA. DID THE COUNCIL SEND YOU? IS THAT THE DEPTHS THEY'RE FALLING TO NOW?
NO.
I COULDN'T LET MORE TIME PASS.
...I NEED YOU.
I THOUGHT I... I THOUGHT YOU AND I WEREN'T MEANT FOR EACH OTHER. BUT AS MORE TIME PASSED, I COULDN'T LET YOU GO.
THE COUNCIL?
EVERYTHING YOU'VE DONE-- IT'S ALL THE MORE CLEARER NOW AFTER WHAT THE COUNCIL'S DONE TO MY FATHER.
HE GAVE HIS LIFE TO THEM-- TO THE ENTIRE CITY! AND THEY'VE REPAID HIM BY MAKING A MOCKERY OF HIS LIVELIHOOD-- OF HIS FAMILY... OF ME...
...NOW THOUGH, MORE THAN HIS POLITICAL CAREER IS PASSING.

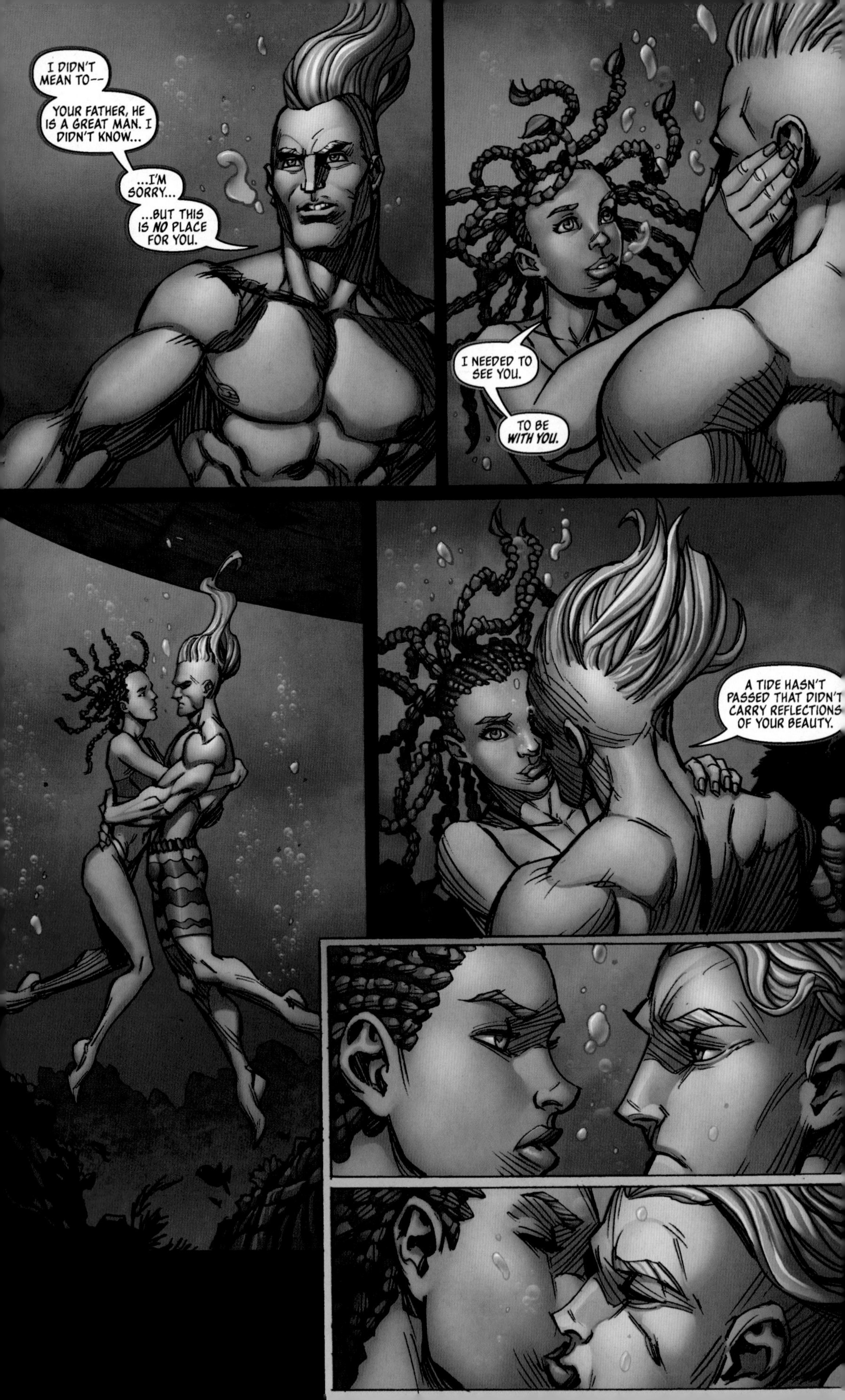
I DIDN'T MEAN TO--
YOUR FATHER, HE IS A GREAT MAN. I DIDN'T KNOW...
...I'M SORRY...
...BUT THIS IS NO PLACE FOR YOU.
I NEEDED TO SEE YOU.
TO BE WITH YOU.
A TIDE HASN'T PASSED THAT DIDN'T CARRY REFLECTIONS OF YOUR BEAUTY.

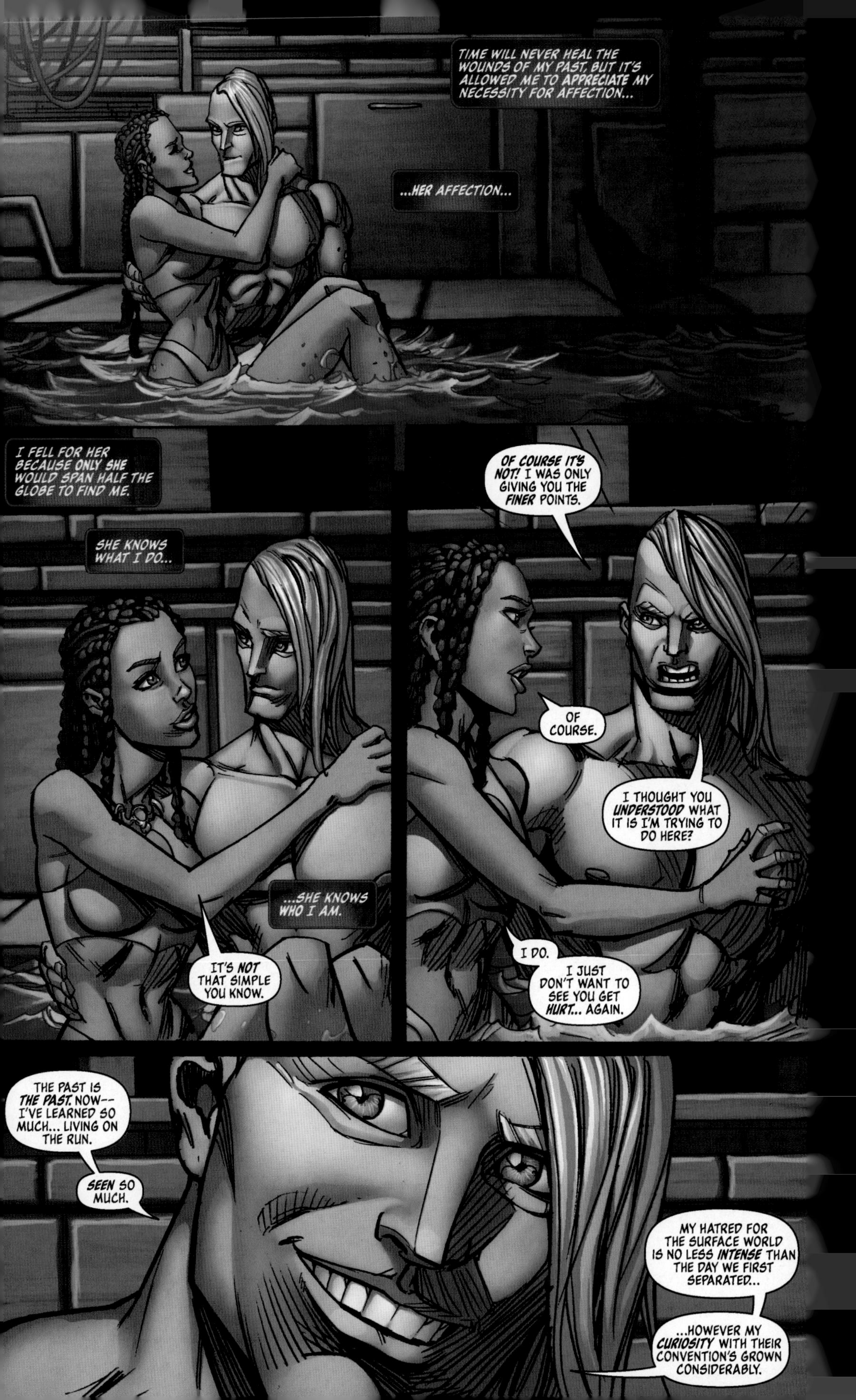
TIME WILL NEVER HEAL THE WOUNDS OF MY PAST, BUT IT'S ALLOWED ME TO APPRECIATE MY NECESSITY FOR AFFECTION...
...HER AFFECTION...
I FELL FOR HER BECAUSE ONLY SHE WOULD SPAN HALF THE GLOBE TO FIND ME.
SHE KNOWS WHAT I DO...
...SHE KNOWS WHO I AM.
IT'S NOT THAT SIMPLE YOU KNOW.
OF COURSE IT'S NOT! I WAS ONLY GIVING YOU THE FINER POINTS.
OF COURSE.
I THOUGHT YOU UNDERSTOOD WHAT IT IS I'M TRYING TO DO HERE?
I DO.
I JUST DON'T WANT TO SEE YOU GET HURT... AGAIN.
THE PAST IS THE PAST. NOW-- I'VE LEARNED SO MUCH... LIVING ON THE RUN.
SEEN SO MUCH.
MY HATRED FOR THE SURFACE WORLD IS NO LESS INTENSE THAN THE DAY WE FIRST SEPARATED...
...HOWEVER MY CURIOSITY WITH THEIR CONVENTION'S GROWN CONSIDERABLY.

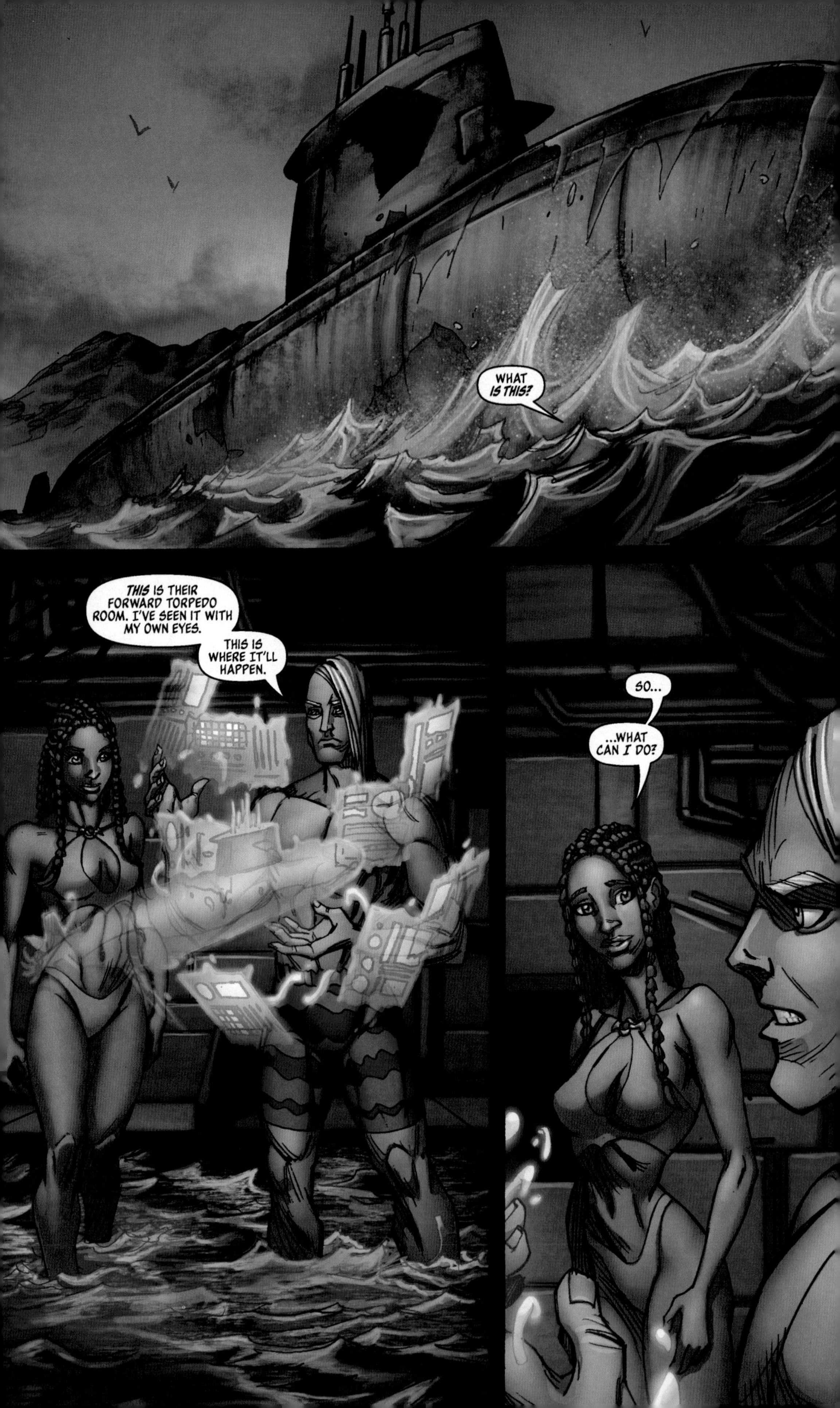
WHAT *IS THIS?*
THIS IS THEIR FORWARD TORPEDO ROOM. I'VE SEEN IT WITH MY OWN EYES.
THIS IS WHERE IT'LL HAPPEN.
SO...
...WHAT CAN *I* DO?

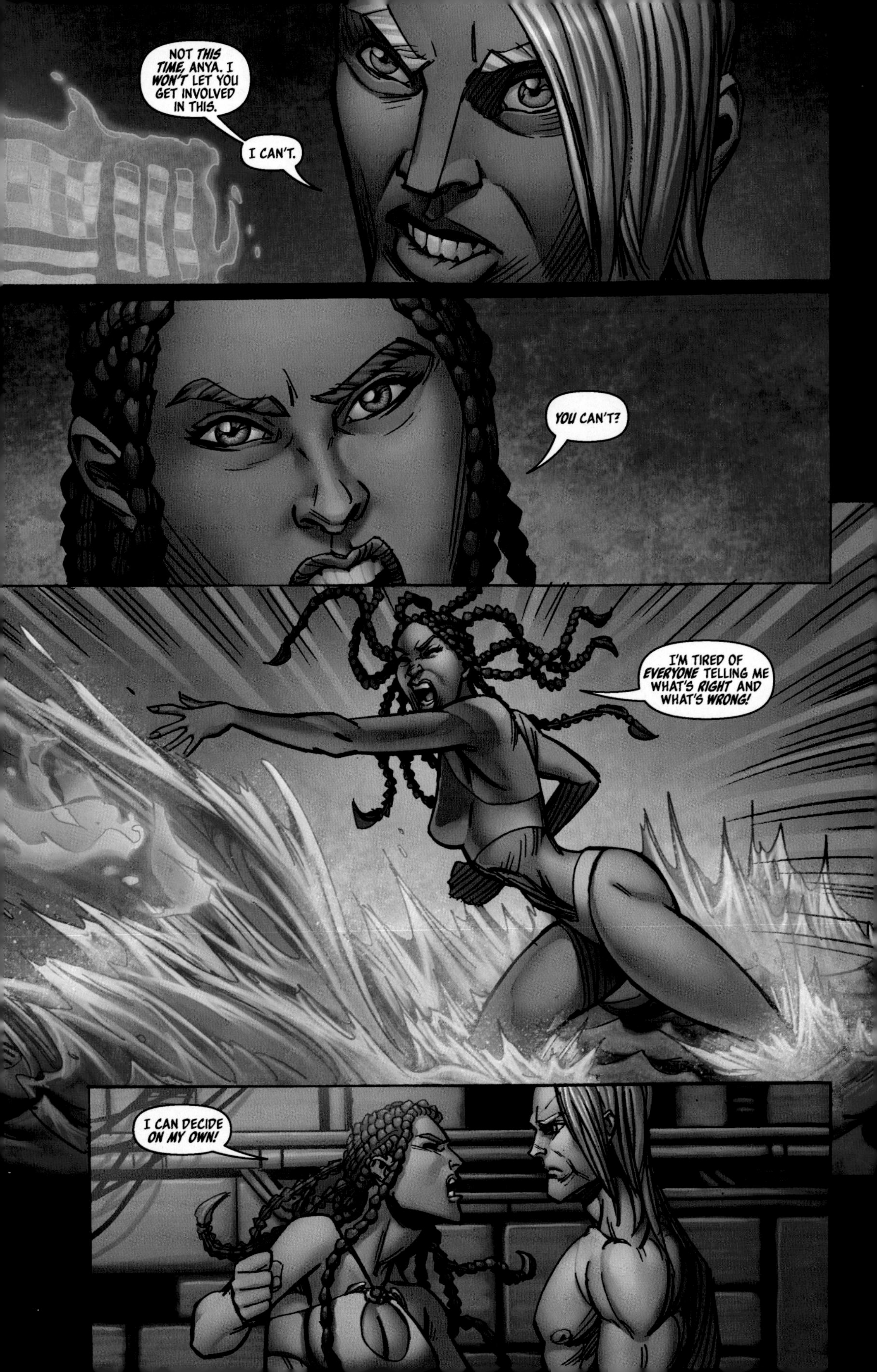
NOT THIS TIME, ANYA. I WON'T LET YOU GET INVOLVED IN THIS.
I CAN'T.
YOU CAN'T?
I'M TIRED OF EVERYONE TELLING ME WHAT'S RIGHT AND WHAT'S WRONG!
I CAN DECIDE ON MY OWN!

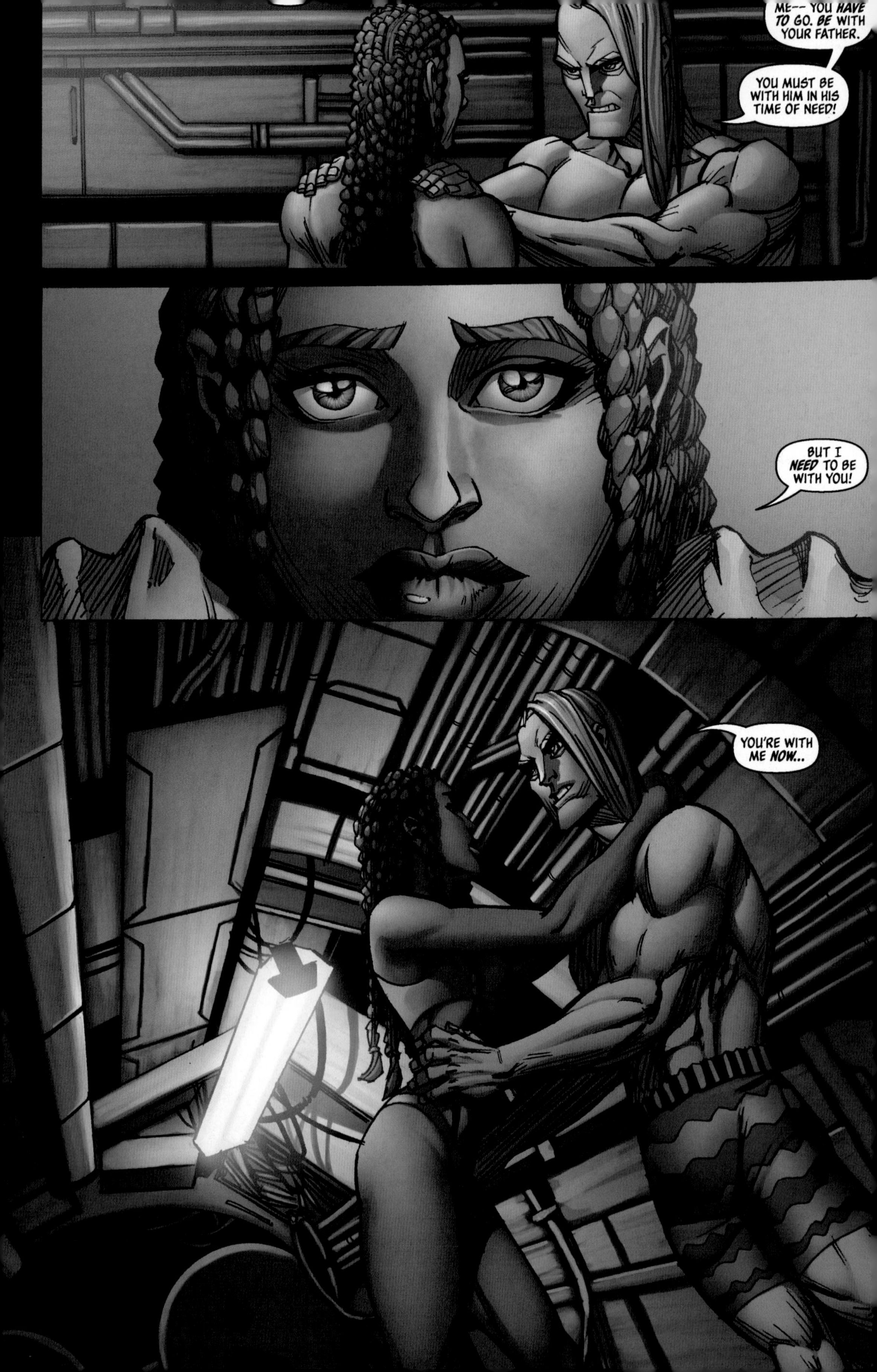
ME-- YOU *HAVE* TO GO. *BE* WITH YOUR FATHER.
YOU MUST BE WITH HIM IN HIS TIME OF NEED!
BUT I *NEED* TO BE WITH YOU!
YOU'RE WITH ME *NOW*...

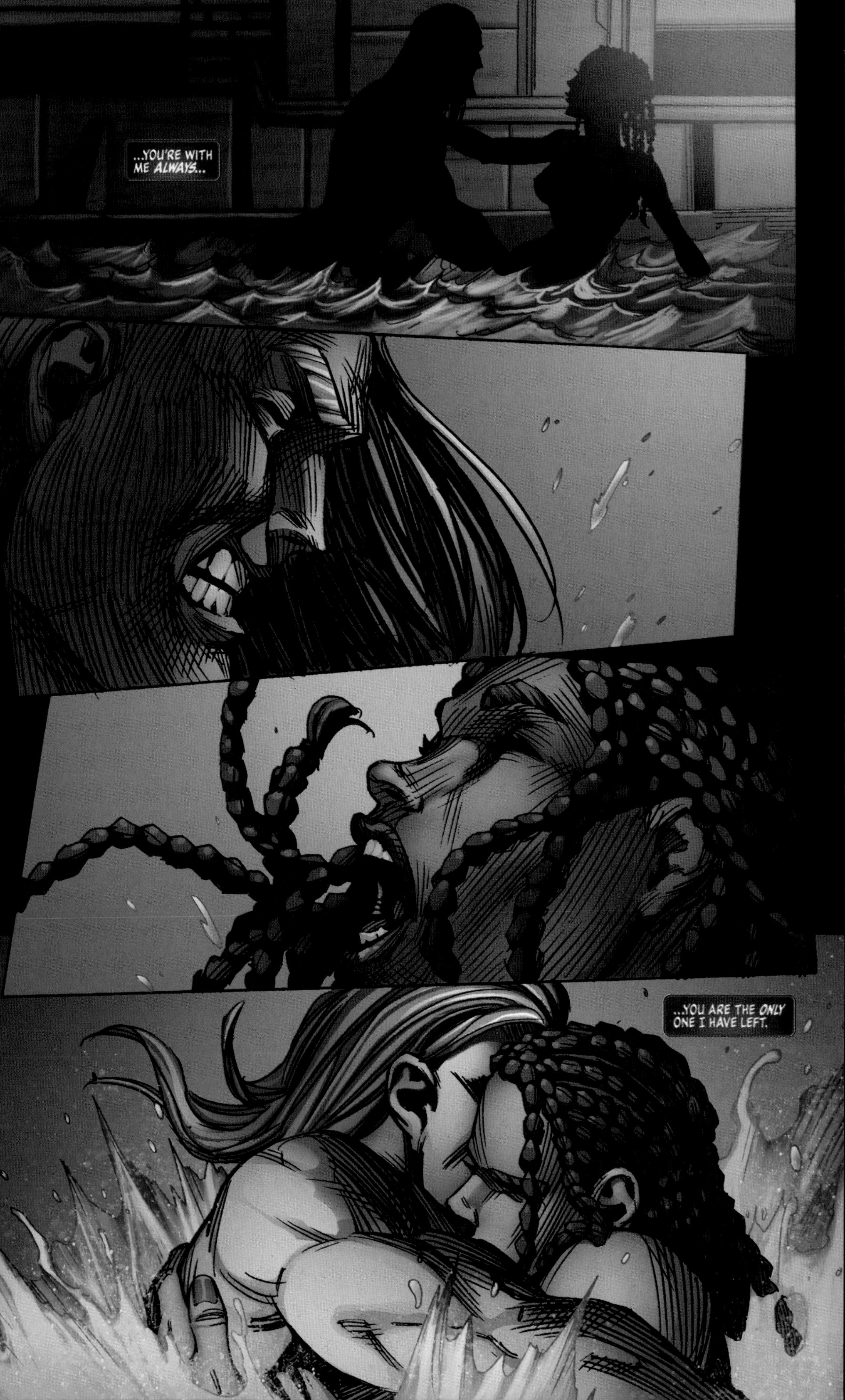
...YOU'RE WITH ME ALWAYS...
...YOU ARE THE ONLY ONE I HAVE LEFT.

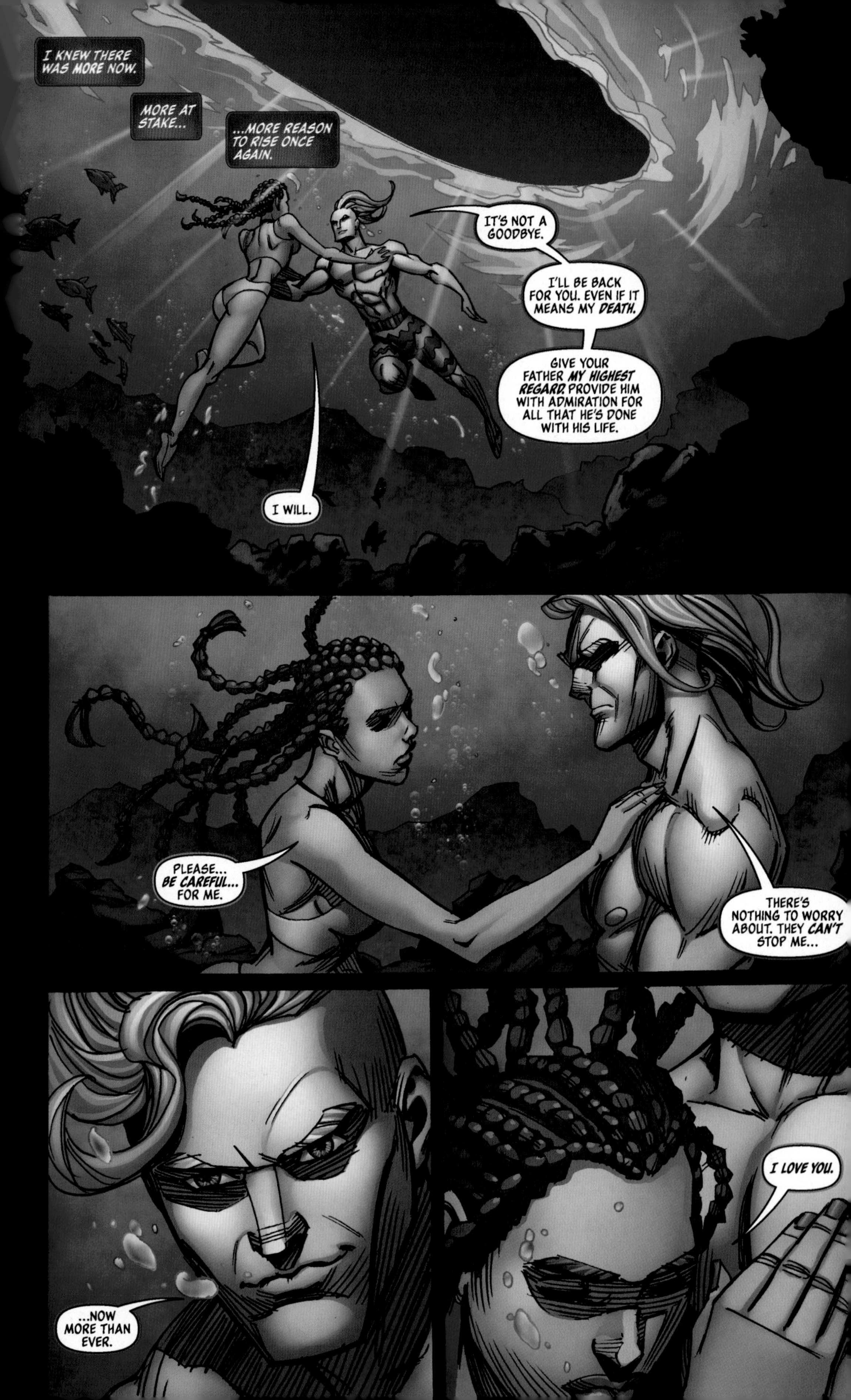

I KNEW THERE WAS MORE NOW.
MORE AT STAKE...
...MORE REASON TO RISE ONCE AGAIN.
IT'S NOT A GOODBYE.
I'LL BE BACK FOR YOU. EVEN IF IT MEANS MY *DEATH.*
GIVE YOUR FATHER ***MY HIGHEST REGARD.*** PROVIDE HIM WITH ADMIRATION FOR ALL THAT HE'S DONE WITH HIS LIFE.
I WILL.
PLEASE... ***BE CAREFUL...*** FOR ME.
THERE'S NOTHING TO WORRY ABOUT. THEY ***CAN'T*** STOP ME...
...NOW MORE THAN EVER.
I LOVE YOU.

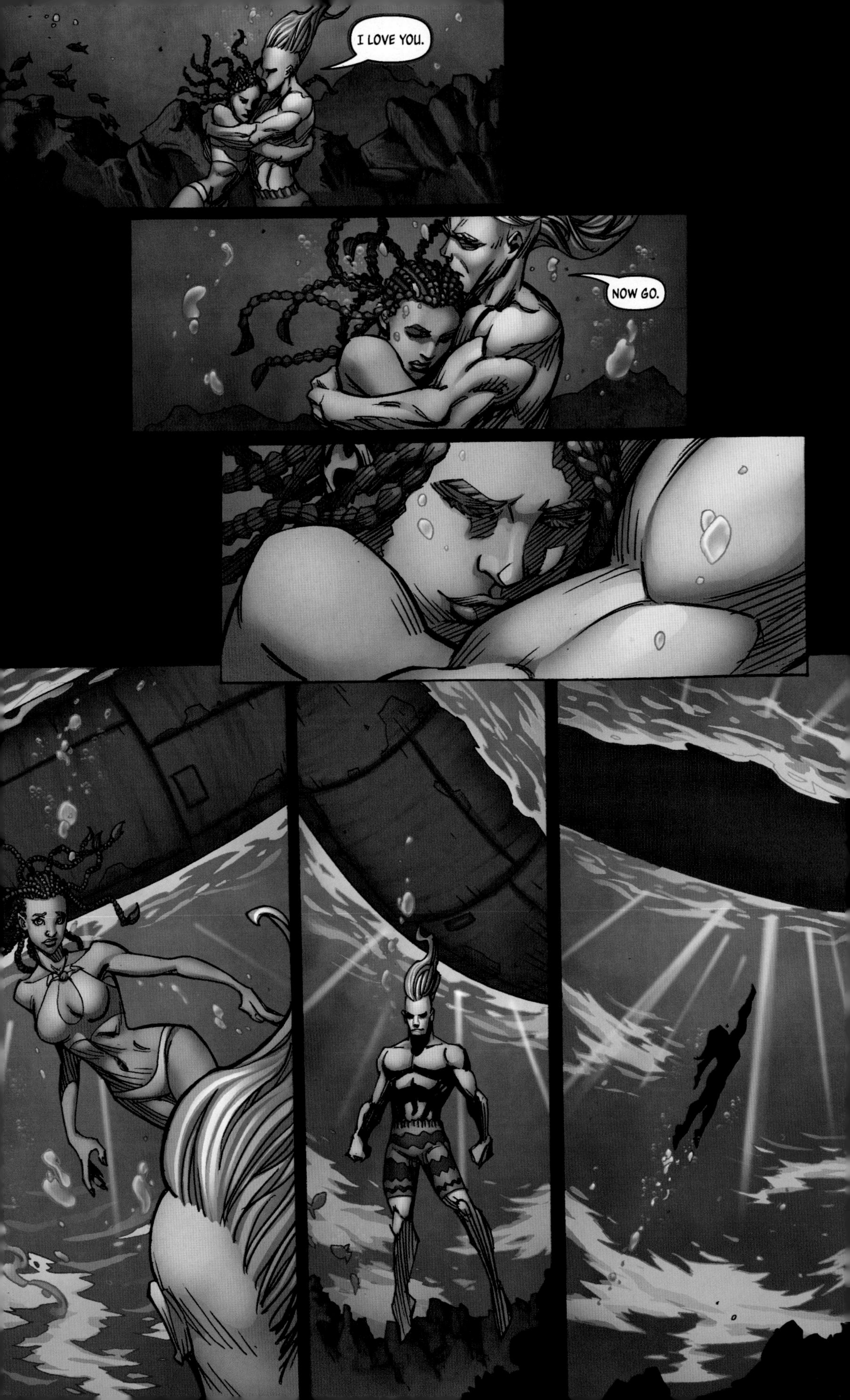
I LOVE YOU.
NOW GO.

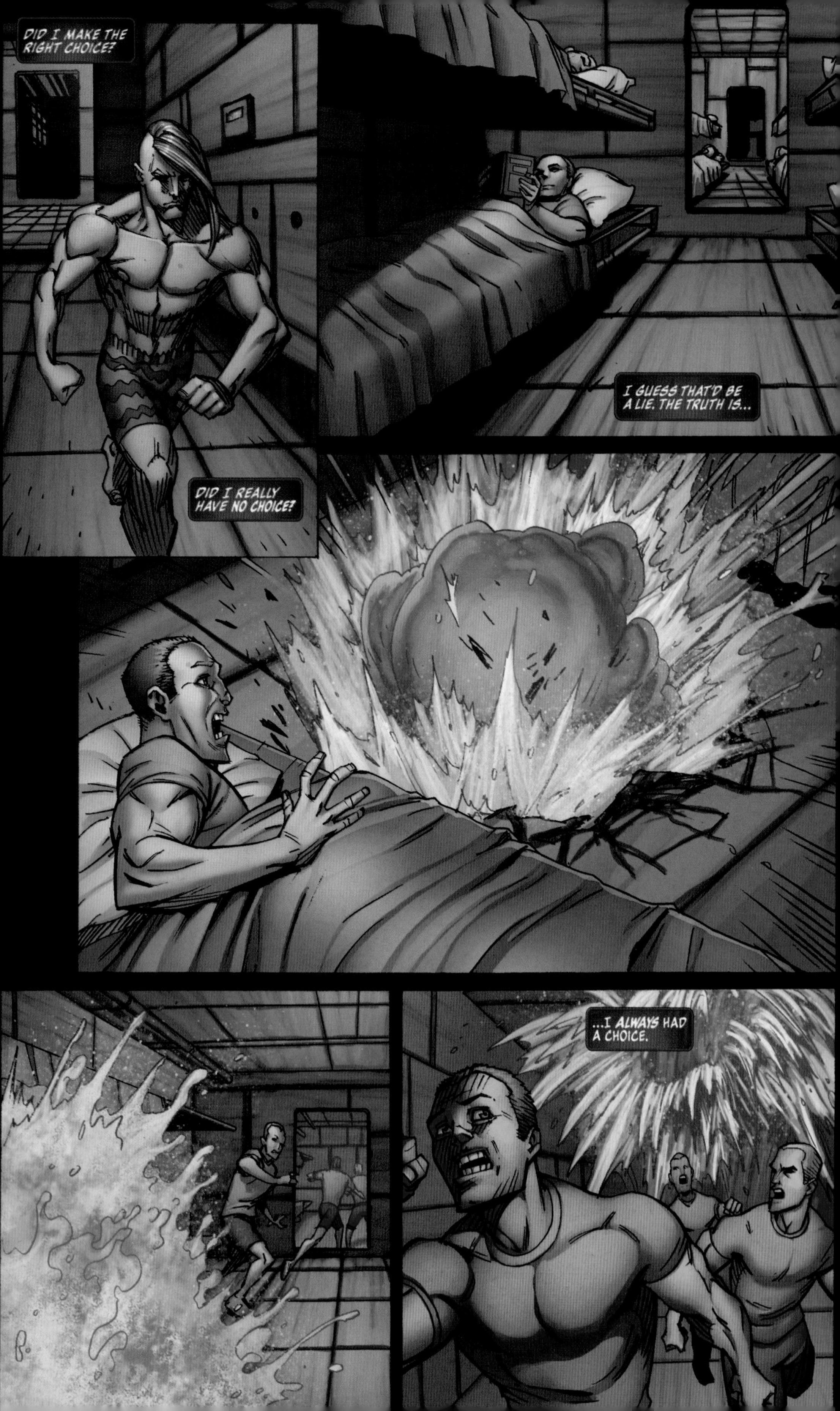
DID I MAKE THE RIGHT CHOICE?
I GUESS THAT'D BE A LIE. THE TRUTH IS...
DID I REALLY HAVE NO CHOICE?
...I ALWAYS HAD A CHOICE.

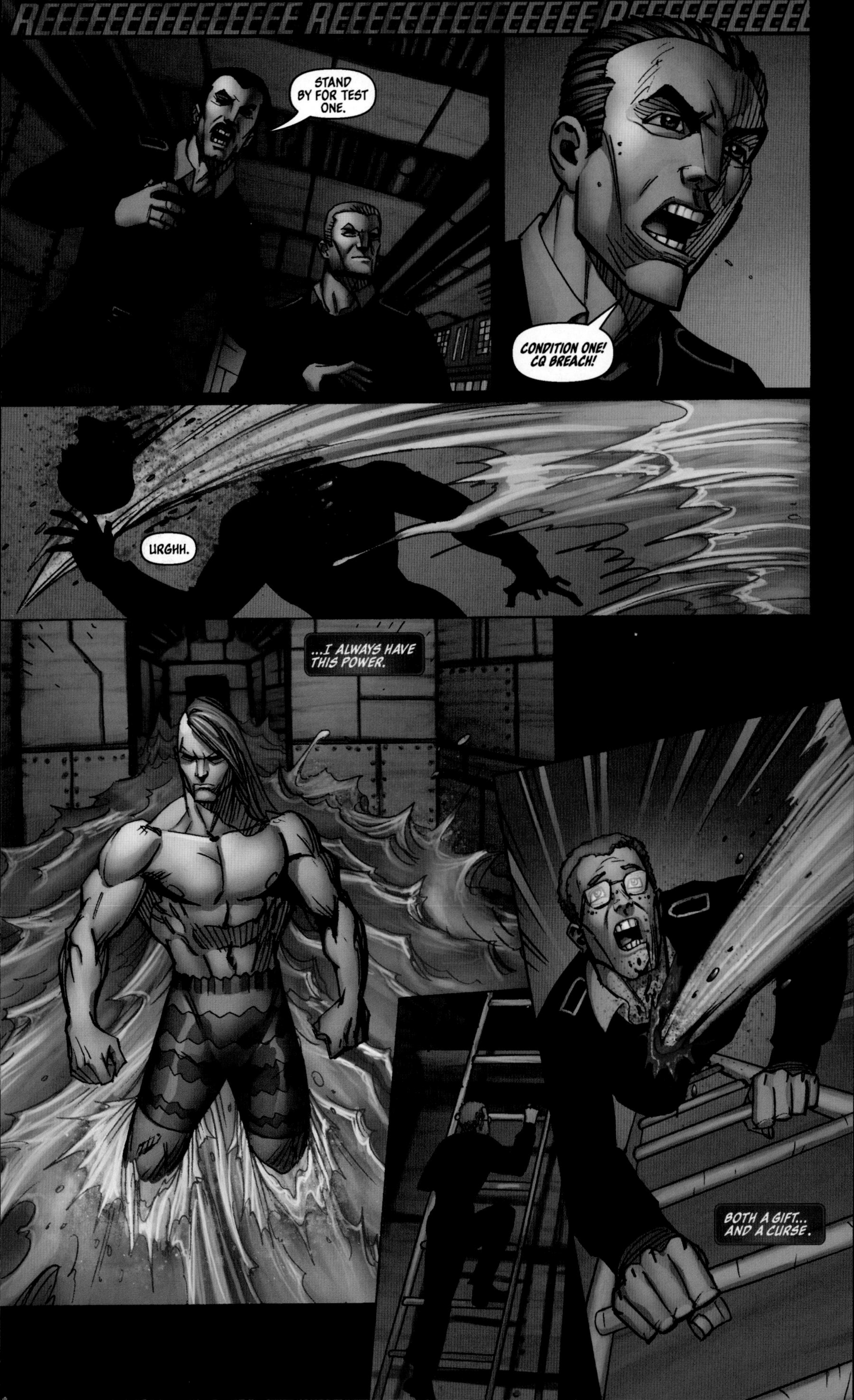
REEEEEEEEEEEEEEEE REEEEEEEEEEEEEEEEE REEEEEEEEEE
STAND BY FOR TEST ONE.
CONDITION ONE! CQ BREACH!
URGHH.
...I ALWAYS HAVE THIS POWER.
BOTH A GIFT... AND A CURSE.

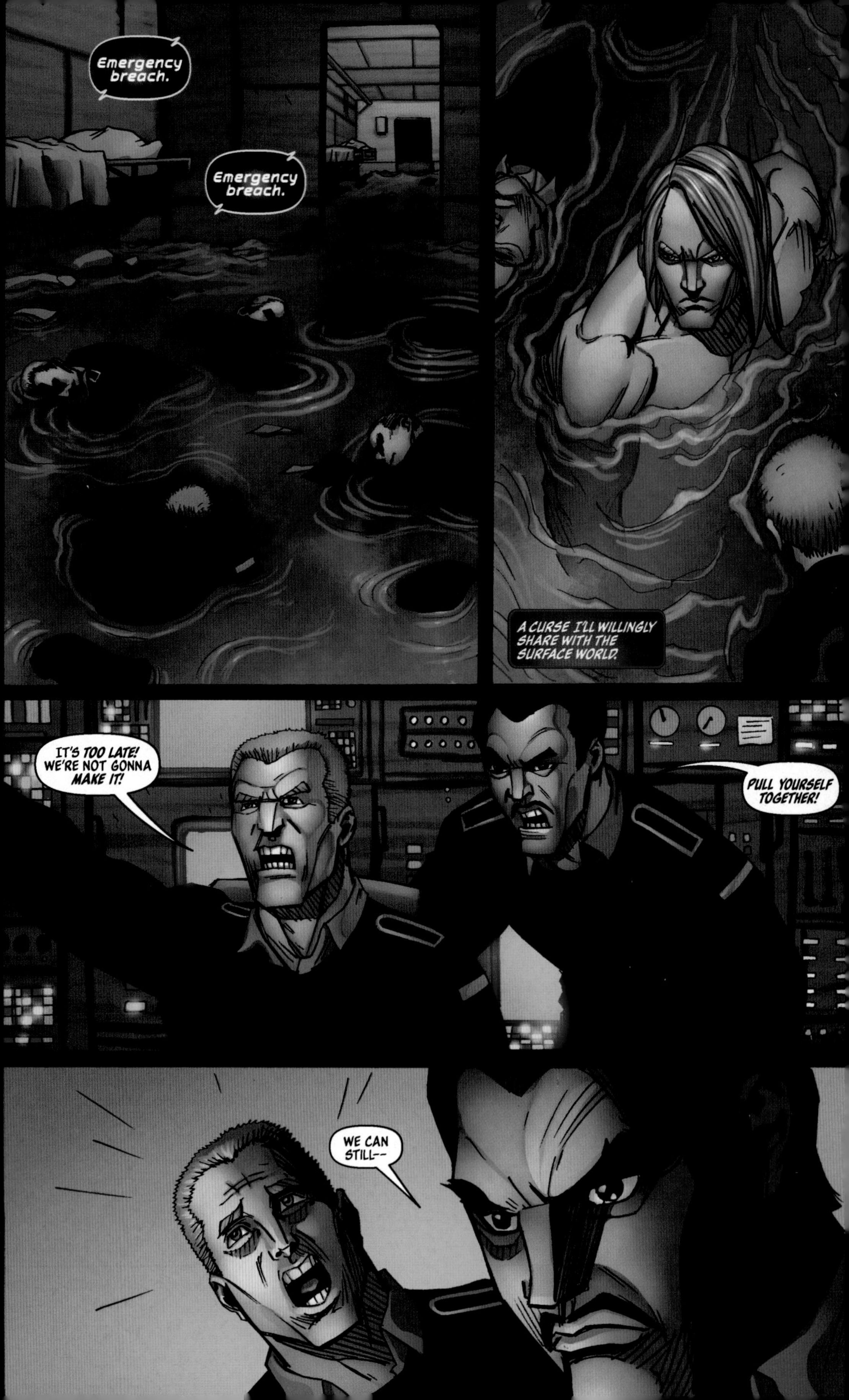
Emergency breach.
Emergency breach.
A CURSE I'LL WILLINGLY SHARE WITH THE SURFACE WORLD.
IT'S TOO LATE! WE'RE NOT GONNA MAKE IT!
PULL YOURSELF TOGETHER!
WE CAN STILL--

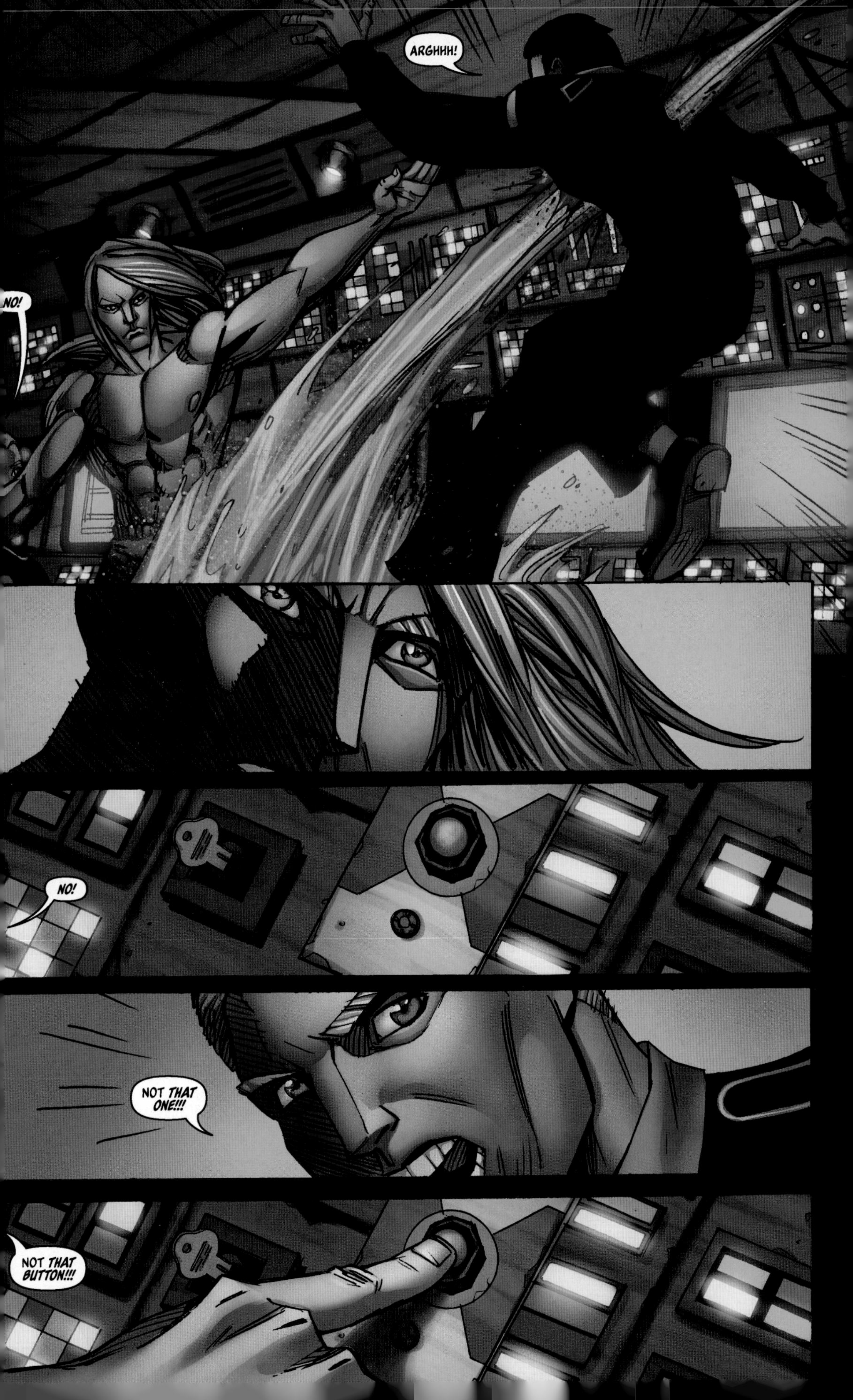
ARGHHH!
NO!
NO!
NOT THAT ONE!!!
NOT THAT BUTTON!!!

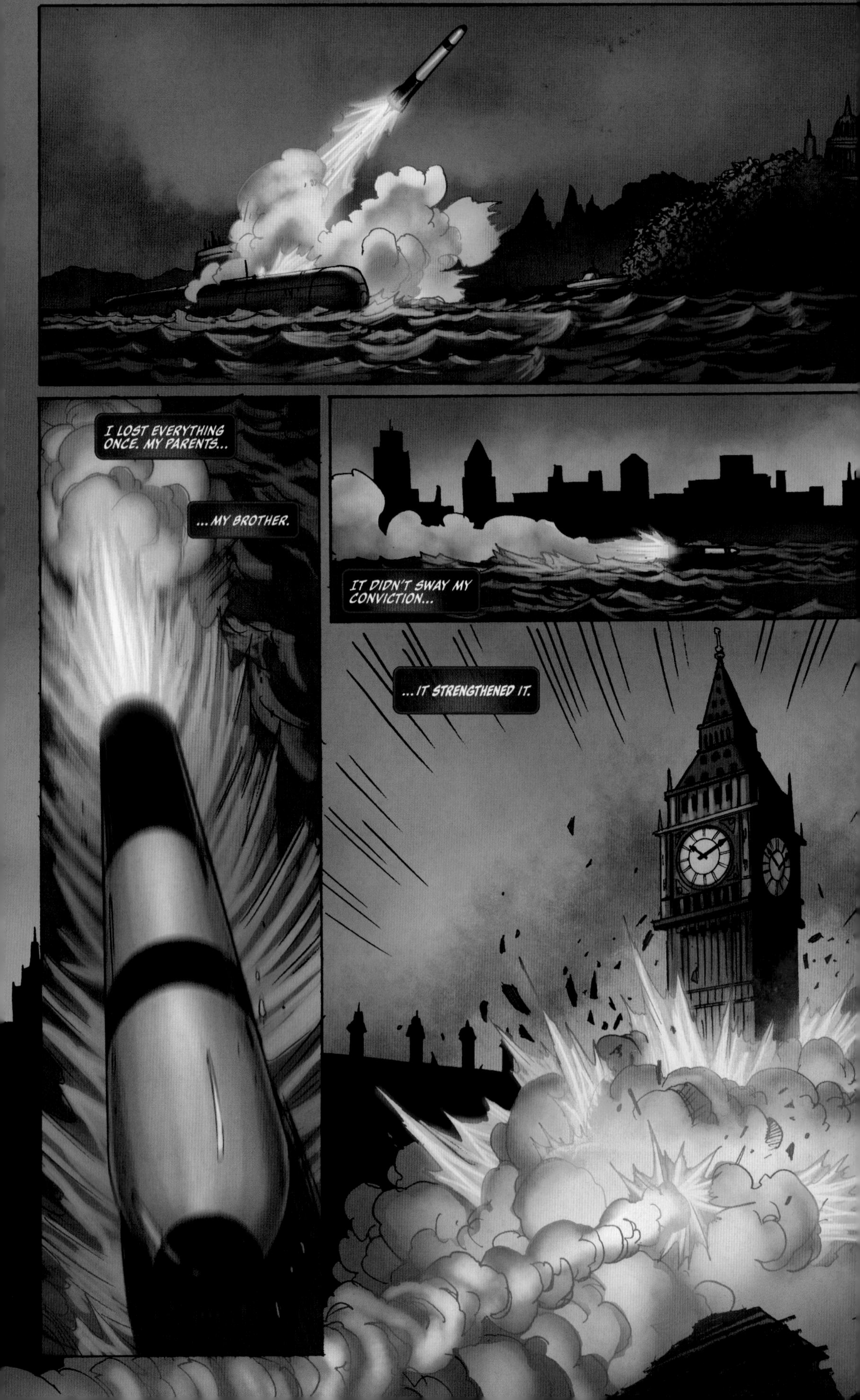
I LOST EVERYTHING ONCE. MY PARENTS...
...MY BROTHER.
IT DIDN'T SWAY MY CONVICTION...
...IT STRENGTHENED IT.

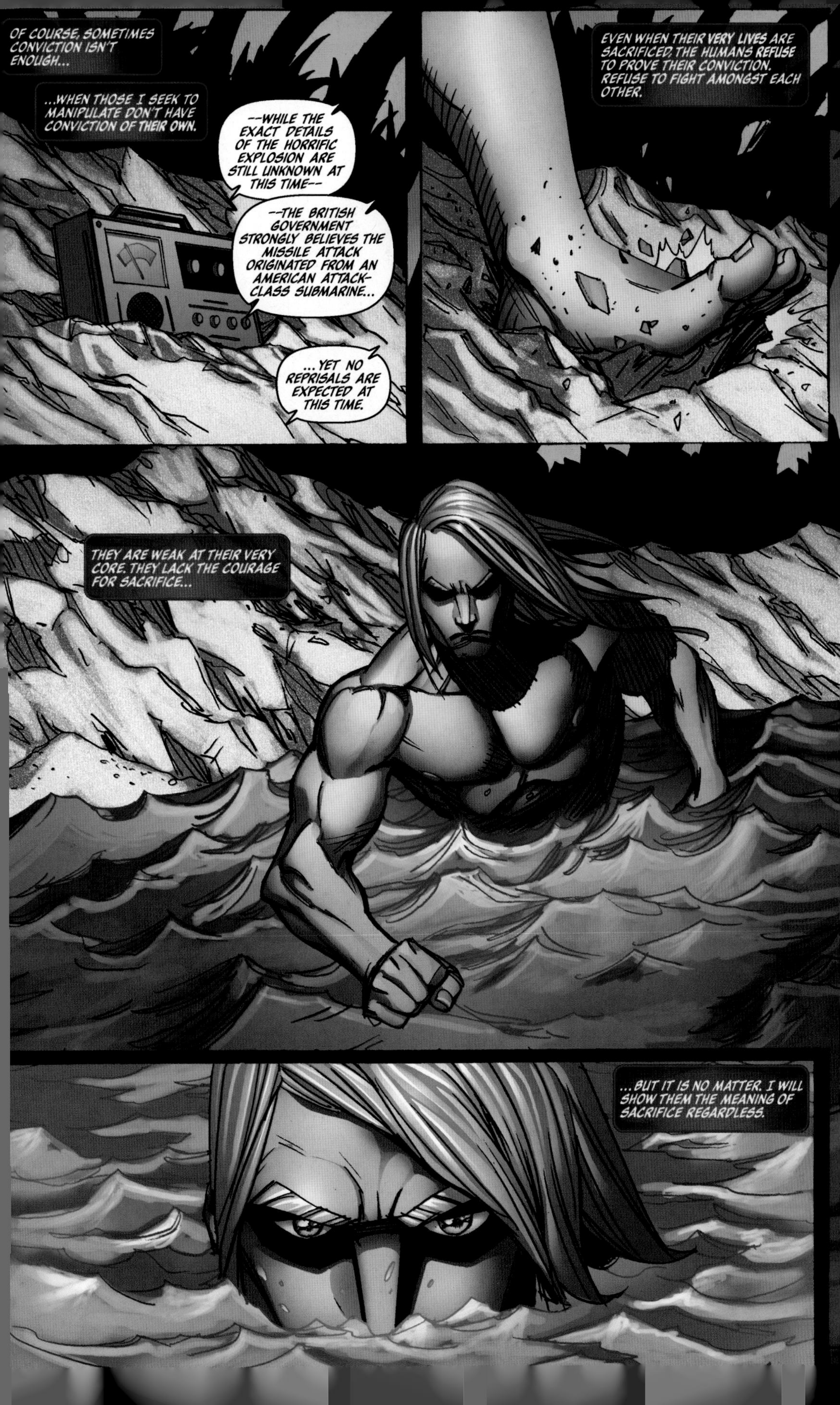
OF COURSE, SOMETIMES CONVICTION ISN'T ENOUGH...
...WHEN THOSE I SEEK TO MANIPULATE DON'T HAVE CONVICTION OF THEIR OWN.
--WHILE THE EXACT DETAILS OF THE HORRIFIC EXPLOSION ARE STILL UNKNOWN AT THIS TIME--
--THE BRITISH GOVERNMENT STRONGLY BELIEVES THE MISSILE ATTACK ORIGINATED FROM AN AMERICAN ATTACK-CLASS SUBMARINE...
...YET NO REPRISALS ARE EXPECTED AT THIS TIME.
EVEN WHEN THEIR VERY LIVES ARE SACRIFICED, THE HUMANS REFUSE TO PROVE THEIR CONVICTION. REFUSE TO FIGHT AMONGST EACH OTHER.
THEY ARE WEAK AT THEIR VERY CORE. THEY LACK THE COURAGE FOR SACRIFICE...
...BUT IT IS NO MATTER. I WILL SHOW THEM THE MEANING OF SACRIFICE REGARDLESS.

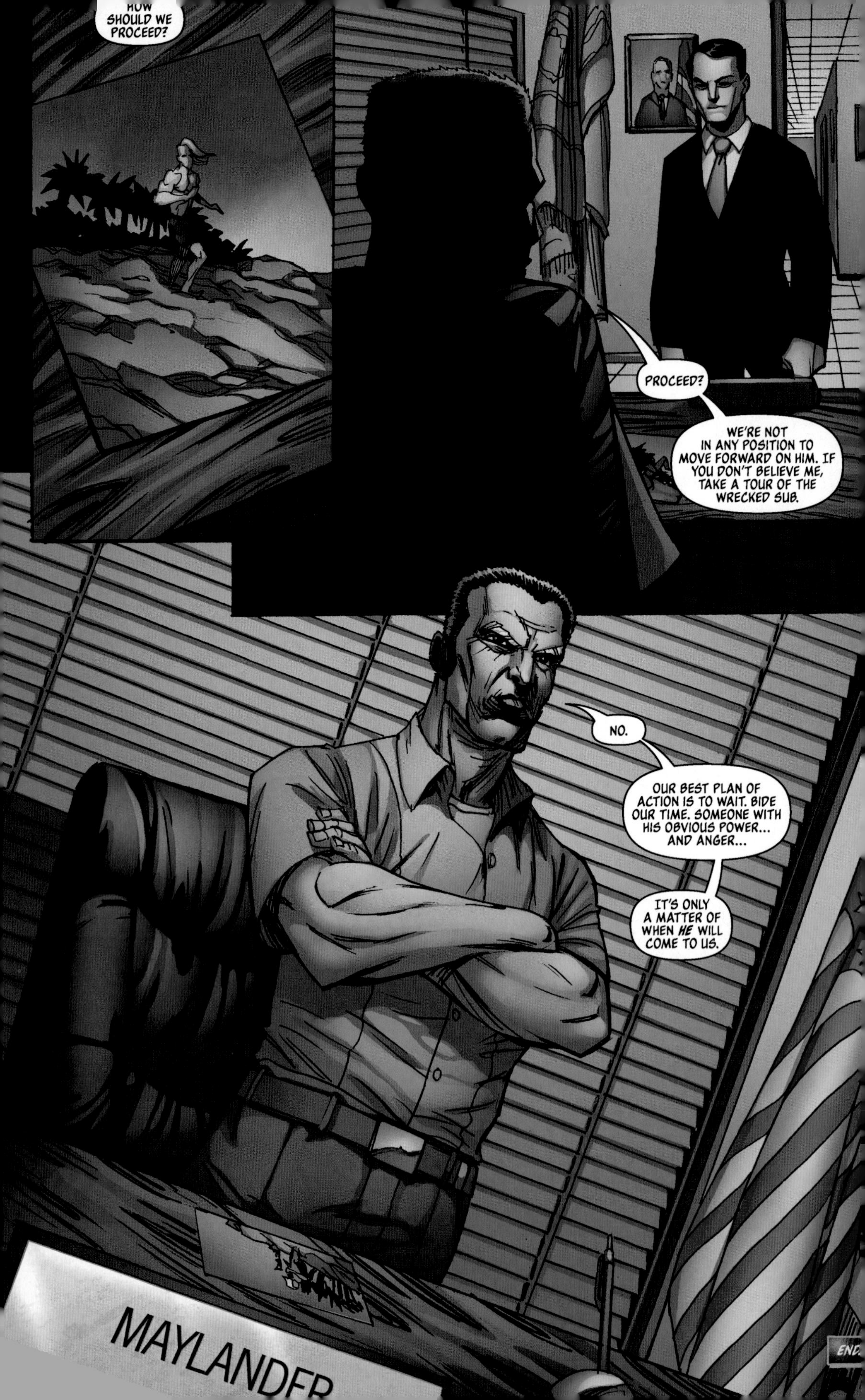
HOW SHOULD WE PROCEED?
PROCEED?
WE'RE NOT IN ANY POSITION TO MOVE FORWARD ON HIM. IF YOU DON'T BELIEVE ME, TAKE A TOUR OF THE WRECKED SUB.
NO.
OUR BEST PLAN OF ACTION IS TO WAIT. BIDE OUR TIME. SOMEONE WITH HIS OBVIOUS POWER... AND ANGER...
IT'S ONLY A MATTER OF WHEN *HE* WILL COME TO US.
MAYLANDER
END

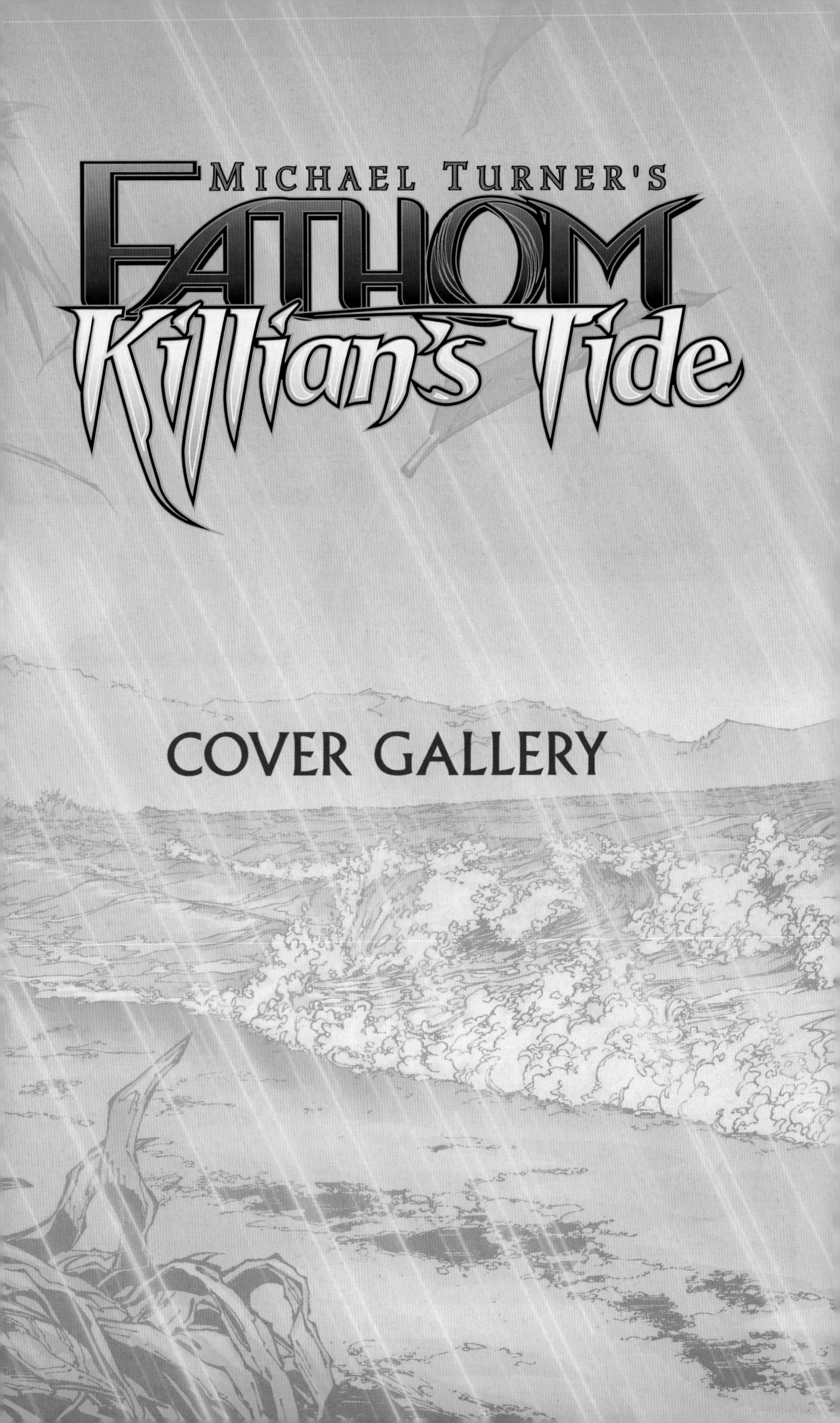

MICHAEL TURNER'S FATHOM
Killian's Tide

COVER GALLERY

COVER A TO MICHAEL TURNER'S:
KILLIAN'S TIDE #1 BY
• Talent CALDWELL • Victor LLAMAS • Dan KEMP •

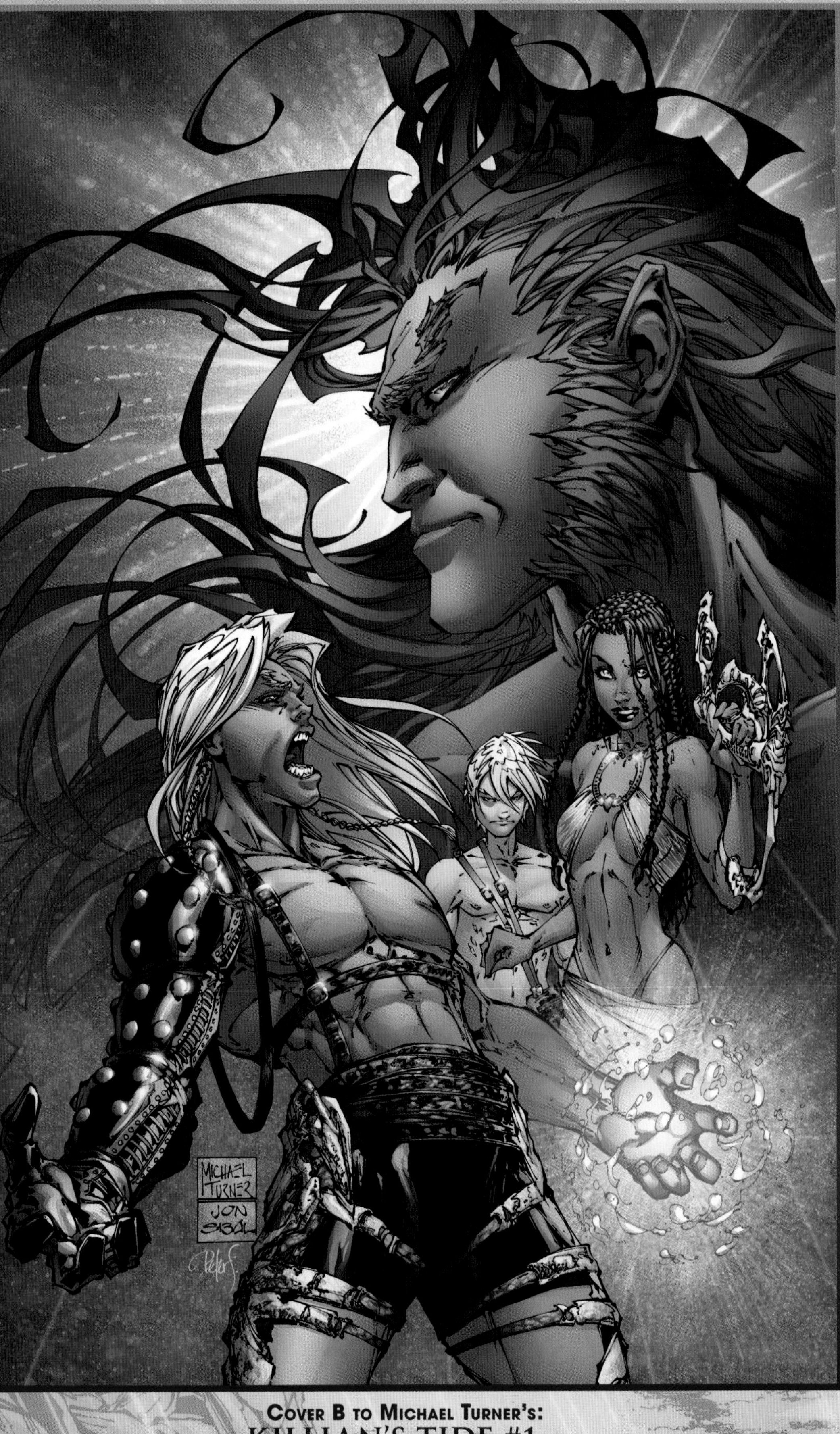
MICHAEL TURNER
JON SIBAL

COVER B TO MICHAEL TURNER'S:

KILLIAN'S TIDE #1 BY

• MICHAEL TURNER • JON SIBAL • PETER STEIGERWALD •

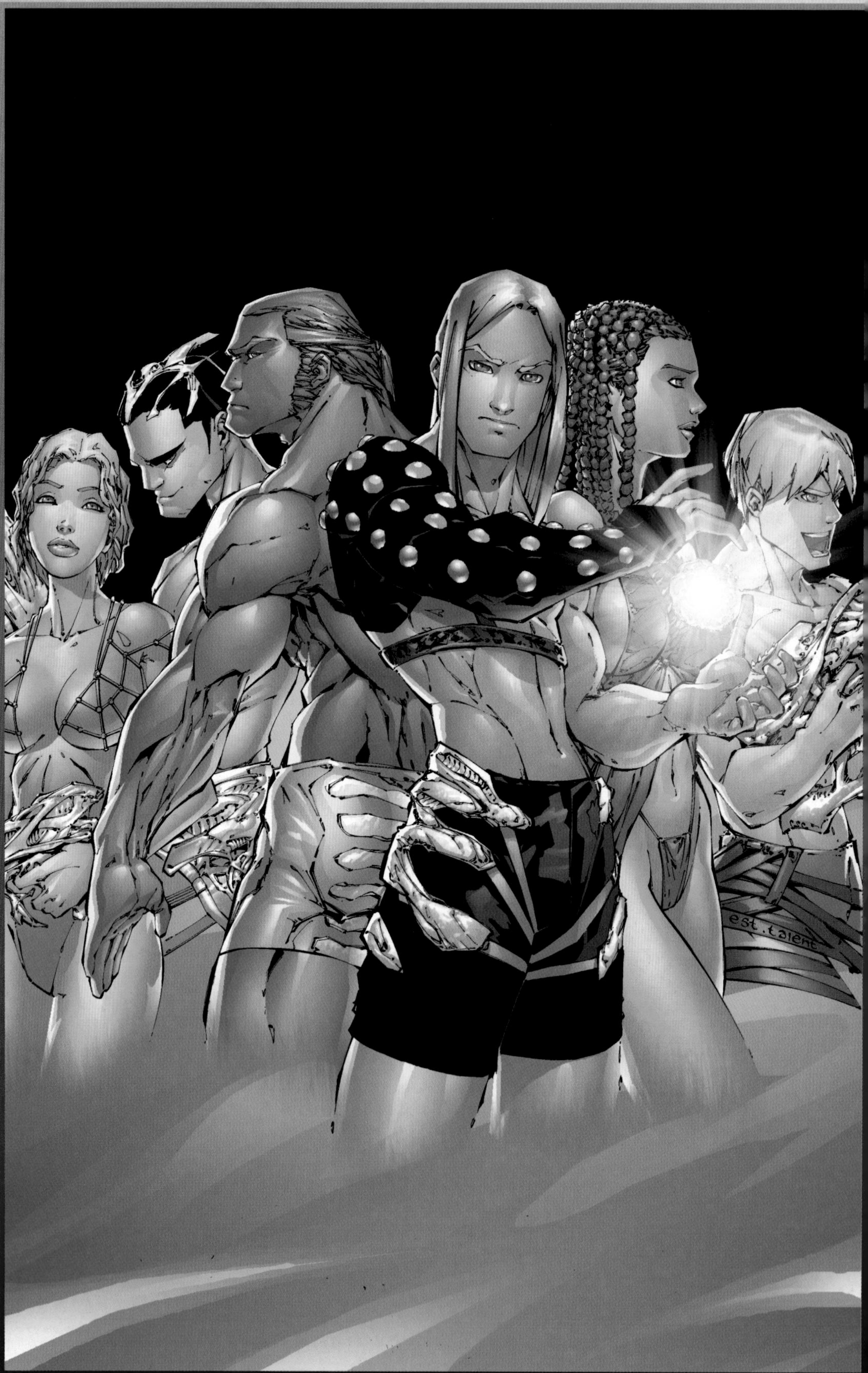
est. talent

Cover A to Michael Turner's:
KILLIAN'S TIDE #2 by
• *Talent CALDWELL* • *Jason GORDER* • *Dan KEMP* •

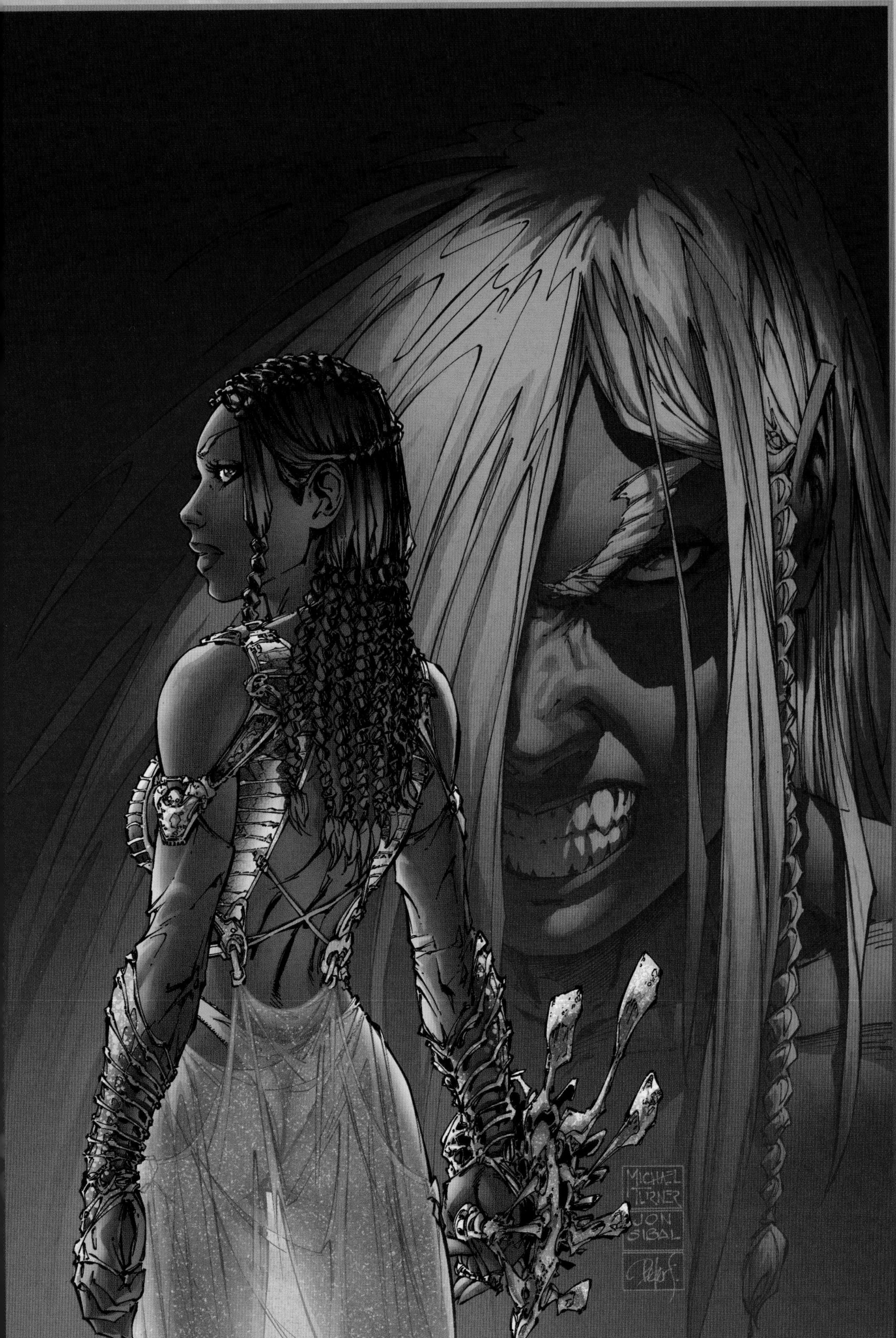
MICHAEL TURNER
JON SIBAL

Cover B to Michael Turner's:
KILLIAN'S TIDE #2 by
• Michael TURNER • Jon SIBAL • Peter STEIGERWALD •

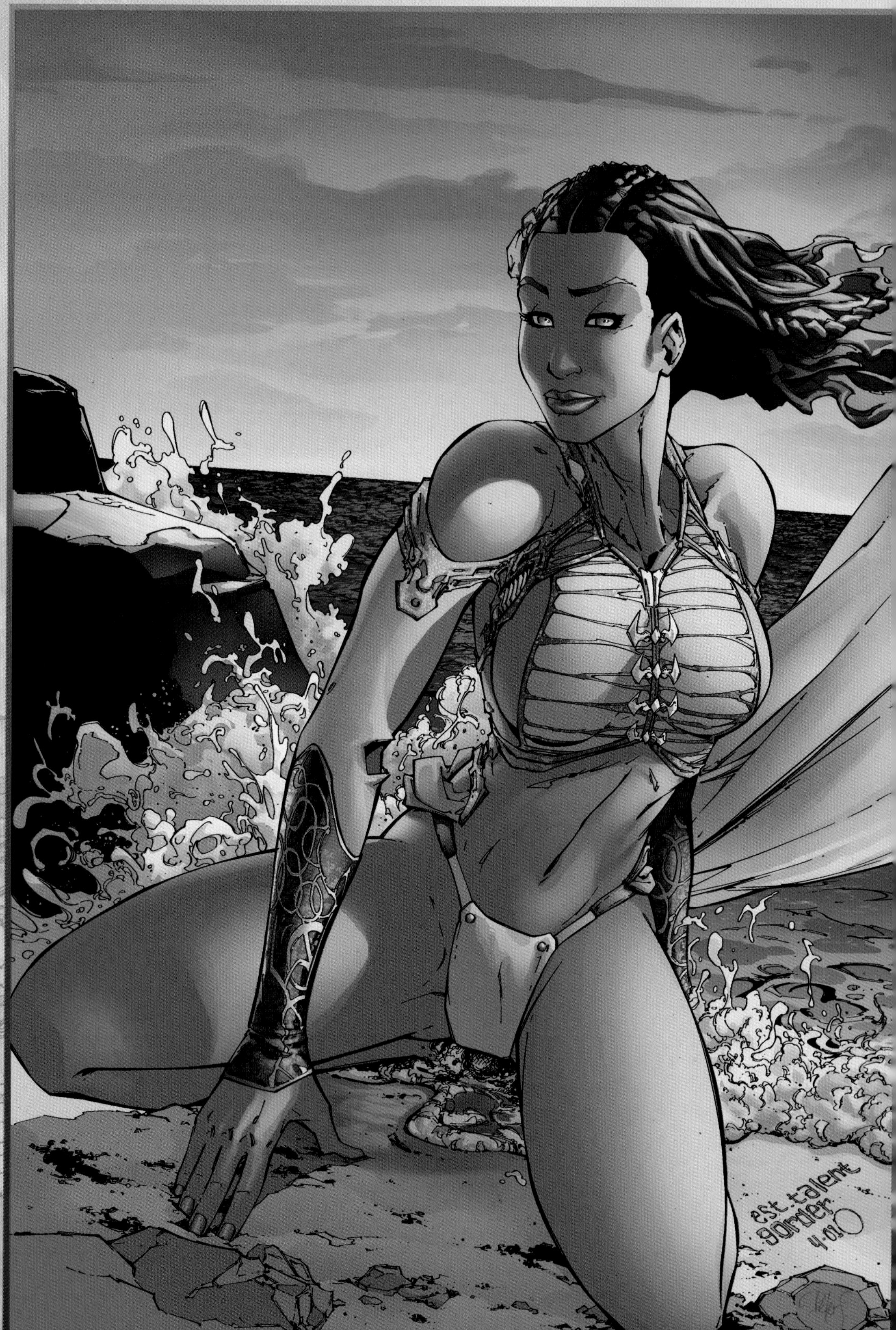

Cover C to Michael Turner's:

KILLIAN'S TIDE #2 by

• *Talent CALDWELL* • *Jason GORDER* • *Peter STEIGERWALD* •

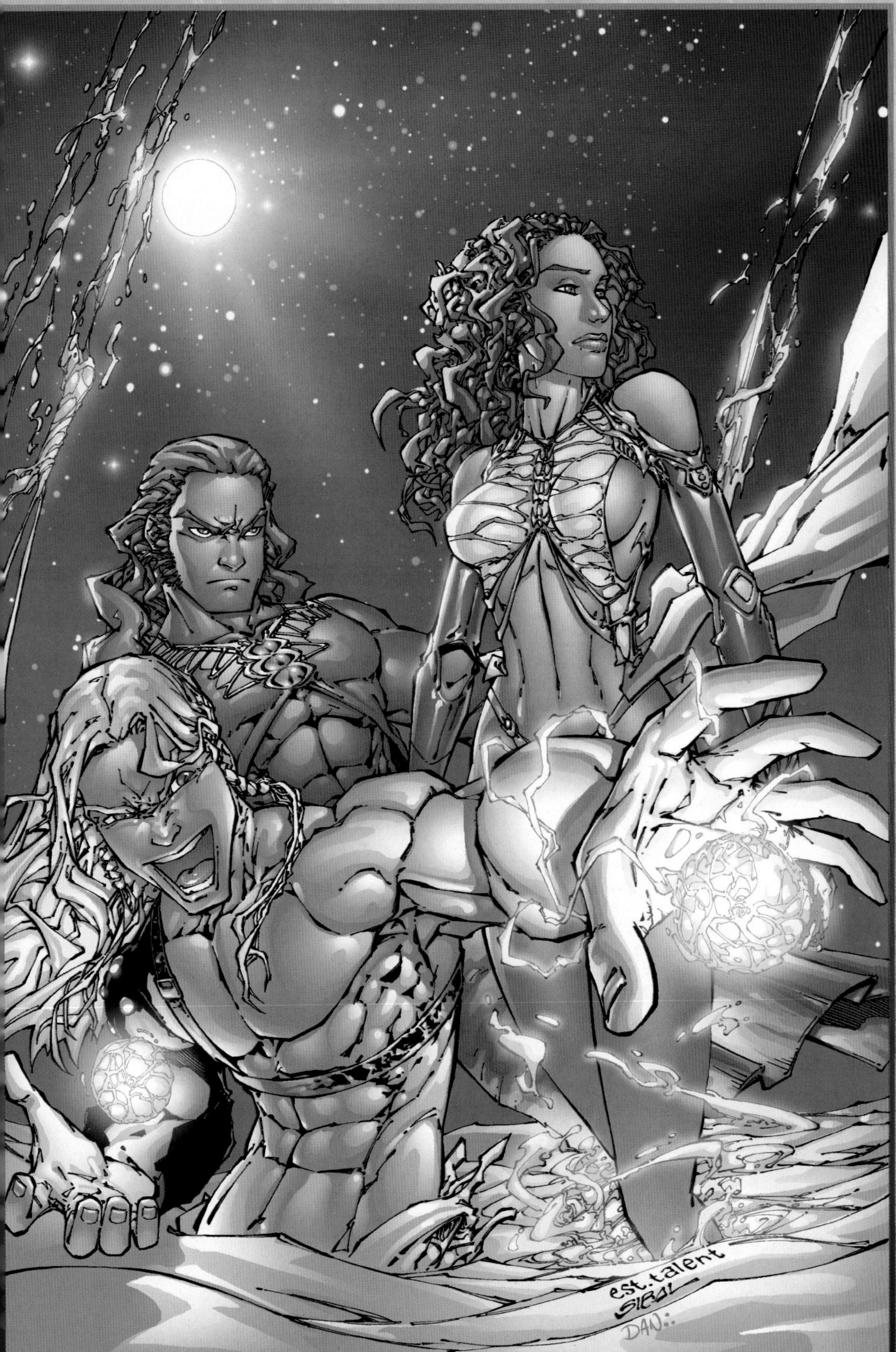
est. talent
SIBAL
DAN

Cover A to Michael Turner's:
KILLIAN'S TIDE #3 *by*
• Talent CALDWELL • Jon SIBAL • Dan KEMP •

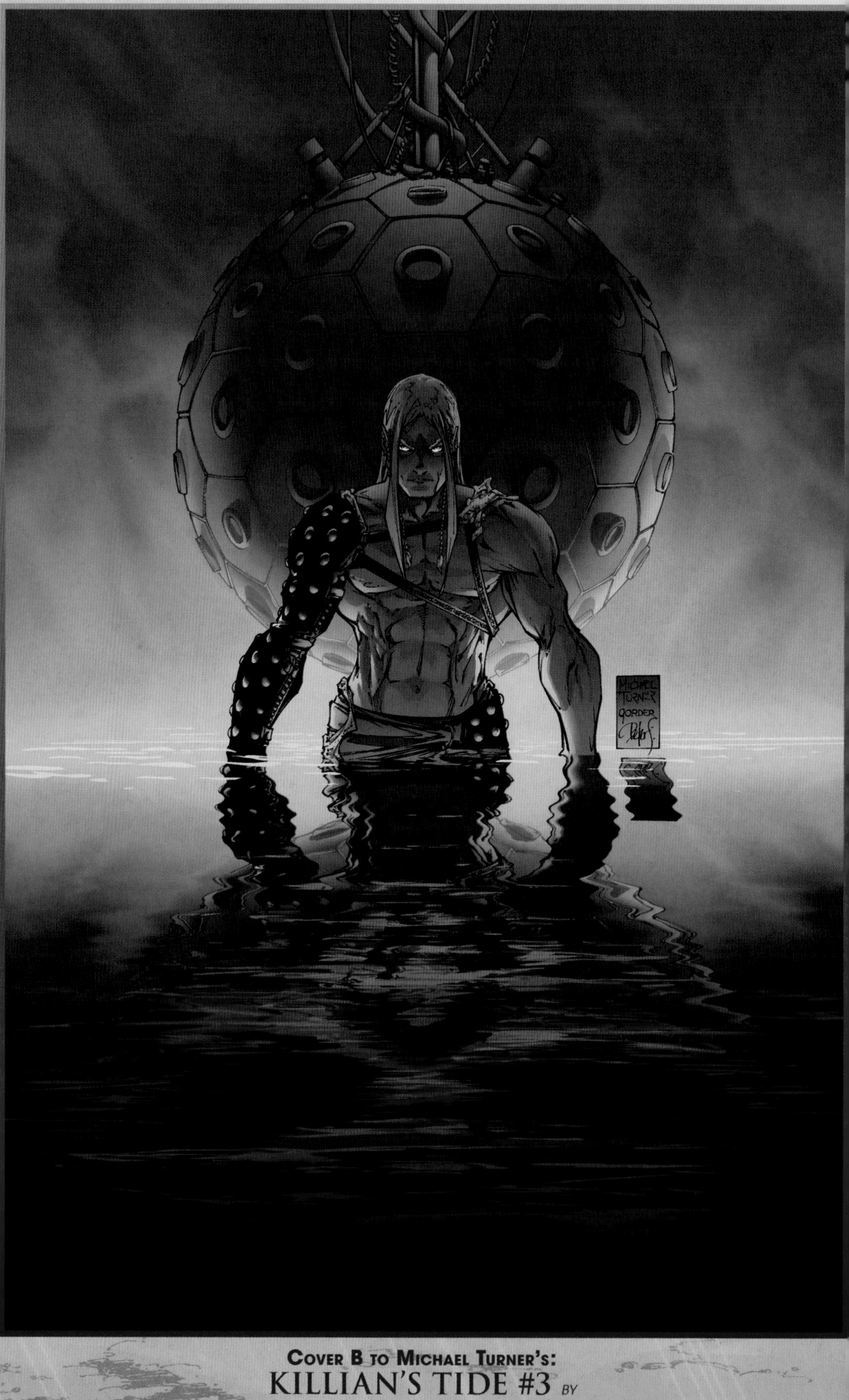
MICHAEL TURNER
GORDER

COVER B TO MICHAEL TURNER'S:
KILLIAN'S TIDE #3 BY
• MICHAEL TURNER • JASON GORDER • PETER STEIGERWALD •

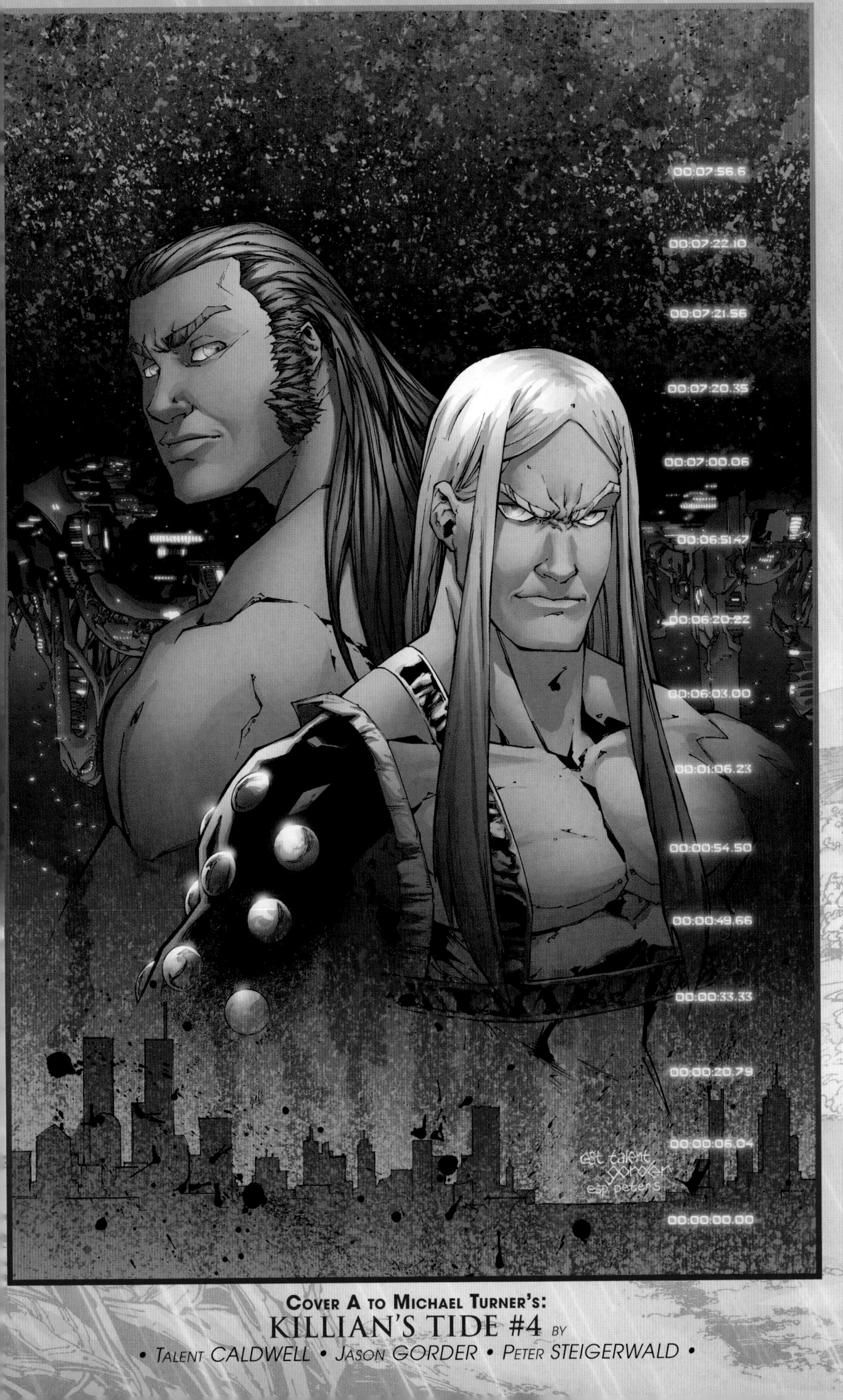

00:07:56.6
00:07:22.10
00:07:21.56
00:07:20.35
00:07:00.06
00:06:51.47
00:06:20.22
00:06:03.00
00:01:06.23
00:00:54.50
00:00:49.66
00:00:33.33
00:00:20.79
00:00:06.04
00:00:00.00

Cover A to Michael Turner's:

KILLIAN'S TIDE #4 *by*

• *Talent* CALDWELL • *Jason* GORDER • *Peter* STEIGERWALD •

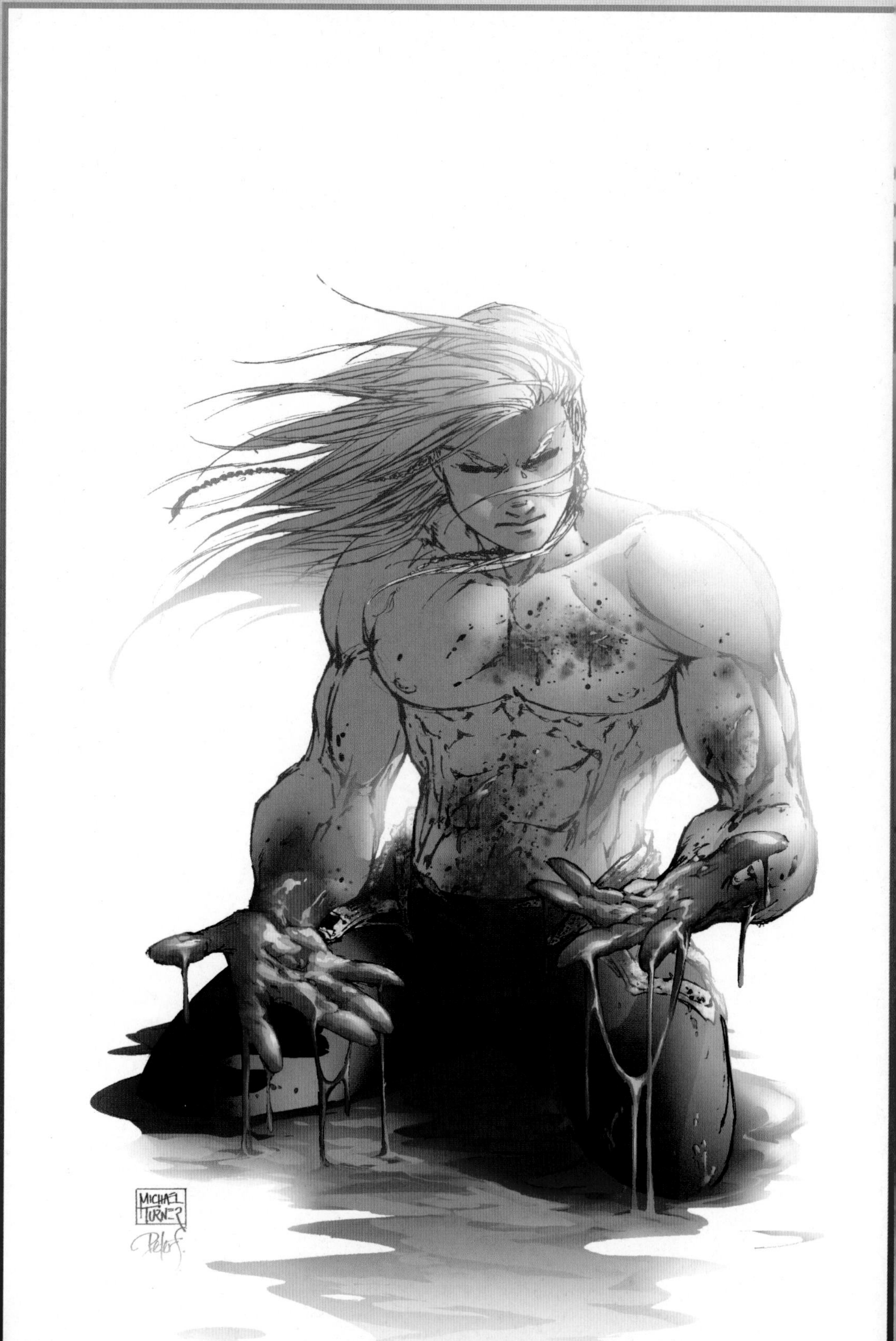

Cover B to Michael Turner's:

KILLIAN'S TIDE #4 BY

• *Michael* TURNER • *Peter* STEIGERWALD •

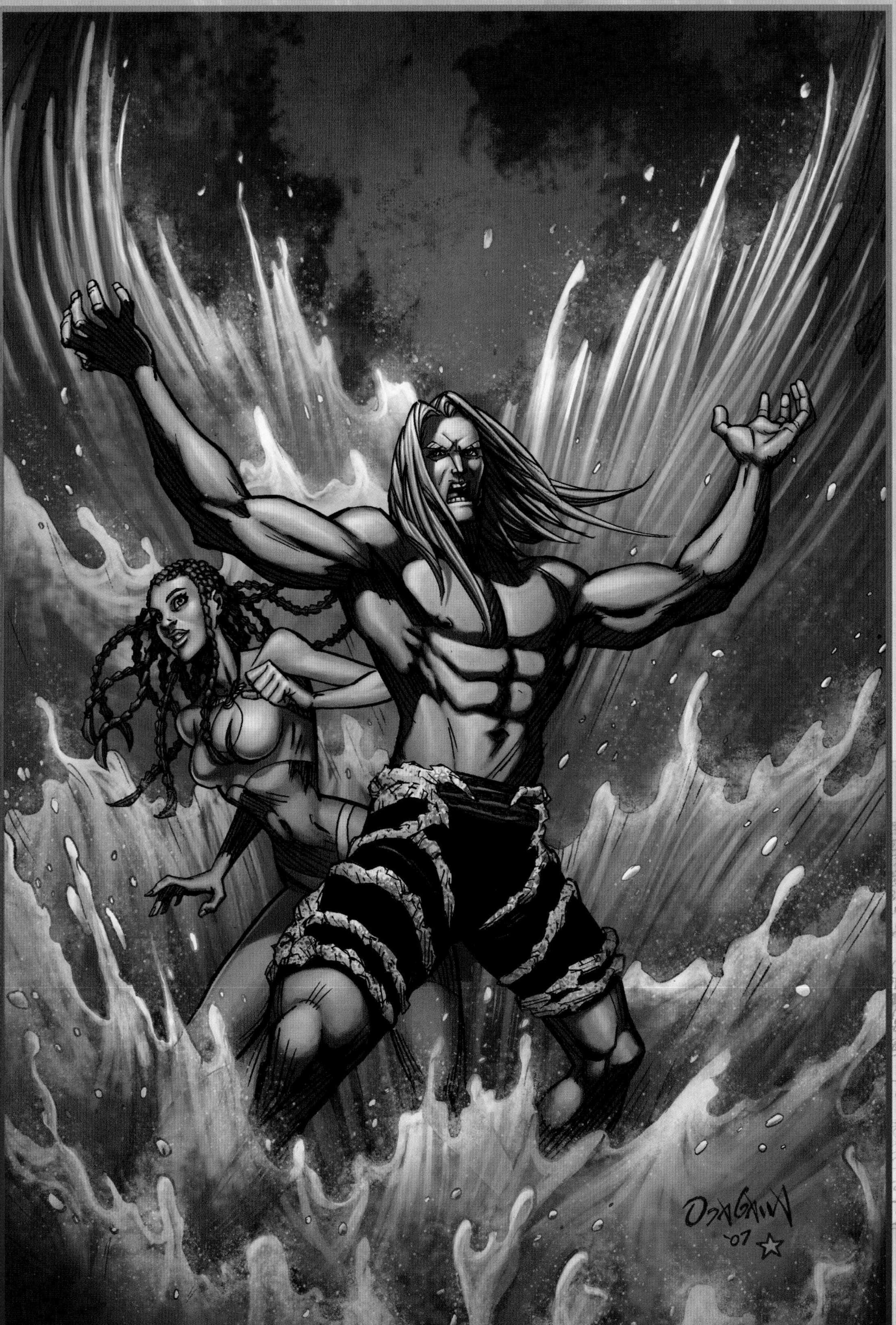

Cover A to Michael Turner's:

KILLIAN'S VESSEL #1 by

• Ryan ODAGAWA • John STARR •

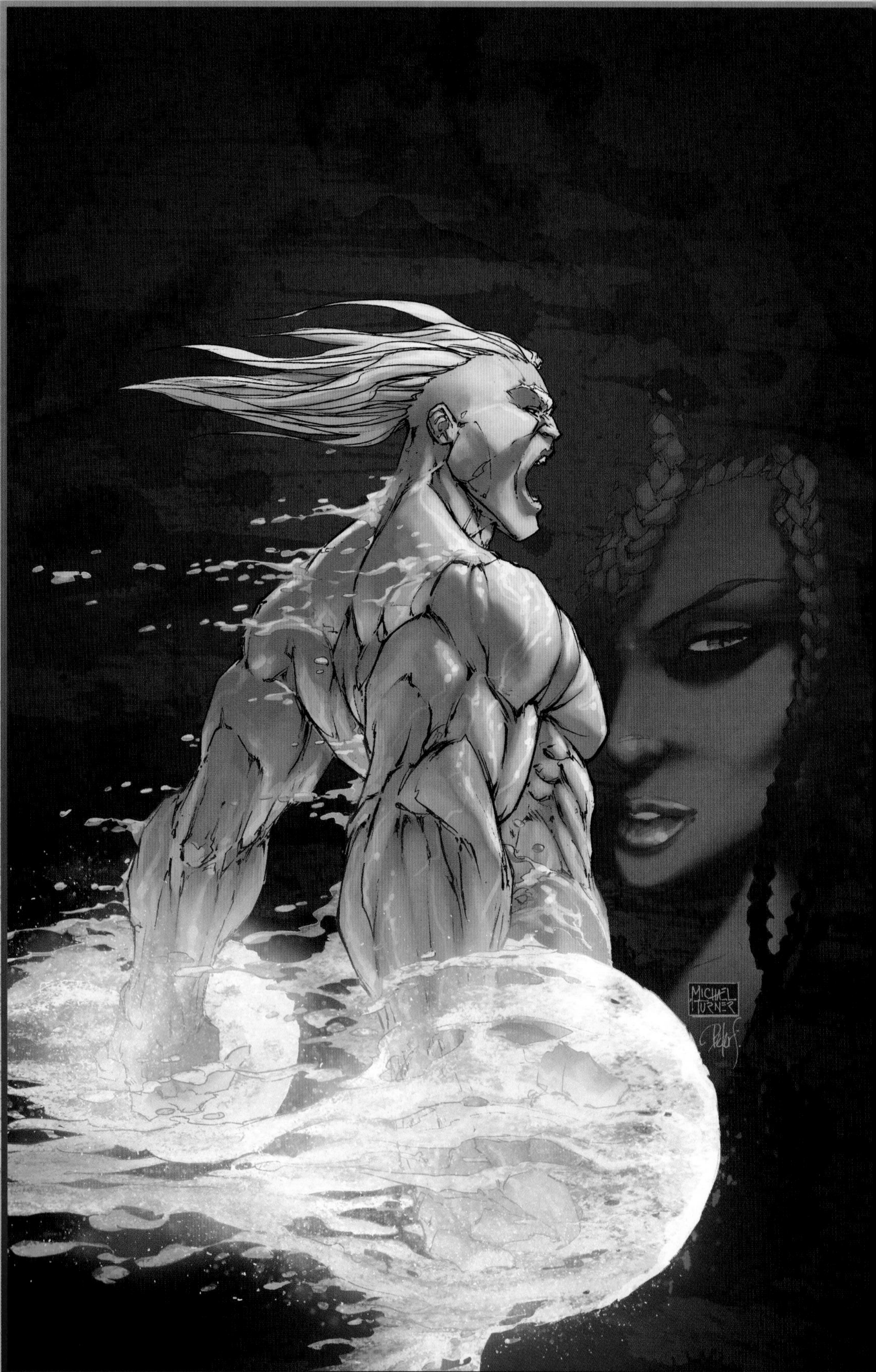
MICHAEL TURNER

Cover B to Michael Turner's:
KILLIAN'S VESSEL #1 by
• Michael TURNER • Peter STEIGERWALD •

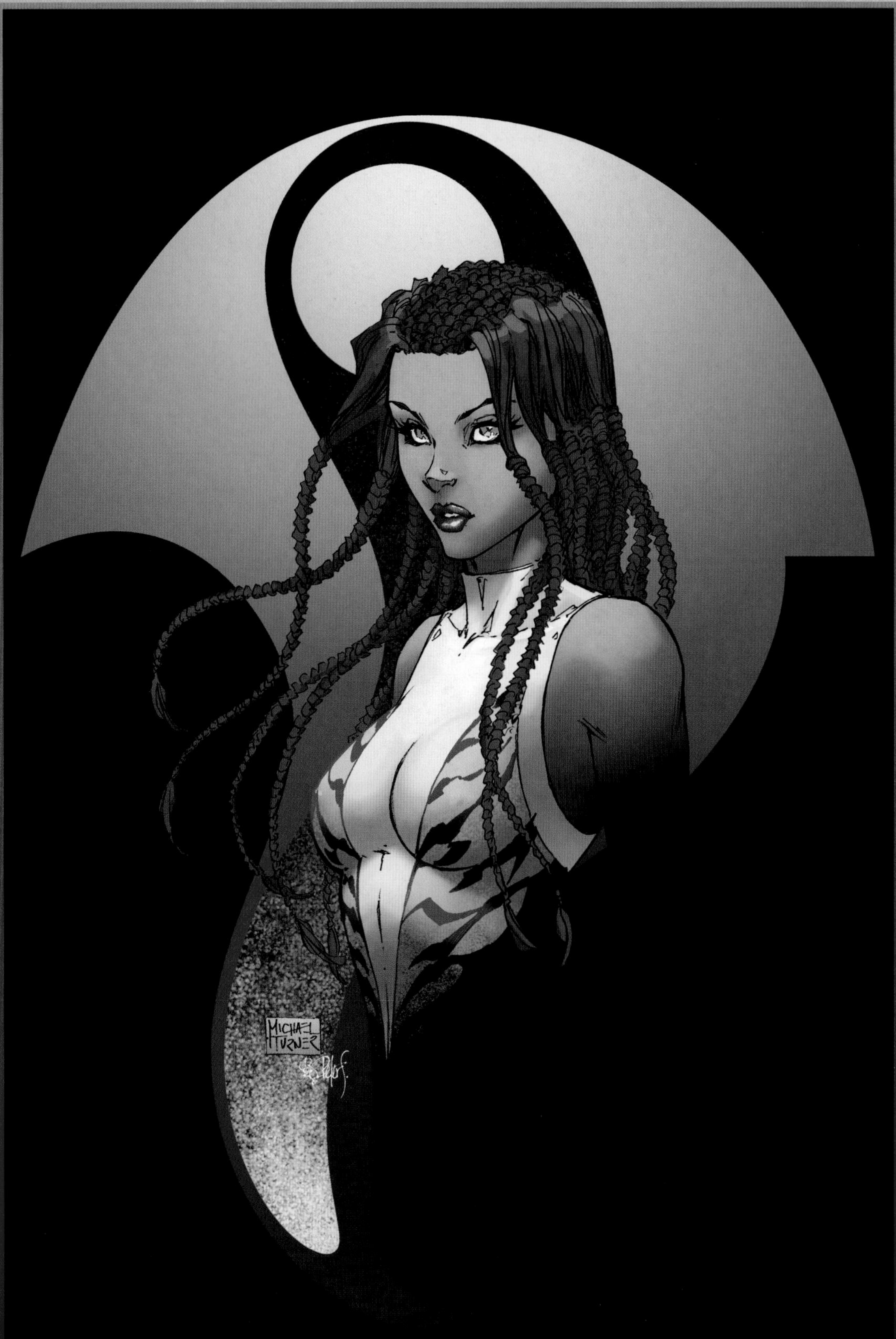
MICHAEL TURNER

Cover C to Michael Turner's:
KILLIAN'S VESSEL #1 *by*
• *Michael TURNER* • *Peter STEIGERWALD* •

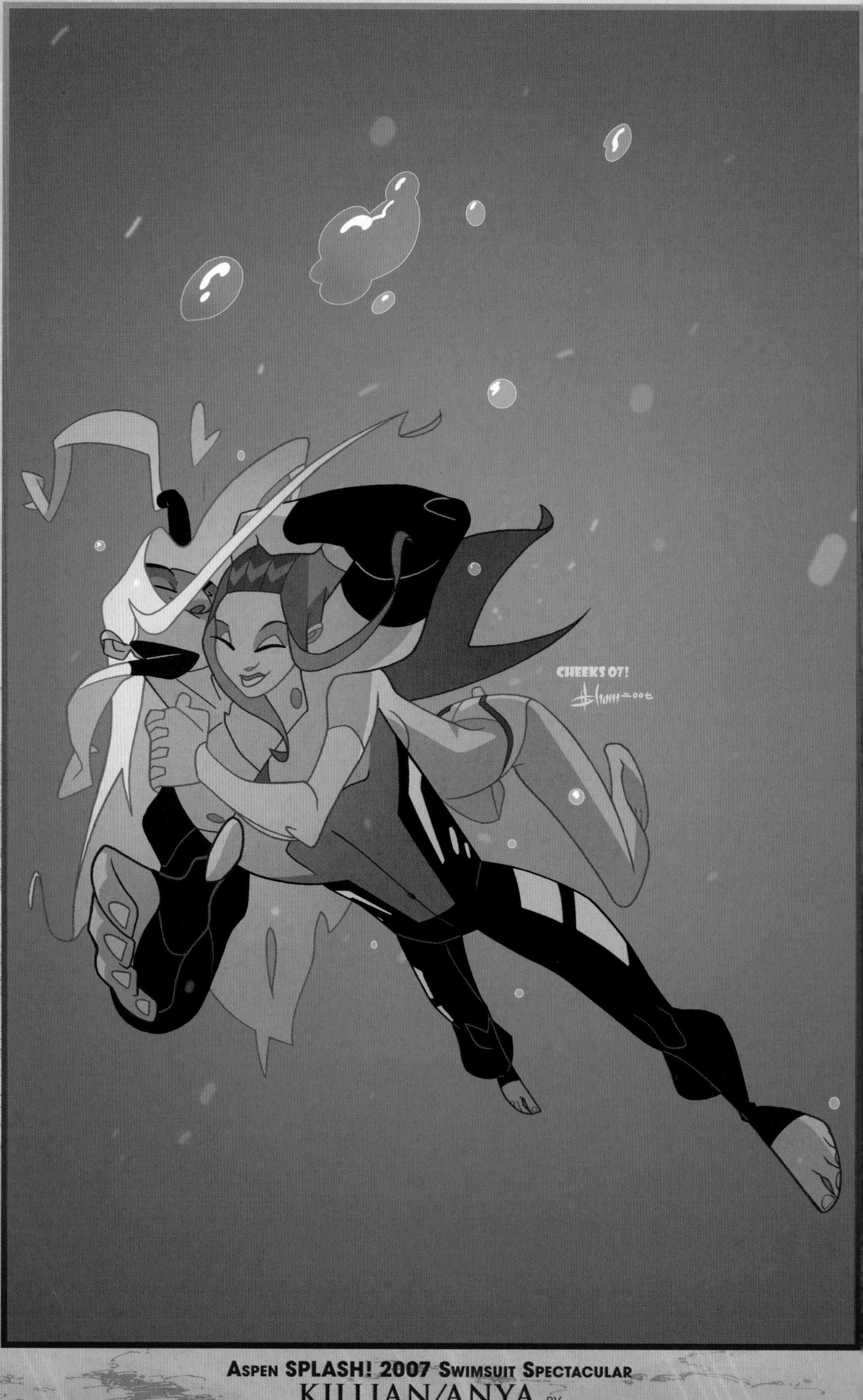
CHEEKS 07!

Aspen SPLASH! 2007 Swimsuit Spectacular
KILLIAN/ANYA *by*
• *Sean "Cheeks" GALLOWAY* • *Howard SHUM* •

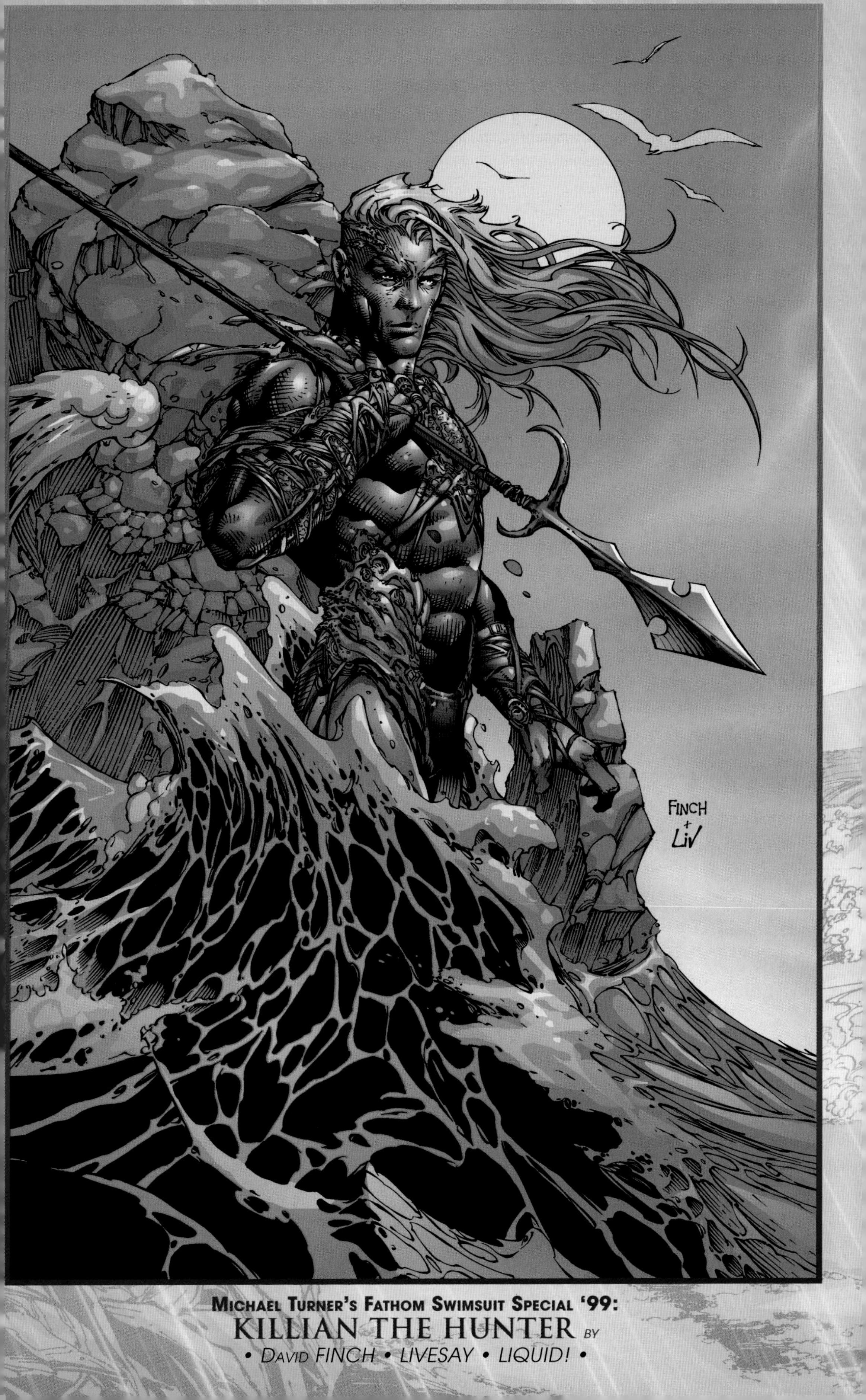
FINCH
+
LiV

Michael Turner's Fathom Swimsuit Special '99:
KILLIAN THE HUNTER *by*
• *David FINCH • LIVESAY • LIQUID!* •